Using Nonfiction Trade Books in the Elementary Classroom

Using Nonfiction Trade Books in the Elementary Classroom

From Ants to Zeppelins

Edited by

Evelyn B. Freeman
The Ohio State University at Newark

Diane Goetz Person
Columbia University

National Council of Teachers of English
1111 Kenyon Road, Urbana, Illinois 61801

To my father, a voracious reader of nonfiction, and to the memory of my mother. EBF

To my husband, all my children, and my friends, who were so supportive, and to my mother, who promised me. DGP

Grateful acknowledgment is made for permission to reprint excerpts from *Operation Grizzly Bear* by Marion Calabro. Copyright © 1989 by Marian Calabro. Reprinted with the permission of Four Winds Press, an imprint of Macmillan Publishing Company.

NCTE Editorial Board: Richard Abrahamson, Celia Genishi, Joyce Kinkead, Louise Wetherbee Phelps, Gladys V. Veidemanis, Charles Suhor, *ex officio*, Michael Spooner, *ex officio*

Manuscript Editor: Jane M. Curran

Production Editor: Rona S. Smith

Cover Design: R. Maul

Interior Design: Doug Burnett

NCTE Stock Number 18119-3050

Library of Congress Cataloging-in-Publication Data

Using nonfiction trade books in the elementary classroom: from ants to
    zeppelins/edited by Evelyn B. Freeman, Diane Goetz Person.
        p. cm.
    Includes bibliographical references.
    ISBN 0-8141-1811-9
        1. Education, Elementary—United States—Curricula. 2. Children—
United States—Books and reading. 3.Teaching—Aids and devices.
I. Freeman, Evelyn B. (Evelyn Blossom), 1948–. II. Person, Diane Goetz.
III. National Council of Teachers of English. IV. Title.
LB 1570.U49   1992   92–4777
372.13'2—dc20   CIP

Contents

Introduction   vii

I. Understanding the Genre of Nonfiction

1. Fact or Fiction?   2
    Russell Freedman

2. The Evolution of a Science Writer   11
    Patricia Lauber

3. The Rise and Fall and Rise of Juvenile Nonfiction,
    1961–1988   17
    James Cross Giblin

4. The Nonfiction Scene: What's Happening?   26
    Barbara Elleman

5. Trends and Evaluative Criteria of Informational Books for
    Children   34
    Frances Smardo Dowd

II. Linking Nonfiction to the Elementary Curriculum

6. The Voice of Learning: Teacher, Child, and Text   46
    Bette Bosma

7. On the Road to Literacy: Pathways through Science Trade
    Books   55
    Marjorie Slavick Frank

8. Windows through Time: Literature of the Social Studies   65
    Diane Goetz Person and Bernice E. Cullinan

9. Reading Aloud and Responding to Nonfiction: Let's Talk
    about It   76
    Sylvia M. Vardell and Kathleen A. Copeland

10. Reading and Writing Connection: Supporting Content-Area
    Literacy through Nonfiction Trade Books   86
    Rosemary A. Salesi

11. Invite Children to Respond Using the Fine Arts   95
    Patricia Grasty Gaines

III. Finding a Place for Nonfiction in the Elementary Classroom

12. Nonfiction Books in the Primary Classroom: Soaring with the Swans   106
    Peter Roop

13. Get Real, Teacher! What Happens When At-Risk Middle-School Readers Become Involved with Nonfiction   113
    Nancy DeVries Guth

14. Using a Nonfiction Author Study in the Classroom   123
    Judith W. Keck

15. Using Informational Books to Develop Reference Skills   131
    M. Jean Greenlaw

16. Putting It All Together: Theme Teaching with Nonfiction Books   146
    Evelyn B. Freeman

Reference Works Cited   153

Children's Books Cited   159

Nonfiction Book Awards   170

Sources for Selecting Nonfiction Titles   173

Index of Authors of Children's Books   175

Index of Titles of Children's Books   177

Editors   181

Contributors   182

Introduction

The Committee on Using Nonfiction in the Elementary Language Arts Classroom was established by the National Council of Teachers of English several years ago to promote the use of children's nonfiction literature. One of the charges of our committee was to prepare publications that could be disseminated widely to teachers. This book is the result of the efforts of committee members and others who advocate that nonfiction share an equal status with picture books and fiction in the elementary classroom. Authors, librarians, university professors, and classroom teachers have contributed their knowledge and ideas on all facets of nonfiction, its relationship to the elementary curriculum, and the myriad possibilities for its use with children.

We have struggled in our committee with the term *nonfiction*. Some prefer this term since it represents the generally accepted Dewey decimal classification of the books we are discussing. Others, however, take umbrage with the term and feel it connotes an inferior relationship to fiction. They would substitute the term *informational books* since it is this kind of book, along with biography, that we are discussing. Indeed, the Dewey decimal classification of nonfiction also includes poetry and folklore, which we do not address in this book or in our committee. Recent library publications have raised questions about the arbitrary division of books into fiction and nonfiction categories created by Dewey's numerical system for shelving books. These questions arise from the proliferation of information, new perspectives on what is meant by information, and the technology for storing and disseminating books. Therefore, we will use the terms *informational books* and *nonfiction* interchangeably to mean those books in the Dewey decimal classification that have numerical or biographical designation, with the exception of poetry and folklore.

This book includes three sections: Understanding the Genre of Nonfiction, Linking Nonfiction to the Elementary Curriculum, and Finding a Place for Nonfiction in the Elementary Classroom. In part I, Understanding the Genre of Nonfiction, noted authors of children's nonfiction and librarians explore nonfiction as a literary genre. Authors Russell Freedman and Patricia Lauber reflect on their experiences in writing award-winning nonfiction for children. James Cross Giblin provides a historical perspective on the genre, while Barbara Elleman describes current trends in nonfiction for children. Frances Smardo Dowd gives us evaluative criteria by which to review books based on their literary merit.

In part II, Linking Nonfiction to the Elementary Curriculum, authors discuss the important role that nonfiction can play in developing concepts in science and social studies, in stimulating creative responses to books, and in supporting oral and written language growth. Bette Bosma's chapter sets the tone for this section by pointing out the voice of the author in nonfiction. The importance of the author's voice is further emphasized in chapters by Marjorie Slavick Frank and by Diane Goetz Person and Bernice E. Cullinan, who describe the values of nonfiction in the science curriculum and the social studies curriculum, respectively. Because of the author's voice, nonfiction can introduce and reinforce concepts in these disciplines in ways far more effective than a textbook. Sylvia M. Vardell and Kathleen A. Copeland provide a framework for using nonfiction to foster oral language experiences in the classroom, while Rosemary Salesi demonstrates how nonfiction can support the reading-writing connection. The final chapter in this section, written by Patricia Grasty Gaines, discusses how children can respond to nonfiction literature through creative expression.

The chapters in part III, Finding a Place for Nonfiction in the Elementary Classroom, suggest specific ways for integrating nonfiction literature into the elementary classroom. Peter Roop, a primary-grade teacher and author of children's books, describes how he has used nonfiction books with his students, while Nancy DeVries Guth details her success in using nonfiction to motivate reluctant middle-school readers. Judith W. Keck gives suggestions for implementing a nonfiction author study, and M. Jean Greenlaw shows how nonfiction can aid in developing reference skills. The last chapter, written by Evelyn B. Freeman, describes the role of nonfiction literature in supporting theme teaching.

We have written this book primarily for classroom teachers, who we trust will find it useful and interesting. In addition, we hope the book will be enjoyed by librarians and students of children's literature at all levels.

Evelyn B. Freeman
Diane Goetz Person

I Understanding the Genre of Nonfiction

Fact or Fiction?

Russell Freedman
Author of children's literature

A few days ago I told a friend that I'd be speaking at a children's literature conference along with some distinguished novelists, poets, anthologists, and illustrators, and that I'd be the only nonfiction writer among them. My friend said, "Then you're the only one who has to tell the truth!"

When I mentioned that I'd be speaking at 8:30 in the morning, my friend said, "Oh, *never* try to tell the truth at 8:30 in the morning."

So I leave it to you, my audience, to decide. Are my remarks this Friday morning fact—or are they fiction?

Patricia MacLachlan, who won the 1986 Newbery Medal for *Sarah Plain and Tall* (Harper and Row, 1985), must have been thinking along these same lines, because her new book is called *The Facts and Fictions of Minna Pratt* (Harper and Row, 1988). The protagonist, eleven-year-old Minna Pratt, has a mother who is a writer. Pinned above the mother's typewriter are messages like "fact and fiction are different truths," and "fiction is fact's elder sister."

Someone else has said that fiction is a pack of lies in pursuit of the truth. As a corollary, I suppose you could say that nonfiction is a pack of facts in pursuit of the truth. Unfortunately, facts can't always be trusted. Facts can be unreliable, misleading, ambiguous, or slippery.

A few years ago, while I was doing the research for my book *Children of the Wild West* (Houghton Mifflin, 1983), I learned something about the treachery of historical facts. The opening chapter of the book describes wagon-train journeys along the Oregon Trail. Now, the movies and television have taught us that this journey was fraught with peril, since the hostile Indians were likely to attack at any moment. And yet, as I pursued my research, I found that Indian attacks were few and far between. Attacks were infrequent. I began to wonder, how menacing *were* the Indians?

Well, it depends on whom you ask. Pioneers going west kept diaries and journals. If you read the diaries written by men—that's one

This chapter is based on a speech given at the Children's Literature '89 Conference, The Ohio State University, Columbus, February 3, 1989. © Russell Freedman. It is reprinted by permission of the author.

set of historical "facts"—you get one impression. The men almost always emphasized the danger from Indians. They often told of their battles with hostile Indian war parties.

Women's diaries—another set of historical "facts"—tell quite a different story, as Lillian Schlissel has pointed out in her book *Women's Diaries of the Westward Journey* (1982). The women invariably started the journey fearful of the Indians. But they usually ended up describing the Indians as friendly in manner and helpful in deed. The women, it seems, had no need to emphasize Indian ferocity.

So that's something to think about when you're writing, or reading, a nonfiction book. Just because the book is allegedly based on fact doesn't mean that it tells the truth.

The Canadian author Mavis Gallant, in her collection of short stories called *The Other Paris* (1955), says this of one of her characters: "She realized for the first time that something could be perfectly accurate but untrue." Now that's a message that *I* have pinned above *my* typewriter: "Something can be perfectly accurate but untrue." It reminds me that my first responsibility as a writer of nonfiction is not just to be accurate as I muster my facts, but to pursue that elusive quality called the "truth." That uncertain and risky pursuit is what adds a sense of exploration and discovery to a nonfiction book.

Like Minna Pratt's mother, I also have a second message pinned above my typewriter. This one is a quote from the well-known nonfiction writer John McPhee, and it says: "Whatever you're writing, your motive is always to tell a good story while you're sitting around the cave, in front of the fire, before going out to club another mastodon" (McPhee 1977, 50).

Certainly the basic purpose of nonfiction is to inform, to instruct, hopefully to enlighten. But that's not enough. An effective nonfiction book must animate its subject, infuse it with life. It must create a vivid and believable world that the reader will enter willingly and leave only with reluctance. A good nonfiction book should be a pleasure to read. It should be just as compelling as a good story.

After all, there's a story to everything. The task of the nonfiction writer is to find the story—the narrative line— that exists in nearly every subject. Jean Fritz puts it succinctly and well when she speaks of giving dramatic shape to her books. "Nonfiction can be told in a narrative voice and still maintain its integrity," she says. "The art of fiction is making up facts; the art of nonfiction is using facts to make up a form" (Fritz 1988, 759–60).

My recent book *Buffalo Hunt* (Holiday House, 1988) provides an example of presenting facts within a narrative form. The book describes the buffalo culture of the Plains Indians. It tells how the buffalo ruled the Indians' everyday lives and provided almost everything they needed to survive. There are at least two narrative lines that arise quite naturally from this factual material. One is the story of how the Indians discovered the buffalo, how they learned to hunt and utilize and worship the animals, and what happened to the Indians when the buffalo finally disappeared. That's the overall framework of the book—the rise and fall of the buffalo culture. The opening paragraph tells the reader immediately that this is going to be a story about Indians and buffalo:

> Over blazing campfires on winter nights, Indian storytellers spoke of the buffalo. They told tales of buffalo giants and buffalo ghosts, of buffalo that changed magically into men, of children who were raised by buffalo and understood their language. (P. 7)

The book also contains a second narrative line—a story within the story—which focuses on a typical buffalo hunt. Here's how that story begins:

> On the day set for starting a hunt, everyone was up at sunrise. The women went right to work, packing their household belongings and getting everything ready for the move. Youngsters rounded up the horses and dogs. The men gathered in small groups to discuss the day's plans.
> After a quick morning meal, the marshals assembled. They took their feathered banners in their hands, mounted their horses, and gave the signal to break camp.
> With that, the Indian village disappeared almost like a puff of smoke. (P. 25)

And the story goes on from there.

Of course, no form of nonfiction lends itself to narrative more readily than biography—the story of a person's life. I think it can be said that the best biographies have always told wonderful stories. So it's not surprising that biography is one of the oldest and most popular forms of literature for children.

History records countless examples of great men and women who were inspired in their youth by the lives of other great men and women. Napoleon read *Plutarch's Lives* as a lonely schoolboy in France. Harry Truman was nine when his mother gave him a four-volume set called *Great Men and Famous Women*, which he loved. His favorite chapter was the one about Robert E. Lee, which includes a letter that Lee wrote to his son commending certain traits of character to the boy, such as "Frankness is the child of honesty and courage" (Zinsser 1986, 60–61).

Abraham Lincoln was a frontier boy growing up in Indiana when he read *The Life of George Washington* by the Reverend Mason Locke Weems. For the rest of his life, Lincoln referred to that book and sometimes quoted from it in his speeches and public appearances.

This was the book that introduced the story about the cherry tree into American folklore. The first edition of *George Washington*, published in 1800, made no reference whatsoever to little George and the cherry tree. It wasn't until the fifth edition, which appeared in 1806, that Parson Weems made up the cherry tree story and added it to his biography as a moral lesson, along with George's immortal confession, "Father, I cannot tell a lie."

The whimsies of Parson Weems influenced generations of biographers that followed. Fictionalization became an accepted tradition. It was justified on the grounds that it dramatized history for young readers, that it heightened interest and helped clarify complex issues. And along with imaginary scenes and made-up dialogue, children's biographies were characterized by a reverential or adulatory tone, which reflected the educational values of the time. The purpose of biography was to provide young readers with idealized heroes to worship and copy—to copy a life that was exemplary. As a rule, important historical figures were portrayed as romanticized stereotypes, controversy was avoided, and readers were served a sanitized version of history.

One of the most popular children's biographies ever published, for example, is *Abraham Lincoln* by Ingri and Edgar d'Aulaire (Doubleday, 1939), winner of the 1940 Caldecott Medal and still popular today. In this well-loved book there is no mention, no hint, that Lincoln was assassinated. As the book ends, the president simply sits down in his rocking chair for a well-earned rest.

As a result of these twin traditions—fictionalization and idealization—children's biographies were regarded in the not-too-distant past with a degree of condescension. Writing in the *New York Times Book Review* in the fall of 1963, John Garraty reviewed a mixed bag of children's biographies and commented: "These books sometimes make use of imaginary incidents and manufactured dialogue that a respectable author would never include in a work for mature adults" (Garraty 1963, 6).

Since Garraty made that comment some twenty-five years ago, there have been dramatic changes in the way biography, and all nonfiction, is presented to young readers. The biographical hero-worship of the past has given way to a more realistic approach, which recognizes the warts and weaknesses that humanize the great. And the practice of fictionalization is dying, if not dead. Today's youngsters seem to prefer the facts. And today's biographies treat their subjects with respect rather than reverence and, I believe, show a greater respect for the reader, too.

I grew up during the cherry tree era of children's biography. Long after I stopped believing in Santa Claus, I still believed that George Washington never told a lie. And if anyone was more honest than George, it had to be young Abe Lincoln. I still have my boyhood copy of *Abe Lincoln: Frontier Boy*, published by Bobbs Merrill in 1932 and still in print (currently titled *Abe Lincoln: The Great Emancipator* by Augusta Stevenson, Macmillan, 1986). This book contains my favorite example of invented dialogue. Abe is eleven years old in this imaginary scene, and his father is bawling him out:

"Books!" said his father. "Always books! What is all this studying
going to do for you? What do you think you are going to be?"
    "Why," said Abe, "I'm going to be President." (P. 119)

That's the Lincoln I grew up with. Honest Abe—always fair in
games and work, always kind to man and beast. If there was a man
behind the myth, I knew little about him. It wasn't until a few years ago
that a passing remark in a memoir by Mary McCarthy ignited my
interest in Lincoln. Mary McCarthy (1987) wrote that she found Lincoln
a sympathetic character because of his intellect and his melancholy. It
was the word *melancholy* that stopped me as I was reading. Melancholy? That was my first inkling that a complex and paradoxical man—
a believable human being—was hidden behind the layers of historical
makeup.

About that time, I read an article in the *New York Times* about the
night Lincoln was shot. It seems that right after he died, someone
emptied the contents of his pockets and put everything into a small box.
The box was wrapped in brown paper and tied with a string, and so it
remained until 1976, when it was finally untied, unwrapped, and
opened at the Library of Congress as the library staff looked on. As I
read about the contents of Lincoln's pockets the morning he died—I
describe those contents in my book—I felt as though this mysterious
and melancholy man was stepping down from his pedestal at the
Lincoln Memorial, changing before my eyes from an imposing marble
statue to an engaging and approachable fellow. From then on, Lincoln
intrigued me, and when the chance came, I was anxious to write about
him.

There had been plenty of others before me, of course. If you go to
the Library of Congress and look under Biographical Entries, which
name do you think has the greatest number of entries? Can you guess?
The greatest number of entries are listed under Jesus Christ. The second
greatest number are under Napoleon. And the third greatest number of
biographical entries at the Library of Congress are under Abraham
Lincoln.

More biographies about Lincoln than any other American,
thousands of titles covering every aspect of his life and career. You may
be wondering, if there are so many books about Lincoln already on the
shelves, why bother to add another one? Well, I might ask: how many
people here want to read a biography of President James Buchanan?
Lincoln is an irresistible subject because of who he was and what he did.
Since his time, every generation has produced a new crop of Lincoln
scholars, authors, and readers. Each generation interprets Lincoln by its
own lights, according to its own needs, because his life and example
have an enduring meaning. I picked Lincoln as a subject because I felt I
could offer a fresh perspective for today's generation of young readers,
but just as important, I picked him because I wanted to satisfy my own
itch to know.

While I was working on the book (*Lincoln: A Photobiography* [Clarion, 1987]), I had a chance to enjoy the pleasures of on-site research. I followed the Lincoln Trail, visiting most of the major historical sites from Lincoln's logcabin birthplace in Kentucky to Ford's Theatre in Washington, D.C., and the rooming house across the street where the president died. I spent quite a bit of time in Springfield, Illinois, where Lincoln married, raised a family, practiced law, and ran for president. As you may know, his house in Springfield was the only house Lincoln ever owned. He bought it in 1844, soon after his marriage, for $1,500. The National Park Service just spent $2.2 million to renovate the place, and it reopened to the public last summer. One of the people I met during my research will have to remain nameless. I promised not to reveal his identity. This person worked on the Freedom Train that traveled across America some years ago—a traveling museum that included, among other exhibits, the furnishings from the Presidential Box at Ford's Theatre the night Lincoln was shot.

I was talking to my informant when he lowered his voice and said, "I want to tell you something that I've told only two other people in my life—my wife, and my mother." I didn't know whether I wanted to hear it or not, but he continued. "One night, after the Freedom Train had been closed to the public, after the cleaning crew had left, I was the only person still there. I looked at Lincoln's rocker, where he was sitting when he was shot. And I wanted to sit in it myself."

Now I was all ears. "So, I eased myself into the rocker," he continued. "I sat there for maybe two or three minutes, but I was afraid to rock. I was afraid the chair might collapse if I leaned back too far. So I just sat there."

"How did you feel?" I asked.

"I felt like an eyewitness to history," he said. "My heart was pounding. To be honest, I was uncomfortable!"

The image of my anonymous informant sitting in Lincoln's rocker stayed with me as I worked on my book. I wanted to put my reader into Lincoln's rocker, uncomfortably if need be, because the facts of history and the tricks of fate are not always comfortable.

I could have spent a lifetime studying Lincoln—as some people have. But at some point, you have to stop researching and start writing. And that's when you have to start making decisions. What should be included in the type of book I want to write? How much space should I devote to Lincoln's childhood? How much detail should I include about the Civil War? How much background about slavery? How much about Lincoln's marriage, his children, his relationships with other public figures?

Franklyn Branley has said that it is only when he must explain a subject to children that he realizes he doesn't understand it at all. A writer for children is forced to refine his thinking to the point of absolute clarity. And with luck, the result can be a distillation of the subject.

Starting a new book is always like trying to solve a puzzle. You have to decide what to include and what to leave out, how to begin, what to emphasize, how much, and where, how to balance facts and interpretation, and how to breathe life into the subject. The process of viewing the material, of seeing what belongs where, is a mystery I never resolve once and for all.

I spend a lot of time looking for revealing details, for meaningful anecdotes and quotations that will help bring my factual material to life. A truthful anecdote can enliven a text far more convincingly than an imaginary scene. An actual quote is certainly more effective than manufactured dialogue. Here's a passage from my Lincoln biography that combines an anecdote with quotes from the two people who knew Lincoln best, his law partner, William Herndon, and his wife, Mary:

> They [Mary and Lincoln] adored their boys, denied them nothing, and seldom disciplined them. Lincoln liked to take Willie and Tad to the office when he worked on Sundays. Their wild behavior infuriated his partner. "The boys were absolutely unrestrained in their amusement," Herndon complained. "If they pulled down all the books from the shelves, bent the points of all the pens, overturned the spittoon, it never disturbed the serenity of their father's good nature. I have felt many and many a time that I wanted to wring the necks of those little brats and pitch them out the windows."
>
> But as far as Lincoln was concerned, his boys could do no wrong. "Mr. Lincoln . . . was very exceedingly indulgent to his children," Mary remarked. "He always said: 'It is my pleasure that my children are free, happy, and unrestrained by parental tyranny. Love is the chain whereby to bind a child to its parents.'" (P. 41–43)

So said Mary Lincoln about her husband.

I'd like to tell you about one anecdote that I did not include in my book. In February 1862, Lincoln's eleven-year-old son Willie died of a fever. Willie was the second son to be taken from the Lincolns. Mary was overcome by grief, and the president "plunged into the deepest gloom he had ever known. . . . Again and again, he shut himself in his room to weep alone" (p. 80). He was heard to say about Willie: "He was too good for this earth. It is hard, hard to have him die" (p. 81).

Now, all of that is in my book. In early drafts, I had also written that Lincoln twice had his son's body exhumed, so he could gaze upon Willie's face again. I felt that the harrowing image of the grieving president looking into his son's coffin was a powerful and unforgettable representation of Lincoln's profound sorrow. And I thought it said something about Lincoln that could be expressed only by example.

And yet something about the story made me uneasy. My only source was a biography published during the 1930s, and I felt that I needed at least one additional source, and preferably more, for confirmation. When I couldn't find one, I decided to drop the incident from my book. But the image still haunts me, and I still wonder if it's true.

I knew, of course, that Roosevelt was a victim of polio—infantile paralysis. And I have searched my memory, trying to recall if I actually realized back then that the president could not stand on his own feet. On the arm of a son or an aide, he appeared always erect. He was so active, he projected such a dynamic personality, he gave the impression that he had no disability. Lots of people, me included, tended to forget that Roosevelt couldn't walk, or even stand up without help. Some visitors to the White House were ready to swear that as they were ushered into the oval office, the president rose to greet them.

That's one reason why Roosevelt is such a terrific subject for a biography. On the personal level, his life is the dramatic story of his struggle to overcome a crippling handicap. That struggle helped forge his character, just as Lincoln's struggle to overcome his log cabin origins helped form his character.

Lincoln served as president during a critical moment in history when the American system had to redefine itself. The Civil War was, on several levels, a test of American ideals. Roosevelt served during two critical moments. The Great Depression and Hilter's rise to power were also, each in a different way, tests of American ideals. The story of Franklin Roosevelt is the story of how he met those challenges, and why he acted as he did.

Roosevelt died on April 12, 1945. The next morning, Professor Paul H. Buck's class, "The Making of Modern America," met as usual at 9 a.m. at Harvard, Roosevelt's alma mater. The class had been discussing two questions: how to solve economic problems to obtain a more equitable society, and how to secure a peaceful world. Professor Buck faced the class that Friday morning and thought for a moment of what had just happened. Most of the young men before him had been seven or eight years old when Roosevelt entered the White House. What could he tell them?

"As one studies history," he said, "the stature of a man is judged by what he does to build or destroy the faith by which men live. . . . Mr. Roosevelt was great because he, like Lincoln, restored men's faith" (Morgan 1985, 767).

That's one of the themes I tried to bring out in my biography of Franklin Roosevelt. I wanted to give my readers a sense of Roosevelt's life as he actually lived it, an appreciation of his character and personality, and an understanding of his role in American history. But most of all, I tried to tell a good story that would pull my reader into Franklin Roosevelt's world, and keep that reader turning the pages until the story ends.

The Evolution of a Science Writer

Patricia Lauber
Author of children's literature

If, when I was fresh out of college, someone had told me that I would one day be standing here delivering a talk at the Spring Conference of the National Council of Teachers of English, I would have been extremely gratified (as indeed I am) and also willing to consider that the prophecy just might come true. But if the soothsayer had added that I would be talking about my science books for children, I would have dismissed the entire prophecy as rubbish—along with promises of dark, handsome strangers and unexpected inheritances. Yet here I am, talking about the evolution of a science writer (meaning me) and wondering whether a better title might be "Confessions of an English Major." For that is what I was.

Science was never one of my interests in school or college; in fact, I might go as far as to say that I never met a science course I liked. What I liked best was English, both literature and composition.

I had been a small child who adored stories and was fortunate enough to have a mother who liked to read to me. But, perhaps because my appetite for stories was insatiable, there never seemed to be enough time. As a result, first grade was probably the most exciting year of my entire education. I discovered that I knew how to read, and immediately worked my way through the first-grade reader. Now I no longer had to depend on my mother's being free when I wanted a story. Next I learned to print and also to spell a few words. An undreamed-of world appeared: I could make up my own stories and poems and write them down. I knew at once what I was going to be—and I have never looked back, never regretted the choice.

After college I was off into the world of publishing in New York and became a staff writer in *Look* magazine's book department. One day a friend who was working at Scholastic dropped by for a visit, and

This chapter is based on a speech given at the National Council of Teachers of English Spring Conference, April 7, 1989, Charleston, South Carolina. © Patricia Lauber. It is reprinted by permission of the author.

as one that says it was right. A person who is simply reporting on the work, however, is under no such restraints. A writer has an obligation to be fair and accurate and to present opposing points of view. But a writer is also entitled to have a point of view and to care how it all comes out.

This realization freed me up in my handling of subject matter. But I still didn't have an overall point of view. What I had was a number of specific points of view concerning individual subjects. I might have stayed at this point in my thinking, except that many branches of science were changing dramatically. In almost every field that was of interest to me, scientists were moving ahead by giant leaps.

In earth science proof was fast emerging that continents had drifted, that whole oceans had opened and closed, that volcanic eruptions and earthquakes were symptoms of what was happening.

Space exploration moved studies of the rocky inner planets out of astronomy and into geology.

Natural science, in just the time I had been writing, had moved from discovering and naming species and studying anatomy to physiology, to studies of animal behavior, to the study of the complex linkages among living things and between living things and their environments, that is, to ecology, which had the greatest impact on my thinking. It is the science in which Donne's "No man is an Island" is extended to every kind of plant and animal.

I began to glimpse an overall picture, to see how wondrously everything fitted together—how the earth's size, distance from the sun, and internal heat (among other factors) had combined to produce a planet with an atmosphere and oceans, a planet where life could arise, a planet where, as some land eroded into the oceans, new land formed. On this planet evolving life modified the atmosphere and surface, and the planet became in time home to myriad forms of life, none existing independent of others, none existing independent of environment. I perceived that the life of this planet was tough and tenacious, that it would take hold wherever an ecological niche existed, and, simultaneously, that it was fragile in its interdependencies, in its checks and balances; and once a species is gone, it is gone forever.

I had, in short, come to the heart of the matter, a basic understanding and deep caring, caring about the earth as a planet and about its life, caring how the story comes out. It is a point of view and a feeling that infuses much of what I now write, to the considerable satisfaction of the child-who-was.

In choosing the subjects for my books, I am of course mindful of what is suitable for various age groups, but the strongest influence is how I myself feel about a subject. If I think it important and interesting, if I am full of enthusiasm, I write the book. If after some reading, I am less than enthusiastic, I have to say the book is not for me. Overall, my aims are to help children understand how the earth (or its parts) works and to try to imbue them with some of my own sense of wonderment, in the hope that they will grow up to be good stewards, who will take care of the earth, not just use (or abuse) it.

With younger readers I tend to take small bites of subject matter—to consider, for example, how a giant cactus is able to grow in a desert, what desert animals depend on the cactus for food, water, and shelter, what animals the cactus needs if it is to make seeds and reproduce (*Life on a Giant Cactus* [Garrard, 1974]). Or I may look, as I did in my books on seeds and pollination, at the incredible variety of means by which flowers ensure their reproduction, the roles played by animals, and the ultimate benefit to us (*Seeds Pop, Stick, Glide* [Crown, 1981] and *From Flower to Flower: Animals and Pollination* [Crown, 1986]).

At an older level, I take a bigger bite. In *Dinosaurs Walked Here and Other Stories Fossils Tell* (Bradbury, 1987), I wanted not only to tell about the fossils as a means of reading the past, but also to give a sense of the long, long history of the earth, of change, of life continuing even after mass extinctions. *Journey to the Planets* stemmed partly from my own interest in the findings of the space program; I am old enough to remember when other planets were simply blurs seen through a telescope, while today television transports us to those planets. But it stemmed equally from the empathy I felt with the Apollo astronauts who stood on the airless, waterless body that is our moon and looked out into the blackness of space at the blue-and-white planet that is the only outpost of life in the solar system.

When Mount St. Helens erupted, I was interested because I enjoy reading and writing about volcanoes, but I had no thought of doing a book about this particular volcano until I saw a small photograph in a nature magazine. It showed a young fireweed plant poking up through a crack in the thick crust of ash deposited during the eruption. I suddenly knew that I wanted to write a book that would examine the mechanics of a big eruption and put eruptions in perspective as a natural phenomenon that helps to make the earth a planet of life, a book that would also be a celebration of life, of its resiliency, of its ability to survive and come back, of the earth's ability to heal itself.

In writing these books, I have no desire to turn all children into scientists, although I like to think that I may kindle an occasional spark. One of the things I hope to do is to strip away the idea that science is hard and unpalatable, something that only a chosen few can understand, never mind enjoy. Properly presented, science appeals as an interesting and exciting field of *human* endeavor. I hope to show that it is possible to read science for pleasure, that a good science book touches the mind, the heart, the imagination. I hope to show that a well-written science book can stand up to literary evaluation, that it is part of our literature, that it is deserving of a place on reading lists and in classroom libraries.

I hope to encourage children like the child-me, who do not wish to be scientists, to read science and understand its ideas. Equally important, I hope to encourage scientifically minded children to write about

He did the job quickly and, as far as I could tell, carefully. I turned the manuscript over to Gertrude Phillips for design and production. That afternoon she summoned me into her office, and as soon as I saw the expression in her eyes I knew that something was wrong. "Just look," she said pointing to a page in the manuscript. "Here *splendor* is spelled in the American way. But here"—she riffled a few pages ahead—"it's spelled *splendour*. Do you call this copyediting?"

I mumbled an apology, saying I'd go over the manuscript again, but that didn't satisfy Gertrude. Staring out the window, she groaned (more to herself than to me), "What am I going to do? First, I have to work with a kid who doesn't know anything about editing, and now I've got to deal with a copyeditor who doesn't know his job, either!"

Russell's and my fortunes could only rise from that low point, and they did. *The Road to Agra* was published in the fall of 1961, no one found any copyediting errors, and the book went on to win the Child Study Association Award and several other honors. Russell's *Teenagers Who Made History* appeared in that same fall season, received excellent reviews, and launched Russell on the writing career that culminated in *Lincoln*.

Back at Criterion, I found myself spending much more time editing nonfiction than fiction. For this was the era of the National Defense Education Act enacted by Congress to provide funds for the purchase of science books by libraries to help counter the threat posed by Soviet scientific successes, such as Sputnik. Publishers everywhere jumped on the science bandwagon, and the first government-supported boom in juvenile nonfiction was on.

From this period emerged such innovative programs as Crowell's Let's Read and Find Out series of science concept picture books, launched by the pioneering editor Elizabeth M. Riley. This series was in many ways the nonfiction counterpart of Harper's I Can Read series, for it employed topflight writers like Roma Gans, Paul Showers, and Franklyn Branley, and their texts were assigned to illustrators like Paul Galdone and Ed Emberley. The result was a line of books that combined solid information with lively, colorful graphics, books that entertained young readers even while educating them.

At Criterion, we were concentrating on a nonfiction series of British science books for older children that had its own unique problems. The information in the books was accurate and well-written, and they were illustrated with appropriate black-and-white photos, but the texts were filled with passages like the following from the original version of J.G. Crowther's *Radioastronomy and Radar*: "On some fair Sunday, maybe you can persuade your Mum and Dad to drive you down to Jodrell Bank for a firsthand look at the radar installations there."

The trick, of course, was to edit such passages for the American audience, and inject additional information about installations in the United States and Canada while maintaining the tone of the British original. We also had to locate photographs of American sites. This was no easy task. To perform it we hired freelance editors, such as Iris Vinton and Edith Patterson Meyer (but not Russell, who no longer needed as much part-time work).

In coordinating the freelancers' work as in-house editor, I learned a great deal about the basics of nonfiction that have stood me in good stead ever since: the need for liveliness, clarity, and sound organization in the text, as well as accuracy; the importance of the illustrations and the need to relate them as closely as possible to the text: the added importance of well-written captions to help the reader's understanding. In addition, there is a need for such aids as an index, a list of suggestions for further reading, and perhaps a glossary of unfamiliar terms. All of these fundamentals of juvenile nonfiction became ingrained in me as a result of my editing *Radioastronomy and Radar* and the other titles in that science series.

However, the graphic standards for nonfiction that prevailed in the early 1960s were very different from those that have characterized the best nonfiction of recent years. *Radioastronomy and Radar,* for example, was published in a trim size of 5½" × 8¼", which meant that the type had to be small and few of the photographs could be given large-scale treatment. Even so, it included more illustrations than most nonfiction titles of the day. Elizabeth Ripley's popular series of artists' biographies (Lippincott) contained a mere smattering of black-and-white illustrations, and they were poorly reproduced. Russell's *Teenagers Who Made History,* which included brief biographies of eight young people from Toscanini to Galileo to Edna St. Vincent Millay—all of whom accomplished great things while still in their teens—featured only a single line drawing of each subject.

When I decided, in 1962, to move on from Criterion, my experience with nonfiction helped me to get my next editorial job at Lothrop, Lee and Shepard. As a tryout for the position, I was asked to do a detailed report on J.J. McCoy's *Animal Servants of Man,* a project that Lothrop's editor- in-chief, Beatrice Creighton, had contracted several years earlier, but had not had a chance to edit. I pointed out that the manuscript was basically solid but would benefit from revision, so after I was hired I was assigned *Animal Servants of Man* as my first Lothrop book.

Encouraged by Creighton, who believed that all children's books should be attractive, we did *Animal Servants of Man* in an oversize 8" × 10" format with black-and-white wash illustrations. The book generated considerable review and sales interest, and several years later Joe McCoy proposed that we do another natural history title about the years-long search for the nesting grounds of the whooping crane.

Even though nonfiction in general seemed to be at a low ebb in the mid 1970s, there were a few signs that pointed to a revival of interest in the genre. Milton Meltzer's 1976 *Horn Book* article, "Where Do All the Prizes Go? The Case for Nonfiction," attracted considerable attention. And a new type of nonfiction book, the photo essay, made a tremendous impact when the first examples appeared on the scene in the late 1970s.

Actually, the concept of the photo essay was not new. *Life* magazine had pioneered the approach with its photo feature stories, and adult publishers had long employed it in art and travel books. It wasn't unknown in the children's field, either. At Lothrop, Beatrice Creighton had used carefully chosen photographs and spacious layouts in such classic nonfiction books of the 1940s as *One God: The Ways We Worship Him* by Florence Fitch (1944) and *Discovering Design* by Marion Downer. Closer in time, author Carla Stevens and photographer Leonard Stevens had collaborated on their sensitive study, *The Birth of Sunset's Kittens* (Young Scott, 1969). But it was really Norma Jean Sawicki, then editor of children's books at Crown, who established the photo essay as a genre unto itself with such titles as *Small Worlds Close Up* by Lisa Grillone and Joseph Gennaro (1978), *The Hospital Book* by James Howe (1981), and *Journey to the Planets* by Patricia Lauber (1982, rev. ed. 1987, 1990). For each of these, and other photo essays she published, Norma Jean insisted on top-quality photographs, reproduced in handsome formats on heavy, expensive paper. As a result of her efforts, the Crown photo essays made a major splash in both the institutional and retail markets, and other publishers soon imitated them.

The timing couldn't have been better for the photo-essay approach. Accustomed to seeing a topic explored largely through visual images on television, youngsters were far more likely to respond to a photo essay than to a typical nonfiction book of the past with its large chunks of type, interrupted only by an occasional line drawing. The photo-essay format not only suited the TV-acclimated attention span of these youngsters, but it fitted neatly into the fast pace of their lives.

Not everyone admired photo essays, however. Some critics felt that by emphasizing the visual and downplaying the verbal, the style pandered to youngsters' tastes instead of attempting to elevate them. Perhaps the term *photo essay* itself was partly to blame. Like all labels, it was often applied indiscriminately to everything from photographic picture books for the very young, to books for the middle grades where the text and the illustrations were in balance—the true photo essay—to heavily illustrated books for older children.

I disagreed then with the critics of photo essays, as I do now, both as an editor and as an author. Perhaps the strength of my feelings stems from the fact that the first book I wrote for children, *The Scarecrow Book* (Crown, 1980), was a photo essay, and it was edited by Norma Jean Sawicki. I often bristled when Norma Jean slashed through some of my favorite passages in the early drafts and scrawled in the margins, "Compress: this rambles too much," or "Cut: not necessary; the illustrations will convey this." But by the time the book reached the final stages of production, I realized she was right. The text hadn't lost anything by being tightened; instead, I could now see that it was stronger than before.

The *Scarecrow Book* certainly wasn't unique. In my opinion, all of the best photo essays and heavily illustrated nonfiction books of recent years display the same sort of tight, economical writing. It's a case where, as Mies van der Rohe claimed of modern architecture, less truly is more.

Led by the interest in photo essays, the juvenile nonfiction area made a quiet but steady comeback in the early 1980s. Unlike the era of the National Defense Education Act and, later, Lyndon Johnson's Great Society programs, this revival wasn't occasioned by any single government act, but rather by a combination of circumstances. Educated young parents were eager to expose their children to challenging books, and these included nonfiction titles as well as fiction. Although national programs dwindled during the Reagan administration, school and public library budgets rose in many localities in the face of pressure from parents, and specialized children's bookstores sprang up across the country to cater to their needs and wants.

Perhaps most significant of all, children in school were still assigned to do book reports on whatever they were studying at the moment—the workings of the sanitation department, life in ancient Egypt, the American Civil War—but many of the standard nonfiction titles from the past had gone out of print in the lean years of the 1970s. Now there was room for good new books to replace them in all of the major subject areas, from natural history to history to pure science to biography.

Both new and experienced authors responded to the call for more nonfiction material. Aiming at the picture-book audience, author-illustrator Gail Gibbons covered a wide range of topics from locks and keys to the development of the modern highway system, and Betsy and Giulio Maestro offered simple but not simplistic treatments of such complex subjects as the framing of the U.S. Constitution. For older children, Jean Fritz examined her Chinese roots; Brent Ashabranner confronted some of American's most pressing social problems; Dorothy Hinshaw Patent brought careful scholarship to a series of books about wild and domestic animals; Milton Meltzer pursued a variety of topics, from a biography of Winnie Mandela to a study of Gentile heroes of the Holocaust; Russell Freedman went from highly visual accounts of sharks and rattlesnakes to equally visual explorations of immigrant kids on city streets and children in the Old West; and I had great fun delving into such offbeat subjects as milk, defensive walls, and the history of eating utensils and table manners.

A few months later, in the spring of 1984, Russell Freedman delivered the manuscript and photographs of *Cowboys of the Wild West* (Clarion, 1985). His editor, Ann Troy, and I took him to a celebration lunch, and over dessert, we discussed ideas for possible future books. We told Russell of our desire to do a group of biographies illustrated with photographs—specifically, biographies of the presidents. Russell's eyes brightened immediately. "I like that," he said, "and Lincoln should definitely be the first. He was a fascinating man, and he was also the first president to be widely photographed."

Delighted by his enthusiasm, we offered Russell a contract then and there. He went on to write the book, and the rest is history, as they say.

Why did *Lincoln* make such an impact? For a combination of reasons, in my opinion. First, it offered—as did the Barth holiday books—a fresh approach to familiar material, demythologizing Lincoln without debunking him, as Mary Burns said in her introductory remarks at the Newbery/Caldecott banquet. Second, like *The Hunt for the Whooping Cranes* and other noteworthy examples of juvenile nonfiction, it told a dramatic true story, recounting the life of one of the most compelling and contradictory figures in American history. And third, its emphasis on the visual, starting with the subtitle, *A Photobiography*, not only reflected Russell's skills as a photo researcher, but also carried forward and developed the best features of the photo-essay approach to nonfiction.

The most significant factor in the book's success was, of course, Russell's accessible yet literate text. In just seventy-four manuscript pages, he offered a many-sided portrait of Lincoln, his family, his colleagues, and his times, proving—if any proof was still required—that the tight, compressed writing style so characteristic of the new nonfiction can result in a profoundly satisfying book. A book that, in the opinion of the Newbery committee, made the year's "most distinguished contribution to American literature for children."

While *Lincoln* is certainly a benchmark in juvenile nonfiction, it's by no means the last word—neither for Russell Freedman nor anyone working in the field. From biography to history to science, the possibilities for entertaining and informative books have barely begun to be tapped. And, with the new emphasis on quality education, the desire of parents to help their children get a leg up on learning, and the increasing use of children's trade books in the classroom, there are thousands of teachers and librarians ready and eager to introduce nonfiction material to young people in stimulating and imaginative ways. All they need are the books.

As a publisher and as an author, I want to help provide these books in the years ahead. It promises to be an exciting time for everyone concerned.

The Nonfiction Scene: What's Happening?

Barbara Elleman
American Library Association

In a speech I gave a few years ago, I likened nonfiction to Cinderella. I said that while picture books are touted for their beauty and design, and fiction is praised for its insights and ingenuity, nonfiction is shunted aside—the stepchild, so to speak, relegated to be the workhorse in the kitchen. And when awards are given out, nonfiction has rarely been at the ball.

While I think this analogy still holds to some extent, there is much evidence of change. If we consider poetry as nonfiction, then one can point to two recent Newbery winners, *A Visit to William Blake's Inn: Poems for Innocent and Experienced Travelers* by Nancy Willard (Harcourt Brace Jovanovich, 1981) and *Joyful Noise: Poems for Two Voices* by Paul Fleischman (Harper and Row, 1988). And Russell Freedman recently captured a Newbery Award for *Lincoln: A Photobiography* (Clarion, 1987), the first biographer to do so since Jean Latham won for *Carry On, Mr. Bowditch* (Houghton Mifflin, 1955) in 1956. Nonfiction has also worked its way into the Newbery Honor Book listings: Patricia Lauber's *Volcano: The Eruption and Healing of Mount St. Helens* (Bradbury, 1986), Rhoda Blumberg's *Commodore Perry in the Land of the Shogun* (Lothrop, Lee and Shepard, 1985), and Kathryn Lasky's *Sugaring Time* (Macmillan, 1983), to name a few. Author Bill Peet's autobiography, *Bill Peet: An Autobiography* (Houghton Mifflin, 1989), joins a few other select nonfiction titles in the Caldecott lineup. Some awards, such as the Society of Children's Book Writers' Golden Kite Award and the Boston Globe–Horn Book Award, have a regular category for nonfiction, and the inauguration of the National Council of Teachers of English Orbis Pictus Award, dedicated to nonfiction, is heartening. Jean Fritz's *The Great Little Madison* (Putnam, 1989) was given the first honor in 1990. It is also satisfying to note that *Publisher's Weekly* now has a category for nonfiction in their monthly listing of children's best-sellers.

By all indications, nonfiction is on its way, and though some of the accolades and attention are still missing, it is surely poised for a grand entrance.

Series Books

While we wait for that to happen, let us look at trends in nonfiction, beginning with series books. In general, these books serve a necessary function in helping children and young people complete their reports, research, and homework assignments. Although often dry and written to a formula, they are organized in a way that allows easy access to facts and information. Their usually straightforward presentations provide much curriculum-matched material that is studded with graphs, charts, time lines, glossaries, and bibliographies. Their prespecified format and style, which may make them tedious and repetitive for reviewers who see them over and over again, are, nevertheless, the meat and potatoes for librarians and teachers meeting students' demands for reports and research material.

As series increase in number, both in the number of series and in the number of titles within a series, it becomes even more important that selectors evaluate each title individually; the reputation of a series is not enough. After analyzing series books for as many years as I have, one notes the same problems cropping up again and again: awkward, simplistic writing; meaningless, poorly reproduced graphics; inaccurate data; and a mismatching of audience to format.

In addition, other, more subtle negatives too often occur. A page full of photographs looks impressive at first glance, but careful scrutiny may yield only superficial or obvious information. Rambling personal accounts may produce some laughs or thoughtful moments, but solid facts will be hard to extract, disappointing and frustrating the young researcher. In the same way, uncaptioned photographs or drawings may be nice for browsing until a child wants to know specifics about the picture for a report. A great camera shot, left uncaptioned, loses an excellent opportunity to inform students and to capture their interest. And where there are no chapter headings, tables of contents, or indexes, information is lost. These problems, of course, are not necessarily confined to series titles, but they are found there with more regularity.

Another problem with series books is the penchant for taking a cohesive subject, breaking it down into many parts, and then publishing each segment as a separate book. For example, I recall a ten-book set about owls, written by the same person, in which each volume had the identical format and the same approach, and each carried a $10.95 price tag. A more useful and less expensive package could have been offered by combining the information into one book, possibly including a comparison of various owls' lifestyles and habitats. This would have added to the presentation and benefitted the reader.

At the other extreme are books so general that their wide overviews are little help at all. For example, a book on animals of the world, including insects, fish, birds, and mammals, along with their environment, protective mechanisms, and geographic habitats, has space for only a few paragraphs for each entry. Animals that live in the mountains, for example, are limited to a two-page spread, including graphics; the result is superficial coverage. In a library, the Dewey classification number would thrust such a book into a general 500 classification, away from other more specific mountain animal books and making it less likely to be found.

Another problematic element of the nonfiction series is in the overlap of common topics, such as space, dinosaurs, prehistoric times, the earth, the planets, and countries of the world. Although each book generally offers a new perspective or piece of data, much of the material has been recycled several times over. Graphics follow the same pattern. In books about space, which need to rely on NASA for photos and graphs, the same illustration appears in a dozen titles.

Interestingly, many series books originate in Great Britain, although translations from Japan and France also appear. This can be a positive element—British nonfiction tends to be more international in scope (perhaps a holdover from the days of the British Empire)—and a plus when discussing such items as population problems, environmental concerns, and oil spills. On the other hand, children who read a book on butterflies, for instance, only to discover that all the displayed varieties are European, will be disappointed. The same goes for history; a British view of the American War between the States may skew rather than help a child's assignment. While British spellings or idioms may add flavor to a fiction title, in works of nonfiction they tend to dull credibility. Furthermore, the inclusion of British bibliographies or addresses of sources that will not be available to American children is annoying when teachers and librarians constantly try to get researchers to use these appended materials.

Individual Titles

The most exciting trend in nonfiction is the single, or nonseries, title. At their best, these books are personalized by the author's deep-seated interest in his or her subject. Hours of research, thoughtful writing, well-chosen graphics, and careful balance between fact and narrative result in books that can be truly termed *literature*. An author's sincere concern for his or her subject is reflected in the writing, often infectiously effecting the reader.

A few years ago I had the opportunity to correspond with Constance Irwin about her book *Strange Footprints on the Land: Vikings in America* (Harper and Row, 1980), and I was impressed when she told me that she had researched the subject for fourteen years. I had the same feeling when listening to Peter Roop tell how he and his wife and coauthor, Connie Roop, traveled from their home in Wisconsin all the way to the coast of Texas to study the migration routes of the whooping cranes for their book *Seasons of the Cranes* (Walker, 1989). This kind of dedication and passion for a subject comes through the written word in a way that a book written on consignment, as series titles usually are, rarely conveys.

This consuming interest can also be extended to picture research. Author Jim Giblin has said that the work he did on *Let There Be Light: A Book about Windows* (Crowell, 1988) included looking for appropriate illustrations, which took almost as much time as the writing. He went on to say that the time was worthwhile, however, as the research resulted in the discovery of new text information that strengthened his final presentation. Inclusion of graphics selected by the author often produces a closer, more meaningful integration of illustration and text.

As we all know, the best kind of nonfiction takes children from where they are and builds on that information, extending their knowledge and stimulating them to further research. Good writers do this naturally, as evidenced in the first chapter of Milton Meltzer's *Columbus and the World around Him* (Watts, 1990). "When the historians tell us that Columbus 'discovered' America, what do they mean?" asks Meltzer. "Surely not that no one knew America was there. . . . It was Columbus who didn't know where he was." Not only does Meltzer immediately involve children and challenge their thinking powers, but he displays a personal enthusiasm that permeates the entire text.

And think what Jean Fritz does with this one sentence from *The Great Little Madison*: "His whole soul, all his passion, all his will were centered in this hot room in Philadelphia where the flies buzzed and the future of the country lay in the hands of 55 unpredictable men." Through those few well-chosen words she gives readers a deeper sense of James Madison and what was going on in Philadelphia than a whole chapter might in a less skillful author's hands.

Fritz's image-producing presentations are famous; one cannot imagine her sharp portrayals shadowed by phonetically spelled out words in bold type. Instead, she, like other top writers, interweaves new terminology into the text, allowing children to grow in their understanding and interest in the subject. Here is the way Kathryn Lasky, in *Dinosaur Dig* (Morrow, 1990), explains erosion: "It is through erosion that fossils long covered are exposed. They literally 'weather out' from the earth. Erosion, in a sense, is the process by which the book is opened and the pages of the story are turned for reading."

Another change that has improved nonfiction is the turn away from fictionalization. For example, it is no longer in vogue to begin a book on raising sheep by having two children visit a ranch and talk about their experience through fictionalized dialogue. Instead, Catherine Paladino in *Spring Fleece: A Day of Sheepshearing* (Little, Brown, 1990) follows several actual sheepshearers as they ply their trade at two different farms. In *Arctic Memories* (Holt, Rinehart and Winston, 1990), author Normee Ekoomiak, an Inuit who grew up on James Bay in northern Quebec, describes his boyhood world of ice fishing, traveling by dog sled, hunting on ice floes, and playing games of blanket toss, using his own words and illustrations that he made of felt appliqués and embroidery to retell legends of his people.

Often books today are written with a you-are-there approach. A visit to the zoo is made real by depicting an actual zoo, with readers following the zookeeper's every step. Ginny Johnston and Judy Cutchins's *Windows on Wildlife* (Morrow, 1990) is such a title, which also has great potential as a read-aloud book. Individual chapters describe how the people at zoos and wildlife parks are working to create natural spaces for the animals. The opening chapter, "Forest for Gorillas," reads with the excitement of a novel.

> Slowly the square, white door of the gorilla building slid open. A huge head appeared, and two dark eyes scanned quickly in every direction. It was the gorilla's first look outside in his twenty-seven years at the zoo in Atlanta, Georgia. Captured as a three-year-old in Africa, the male lowland gorilla had lived alone since then in an indoor cage with bars. Now he was about to enter the outdoor area of his new habitat exhibit. . . . the zoo director, exhibit designers, keepers, and news reporters watched anxiously. They wondered what the gorilla's first reaction to the outdoors would be. (P. 10)

Another example is Helen Roney Sattler's book *Giraffes: The Sentinels of the Savannas* (Lothrop, Lee and Shepard, 1990), which begins with the author meeting a group of giraffes on the road in Kenya. This personal approach continues through the final chapter, "The Future of Giraffes," where she tells about the special problems of studying these gangly creatures. Too fast to be followed, able to elude jeeps in the bush, and too leery of humans to allow attachment of a radio transmitter, these "walking watchtowers," as she calls them, are hard to track. What an inviting way to start a discussion on how naturalists learn about animals.

Use of Graphics

Whether series books or single titles, an important element in the nonfiction scene today, in addition to the increasing numbers, is the way graphics are employed—and constantly being refined. Many series books have led the way in the use of full-color graphics. Franklin Watts's First Books, for example, are being revised and now feature full-color photographs; many revisions in the HarperCollins I-Can-Read-Science series also contain full-color illustrations.

It is not only the visual countenance of the graphics that has changed, but also the substance. Gone for the most part are the meaningless, decorative illustrations of the 1940s and 1950s. When done well, today's visuals are directly connected to the text, are made up of either meticulous, accurately produced drawings or clear, full-color photographs, and have captions that extend the information. An excellent example is Russell Freedman's *Children of the Wild West* (Houghton Mifflin, 1983). The caption accompanying a photograph of a family seen at the doorway of their Oregon cabin points out that the cradle in which a baby sleeps is made of a split packing crate and that a birdcage hangs in the window. Without that informative note, readers might miss two details that help bring these long-ago pioneers to life.

Placement of illustrative matter is also important; if readers cannot easily identify what an illustration is depicting or how it connects to the text, then the impact is lost. Each of Anne Ophelia Dowden's intricate botanical illustrations in *The Clover and the Bee: A Book of Pollination* (Harper and Row, 1990) is positioned for easy reference. Accentuated by the crisp, creamy paper and surrounded with plentiful white space, the drawings seemingly can be plucked off the paper, grasping readers' attention.

Design has also become an important factor, often integral to the text. For instance, in Seymour Simon's *Storms* (Morrow, 1989), white type reversed out of a black background accentuates the photographs of crackling lightning, and in Barbara Bash's *Tree of Life: The World of the African Baobab* (Little, Brown, 1989), the calligraphic type sometimes echoes the thin, spiny tree branches. The placement of the type on the tree trunk or against the grasslands gives an immediacy to the entire work. This device is often found in picture books, but less so in nonfiction; yet when used with care, it can be effective.

Alignment with Picture Books

Another trend today is nonfiction's close alignment with the picture book. Diane Stanley has done an excellent job of portraying through text and illustration the lives of such personalities as Peter the Great (Macmillan, 1986), Queen Elizabeth I (*Good Queen Bess* [Macmillan, 1990]), and Shaka the Zulu King (Morrow, 1988). Stanley's artwork becomes a part of the presentation; through costume, background detail, and architectural style, she allows us to appreciate not only the subjects, but also the time in which they lived. A series that integrates illustration and information successfully is created by the team of Joanna Cole, author, and Bruce Degen, artist. Their highly lauded Magic School Bus series has taught children about urban waterworks, the human body, the earth, and the solar system with great humor, an element too often ignored in nonfiction. Happily, inroads are beginning to be seen as ingenious writers and illustrators learn how to manipulate humor while still maintaining their books' credibility. One of the first author-illustrators to do this was Tomie dePaola. His clever text in *The Quicksand Book* (Holiday House, 1977) explains the makeup of quicksand while a battle of wits goes on between two jungle children; a secondary story finds a monkey setting up a table for tea.

Evaluating Children's Literature

Anyone who has been involved with children's books knows that in the 1980s the field exploded throughout all the major genres and is continuing to rise. According to statistics, close to 5,000 children's books are now being published annually in the United States. Nearly every week brings a telephone call to me from a new publisher asking for information about submitting its books for review. The major publishers continue to increase their seasonal lists, new lines are begun, small presses are flourishing, and publishers of adult books are starting new children's lines. This escalation can be most clearly seen in nonfiction—and especially in series.

For a book-review journal editor, coping with these multiplying numbers can be daunting, especially when you are trying to be current. But more important than the numbers is the criteria used in evaluating them. There are many sources of current reviews—*Booklist, The Horn Book, School Library Journal, Bulletin of the Center for Children's Books, Language Arts,* and *Appraisal* among them. All offer concise, readable reviews of the new books of the season. With time at an essence, teachers might find relying on one or two more manageable. Picking which ones, of course, can be difficult; individual needs and taste will be the deciding factor.

As teachers move more into using children's trade books in the classroom, locating the best of this multitude of books will be a high priority. A new magazine designed around themes can help in this selection process. Published by the American Library Association, *Book Links: Connecting Books, Libraries, and Classrooms* not only identifies the best books, both current and the "tried and true," but gives concise annotations as to their content and suggests ways they might be used with children.

When choosing books or when reading about books, teachers should be aware of what professional reviewers look for in a good nonfiction book. The uppermost concern must be for accuracy and authenticity. If those factors are missing, it does not matter how well the writing flows or how sharply the artwork has been executed. The materials must be up-to-date, avoid stereotypes, make clear distinctions between fact and theory and opinion, and be cognizant of the intended audience.

Another area of concern is approach; the content should transport children to new horizons, provide diverse viewpoints on controversial matters, and discuss interrelationships between topics. Children should be taught early on that there are nearly always two sides to any issue or event, and opposing viewpoints should be introduced. They should also learn that rarely do events happen or people exist in vacuums and that connections between the two are essential.

Organization in books, of course, is especially important. Young readers who are still learning vocabulary while trying to understand content need to be able to extract material with ease. It is necessary to have complete, detailed indexes, glossaries, maps, bibliographies, and other source materials.

The last evaluative point to consider is style. Whether the information is written in a conversational tone or a more formal one, the book needs to create a feeling of reader involvement. The author's own enthusiasm and attitude toward the subject should come through to stimulate readers, to stir their minds, and to lead them to other books on the subject.

Using Nonfiction in the Classroom

This same enthusiasm is an important aspect when sharing nonfiction with children. Whether it is reading books aloud, book talking, or using books in conjunction with the curriculum, adults need to choose titles that spark youngsters' interest. Interweaving poetry, biography, and fiction with nonfiction can produce an interesting approach, regardless of the subject.

Linking fiction and nonfiction can not only be a stimulating exercise, but it can be a good habit to get into--especially with the implementation of literature-based curricula in schools today. Most importantly, it can trigger children's enjoyment of books. There are many forces in our modern world vying for youngsters' attention, and we need to use all our resources to have reading get its share. Let nonfiction be one of these resources. Though often we think only of fiction and picture books as ways to turn kids on to reading, nonfiction is the genre that some children prefer. When this is the case, take advantage of the opportunity to get kids reading. Introduce them to the best, and in return the best will reach out to children. By necessity, nonfiction will continue to be the workhorse of children's books—there to provide reliable facts and information. But, like Cinderella, nonfiction also deserves a place at the ball; it is up to us to see that the door is open and that nonfiction is ushered in to receive the attention it deserves.

Trends and Evaluative Criteria of Informational Books for Children

Frances Smardo Dowd
Texas Woman's University

Nonfiction or informational books have undergone perhaps the greatest revolution of all genres of children's books, and consequently they are receiving deserved attention and respect (Elleman 1987; Epstein 1987). During the past two years, the Newbery Award was given for Paul Fleishman's *Joyful Noise: Poems for Two Voices* (Harper and Row, 1988) and Russell Freedman's *Lincoln: A Photobiography* (Clarion, 1987). Now the Orbis Pictus Award for Outstanding Nonfiction for Children has been established by the National Council of Teachers of English (NCTE) in commemoration of a work by Johann Comenius, *The Orbis Pictus (The World in Pictures),* published in 1657 and considered the first factual book actually planned for children. The Orbis Pictus Award is designed to promote and recognize excellence in the writing of nonfiction which "in recent years has emerged as an exciting, attractive and popular genre" (NCTE 1990).

Nonfiction titles account for at least 70 percent of most library collections in elementary schools and in children's sections of public libraries and 30 percent of the children's book space in bookstores (Cullinan 1989; Fakih 1987). Parents, alarmed with current illiteracy rates, are eager to stimulate their children with factual books, and there is a greater use of children's trade books in the classroom. Librarians, teachers, and parents should be cognizant of trends in publishing and of the specific criteria used to evaluate nonfiction books.

This chapter describes six trends and five major evaluative criteria of children's nonfiction. Specific titles published in the late 1980s that are appropriate for students in kindergarten through sixth grade are used as examples. The evaluative criteria discussed are applicable to

This chapter is an abridged version of an article that originally appeared in the *Journal of Youth Services in Libraries* 4 (Fall 1990): 65–78. © Frances Smardo Dowd. It is reprinted by permission of the author.

"nonfiction or informational literature which has as its central purpose the sharing of information," excluding "textbooks, historical fiction, folklore, poetry" (NCTE 1990).

Trends in Children's Nonfiction

Humor

The inclusion of humor is one trend exemplified in Joanna Cole's Magic School Bus series as well as in Laurene Krasny Brown and Marc Brown's Dinosaurs series. In *The Magic School Bus inside the Human Body* (Scholastic, 1989), a class field trip turns into a fantastic journey transporting students into the human bloodstream, where they experience capillary action firsthand. *Dinosaurs Travel: A Guide for Families on the Go* (Little, Brown, 1988) offers practical tips on packing, traveling by various methods of transportation, eating out, and so on. Cartoon illustrations depict dinosaurs reading a Camptosaurus Fishing Paradise map and flying on Pterosaurs Air. *Bugs* by Nancy Winslow Parker and Joan Richards Wright (Greenwillow, 1987) intersperses rhymed jokes about insects with factual information and authentically detailed scientific diagrams of various species (Fakih 1988). Since children learn through the interaction of the left-brain and right-brain hemispheres, or through logic and creative experiences, this combination of humor and fact is enjoyable, educational, and appropriate for this audience.

Unusual Formats

Combining an unusual format with high-quality construction, including three-dimensional, movable books with pop-ups, pull-tabs, and lift-flaps pertaining to scientific topics, is a second trend in children's nonfiction (Bohning and Radencich 1989a, 1989b; Brodie and Thomas 1989). *Skyscraper Going Up* by Vicki Cobb (Harper and Row, 1987), *Our Living Earth: An Exploration in Three Dimensions* by Gillian Osband and Richard Clifton Dey (Putnam, 1987), and *Journey to Egypt: A UNICEF Pop-Up Book* by Joan Knight (Viking Penguin, 1986) are representative action-book titles on the topics of technological science, physical science, and social studies, respectively. Braille books are also available, such as *Redbird* by Patrick Fort (Orchard, 1988), which explains the basic parts and functions of an airplane in Braille, printed text, and full-color visuals on vinyl pages. All of these unusual formats rely and build upon children's need to learn by doing and manipulating. Since movable pop-up books allow for a degree of concreteness to accompany print, they serve as excellent transitions between the concrete world and the abstract dimension of reading (Abrahamson and Stewart 1982; National Association for the Education of Young Children 1986).

Simplification of Advanced Topics

A third trend is the simplification of advanced topics (particularly in science) for very young audiences. The Talkabout series and the Knowabout series, including *Talkabout Soil* by Angela Webb (Watts, 1986) and *Knowabout Weight* by Henry Pluckrose (Watts, 1988), as well as *Hide and Seek* and other titles by Oxford Scientific Films, are suitable for kindergartners. These books intersperse questions throughout a minimal amount of text per page, do not get too technical, and include numerous full-color photographs. Books in the National Geographic Society's Books for Young Explorers series, such as *Helping Our Animal Friends* by Judith Rinard (1985), introduce science topics to primary-grade children in an age-appropriate manner ideal for short attention spans and limited reading skills.

Emphasis on Graphics and Illustrations

A visual and colorful approach with greater emphasis on graphics and more space devoted to illustrations that convey complex information is a fourth recent development in children's nonfiction titles (Freedman 1986; Giblin 1988). This is essential since books compete for children's attention along with television and videos. Today's readers expect visual variety (Elleman 1987; Giblin 1987). Typical of this trend are *See inside a Submarine* by Jonathan Rutland (Warwick, 1988), which uses cross-sectional drawings to reveal the compartments of a submarine, and *I Can Be a Reporter* by Christine Fitz-Gerald (Children's Press, 1986), which contains a picture dictionary for such terms as *headline, tape recorder*, and *deadline*.

Evidence of Research

In a fifth trend, children's informational books reveal more evidence of research by the author and/or illustrator (Epstein 1987). Documentation is usually in the form of bibliographies, appendixes, or notes about source materials. Aliki informs readers in *A Medieval Feast* (Crowell, 1983) that many of the illustrations were adapted from tapestries and the artwork of medieval craftspeople and artisans. The final pages of *The Story of the Statue of Liberty* by Betsy and Giulio Maestro (Lothrop, Lee and Shepard, 1986) provide additional information, including a table of important dates and people connected with this monument. Documentation is valuable in nonfiction titles for children because it helps them understand that writers and artists must do research—they do not just "invent" facts.

Focus on One Particular Aspect of a Subject

Finally, the approach of children's nonfiction has changed from that of lengthy formulaic text describing an entire topic, to concise writing focusing on one aspect of a topic in order to reveal other characteristics of that topic (Giblin 1987). In *Deadline! From News to Newspaper,* Gail Gibbons (Crowell, 1987) informs readers about newspaper operations by concentrating on a typical day's activities. Aliki conveys facts about the work of paleontologists in *My Visit to the Dinosaurs* (rev. ed. Crowell, 1985) by presenting a first-person account of a young boy's visit to a museum. In this approach, the author tells a story in order to set the scene or create an interesting atmosphere (Giblin 1988). The characteristic that sets nonfiction apart from fiction is emphasis rather than content.

While informational books as well as fiction may tell a story, in the former the storytelling is incidental and perhaps used as an expressive technique. Both genres may include facts, but in fiction, facts may be used only as supportive material, while the story is paramount (Cullinan 1989). Combining story and fact also adds drama. This new approach in nonfiction writing is ideal for children since they are natural storytellers with great imaginative capabilities. They learn best when they can relate new information to what they already know.

Evaluative Criteria

The best informational books are written by authors who thoroughly research their subjects, write about these topics imaginatively, and understand the needs and abilities of children (Sutherland and Arbuthnot 1986). Children's informational books can be evaluated by five major criteria: (1) accuracy/authenticity, (2) content/perspective, (3) style, (4) organization, and (5) illustrations/format. It is important to remember that all five criteria need not apply to each nonfiction book. Books can be of high quality in different ways, depending upon their function or type, such as a brief survey of a broad topic, a life-cycle book, an identification book, a concept picture book for the very young, or a reference book with many facts easily found (Huck, Hepler, and Hickman 1987). However, the following criteria are generally applicable to most types of informational books.

Accuracy/ Authenticity

In order for the first criterion of accuracy/authenticity to be met, the following six requirements should be satisfied: (1) qualified, competent author or specialist as consultant; (2) accurate and current information without significant omissions; (3) avoidance of stereotypes and inclusion of diversity; (4) generalizations supported by facts; (5) clear distinctions among fact, theory, and opinion; and (6) omission of both anthropomorphic and teleological explanations (Huck, Hepler, and Hickman 1987).

Qualifications of the Author

An author's qualifications or competence to write about a particular subject may be confirmed by a list of credentials, such as degrees earned, positions held, professional affiliations and experiences, and other books written (Sutherland and Arbuthnot 1986). *Storms* by Seymour Simon (Morrow, 1989) states that the author has written over one hundred science books for children, many of which are award-winning titles, including at least one book which received the New York Academy of Sciences Children's Book Award.

When authors do not already possess sufficient knowledge to write about a topic, they may rely upon subject specialists to review their work, or they may interview experts and observe operations to gain a better understanding (Cullinan 1989). Gibbons used the latter technique in *Deadline.* On the title page, she gives special thanks to the staff of the *Valley News* in West Lebanon, New Hampshire, United Press International, and *The Times Argus* in Barre, Vermont.

Accurate Information

Accurate, up-to-date, and complete information is essential in all informational books, especially in science books, which, due to rapid technological advances, quickly become dated. Being current is vital in social studies books, too. Books about minority cultures should include facts about contemporary life as well as about heritage in order to convey a realistic and complete picture of society (Huck, Hepler, and Hickman 1987). Whatever the topic—anatomy, geology, technology—simplified terminology should not be substituted if the correct word is not too difficult for children to grasp, since watered-down substitutions can lead to misconceptions and inaccuracies (Sutherland and Arbuthnot 1986).

Avoiding Stereotypes and Conveying Positive Images

It is not sufficient for children's informational books to avoid stereotypes. They should accentuate the positive by illustrating diversity and conveying multicultural images, since children are just developing attitudes about people who are different from themselves. Quality books depict competent female plumbers (as in Dee Lillegard and Wayne Stoker's *I Can Be a Plumber* [Children's Press, 1987]); scientists without glasses, females successfully performing science projects (as in *Experiments with Water* by Ray Broekel [Children's Press, 1988]), and males enjoying cooking (as in the *Better Homes and Gardens New Junior Cookbook* [Better Homes and Gardens, 1981]). Children need to see ethnic minorities in professional positions (as in Gail Gibbon's *Check It Out! A Book about Libraries* [Harcourt Brace Jovanovich, 1985]) and sharing ethnic recipes (as in Jill Krementz's *Fun of Cooking* [Knopf, 1985]). Disabled people who are competent, dressed fashionably, and in mainstream jobs (such as the deaf people in *Look at Hands* by Ruth Thompson [Watts, 1988] and the editor/reporter in a wheelchair in Gibbons's *Deadline!*) should be portrayed (Kobrin 1988). Critical readers need to be especially alert to blatant misconceptions in social studies books, such as those which erroneously categorize certain ethnic groups or nationalities as easygoing, tough, poor, uneducated, and so on (Huck, Hepler, and Hickman 1987).

Generalizations

Children find it easier to locate the main idea and to gather information from a whole page or chapter when the text combines facts with generalizations. In the book *Ants*, Cynthia Overbeck (Lerner, 1982) proceeds from the general to the specific: "Most ants are helpful to people. They eat many pests. Their underground tunnels help make soil healthy." Similarly, Seymour Simon states in *Icebergs and Glaciers* (Morrow, 1987) that glaciers move in two different ways; then he tells and depicts exactly how they move.

Clear Distinctions

Informational books should make clear distinctions among fact, theory, and opinion since children tend to accept what they read as true. Their inexperience can result in difficulties in differentiating among these three levels of truth and at worst can cause them to misinterpret information. Highly qualified writers state clearly and succinctly what is known and what is conjectured. They do not mislead by stating as fact what is still a theory or merely an opinion. Careful use of qualifying phrases, such as "scientists believe," "probably," and "evidence indicates," conveys that the information—whether it is about the ice age, the extinction of dinosaurs, or black holes—is actually a theory rather than a confirmed fact (Cullinan 1989; Sutherland and Arbuthnot 1986).

Avoiding Anthropomorphism and Teleology

Two rhetorical devices that should be avoided in informational books are anthropomorphism and teleology (Kobrin 1988). Writers of animal books should describe each animal in terms that can be substantiated through careful observation, rather than in anthropomorphic terms that ascribe human characteristics to animals, plants, and other inanimate objects (Norton 1987). Baby foxes described as being lonesome, happy, or sad are anthropomorphic (Kobrin 1988). Although most wildlife books are free of this error, it still can be found (Elleman 1987). Teleology transforms a natural event into one that is planned and attempts to explain natural phenomena by assigning a humanlike purpose to plants, animals, or forces. Two examples of this are suggesting that leaves turn toward the light in order to bask in the sun and that "Mother Nature" paints the flowers (Huck, Hepler, and Hickman 1987). In other words, children's informational books should reflect a scientific attitude not only in regard to what is said but also regarding how it is said. Since young children are animistic and accepting of personification in fictional stories, nonfiction writers have a responsibility to exclude teleological and anthropomorphic aspects in children's books in order to foster accuracy.

Content/Perspective

To meet the second major criterion of content/perspective, children's informational books should (1) contain adequate coverage of material for the intended grade level and purpose; (2) present different viewpoints on controversial issues; (3) foster the use of the scientific method and the spirit of inquiry; and (4) discuss interrelationships between subjects (Huck, Hepler, and Hickman 1987).

Different Viewpoints

Presenting both the pros and cons of debatable topics helps children learn to examine issues critically and to realize that authorities do not always agree (Huck, Hepler, and Hickman 1987). Revealing both sides of controversial topics also helps children see that life is not all black and white and that everyone is entitled to his or her own opinion. Whether oil companies should be permitted to drill in wildlife refuges or whether the Arctic's resources should remain undisturbed to preserve the natural environment are two issues discussed from two vantage points in *The Arctic Fox* by Gail LaBonte (Dillon, 1989).

Scientific Method   Informational books should use the scientific method in order to familiarize students with fact finding by means of observation, hypotheses formulation, experimentation, and recording. Using open-ended questions and encouraging and guiding observations are two strategies which can facilitate this problem-solving process. Webb's *Talkabout Soil,* for instance, motivates and assists preschoolers to look around and talk about what they see: "What is soil? Spread some soil out on paper. What can you see? Roots? Dead Leaves, Rock?" Broekel encourages readers to investigate surface tension in liquids in *Experiments with Water*: "You can explore. . . . What happens when you drop oil into a glass of water?"

Interrelationships   Interrelating subjects—particularly linking social problems with science—helps children put facts into a human perspective and understand how these facts can be affected by external factors. Thus the information has relevance to readers and becomes more than isolated facts. The relationship might focus upon health and technology, as in the case of Lillegard and Stoker's *I Can Be a Plumber,* which notes that sanitation problems and sickness can occur from unclean water. Or the author may integrate ecological factors with geography. Elizabeth Tayntor in *Dive to the Coral Reefs: A New England Aquarium Book* (Crown, 1986) discusses damage to coral life caused by souvenir collectors, oil spills, and ocean dumping.

Styles   Quality nonfiction books for children satisfy the criterion of style when they (1) create a feeling of reader involvement, (2) use vivid and interesting language to present information in a clear and direct manner, and (3) convey a positive tone or attitude toward the subject.

Reader Involvement   Games and puzzles, do-it-yourself activities, questions, and use of the second-person point of view to address readers are four techniques authors use to create reader involvement. Both *Ant Cities* by Arthur Dorros (Crowell, 1987) and *Look at Hands* by Thompson encourage reader involvement by the use of culminating projects which require children to make use of the information that they have read. After describing ants and the communities that they maintain, *Ant Cities* describes how to make an ant farm, while *Look at Hands* illustrates various things to do with hands, including feeling different textures of objects and measuring a cubit. Ulla Andersen's use of quotations from twenty-eight young Danes in *We Live in Denmark* (Bookwright, 1984) is another device used to achieve a sense of immediacy, personal drama, and involvement.

Interesting Language   A lively, direct literary style with a vocabulary which is neither conde-scending nor too advanced helps convey information clearly to children. Imagery can be used effectively to add an exciting flavor to the textual material, as in Kathryn Lasky's *Sugaring Time* (Macmillan, 1983), which compares the sparkling sap running clear and bright to "streams of Christmas tinsel." Charles Oz uses vivid language to emphasize a point in *How Is a Crayon Made?* (Simon and Schuster, 1988): "If all the regular size crayons made in the U.S. last year were laid end-to-end around the equator, they would circle the globe four and one-half times."

Positive Attitude   The tone of the text should create enthusiasm, express appreciation for nature, and stimulate curiosity. Tayntor's *Dive to the Coral Reefs* accom-plishes all of this from cover to cover, from the first sentence, "Did you know that there is a city full of fantastic shapes and structures that lies beneath the surface of the sea?" to the concluding remark, "So maybe someday you, too, can put on scuba tanks and explore this fantastic underwater world." A positive tone may stimulate additional reading on the topic, as in the case of Patricia Lauber's *Volcano: The Eruption and Healing of Mount St. Helens* (Bradbury, 1986), which propels readers into other books about volcanoes (Kobrin 1988).

Organization   The fourth evaluative criterion, organization, refers to whether the information is structured clearly and logically with appropriate sub-headings and whether the book has reference aids, such as a table of contents, index, bibliography, glossary, and appendix (Huck, Hepler, and Hickman 1987). To assist children in understanding factual mate-rial, the information should be presented in a clear and logical manner, such as from the simple to the complex. The *Better Homes and Gardens Step-By-Step Kid's Cookbook* (Better Homes and Gardens, 1984) uses this arrangement. The initial pages discuss measuring ingredients; next comes a section of no-cook recipes and breakfast meals; the book con-cludes with longer and more complicated recipes for junior chefs. Factual material might also be organized in a historical or chronological sequence.

Subheadings should be used to break down information into palatable segments, since children cannot readily assimilate large quantities of material. *Know Your Pet: Hamsters* by Anne and Michael Sproule (Bookwright, 1988) includes major subheadings in large, bold type followed by minor subheadings in smaller type to help readers easily locate facts about hamster health, feeding, mating, and so on.

Reference aids in the front, middle, or back of the book offer help to the reader, such as a combination pronunciation guide and glossary in *Rice* by Sylvia Johnson (Lerner, 1985), which contains words shown in bold type in the text. Jennifer Cochrane provides a list of organizations to contact, along with mailing addresses, and a bibliography of books about the environment in *Urban Ecology* (Bookwright, 1988). *See inside a Submarine* by Rutland has a list of important dates pertaining to submarines. Geography books should contain two other reference aids: a world map and a map of the country or place discussed in the book. Inclusion of these two visual aids sharpens children's understanding of relative location as well as their identification of place within a specific locality. *Take a Trip to Malaysia* by Bruce Elder (Watts, 1985) provides both of these types of maps. Any reference aid, including an index or table of contents, is valuable in helping children develop basic research skills.

Illustrations/Format

In order for the evaluative factor of illustrations/format to receive a high rating, the book must contain illustrations which (1) clarify and extend the text, (2) make size relationships apparent, (3) are clearly explained in captions or labels, and (4) contribute to an attractive overall format (Huck, Hepler, and Hickman 1987).

Extend the Text

The adage "a picture is worth a thousand words" is pertinent in evaluating whether the pictures in children's informational books play a vital function in extending or clarifying the text. Gail Gibbons's *Check It Out!* states that "libraries also have special books, services, and equipment for the handicapped," but the illustrations elaborate and go beyond this fact by depicting cassettes, records, large-print books, a librarian visiting a homebound patron, and books that are borrowed by mail. Because children often learn as much from illustrations as from text, it is essential that the visual components of informational books are not merely colorful insertions, but actually relate facts.

Clarify Size Relationships

One way in which size relationships can be clarified is by placing a familiar object next to an unfamiliar one so that children can compare relative proportions at a glance. In *The Story of the Statue of Liberty* by the Maestros, antlike people are shown on scaffolds dwarfed by the statue's immensity. Jerome Wexler's *Flowers Fruits Seeds* (Prentice-Hall, 1987) depicts a child placing watermelon seeds on one thumb and holding a coconut in two hands. In this same book, readers can easily grasp size relationships in inches of petal extension because Wexler placed a ruler in back of a flower. In *Bugs*, authors Parker and Wright denote the actual size of each insect by drawing a line next to each. Still another method of helping children recognize true dimensions is to present actual life-sized figures, as in Joanna Cole's Large as Life books: *Large as Life: Daytime Animals Life Size* (Knopf, 1985), *Large as Life: Nighttime Animals Life Size* (Knopf, 1985), and *Large as Life: Animals in Beautiful Life-Size Paintings* (Knopf, 1990). Certainly the text should state whether a photograph has been magnified and, if so, how many times. Since quantifications can be very abstract and complex for readers and since in many cases children are unfamiliar with the objects described in informational books, any or all of these techniques of visually explaining size relationships can be helpful.

Clear Captions and Labels   Captions and labels need to explain what is being portrayed in the illustrations. For example, the parts of an oil rig (such as a derrick, pipes, drill, helicopter platform, and buoyancy tanks) are clearly labeled in the sketch in *Oil* by Nigel Hawkes (Glouchester, 1985), and the photographs in Johnson's *Rice* are explained through the use of captions.

Layout   Layout on each page should be pleasing so that the total "look" of a book, including the cover, typesize, width of margins, amount of text per page versus illustrations, placement of the text on the page, paper quality, and arrangement of the front and back matter, is attractive (Huck, Hepler, and Hickman 1987). *A World of Things to Do* by the National Geographic Society (1986) is a wonderful example of a book with an eye-catching appearance. Readers are often "turned off" by a book which contains print that is too small, margins that are too narrow, illustrations that are too few in number, or too much continuous text without segmentation by use of color or subheadings.

Conclusion

Examining the trends and evaluative criteria of recent children's informational books indicates that writers are addressing a broad range of subjects—from the making of a crayon, to coral reefs, to bug collecting. Considering this diversity, as well as the manner in which authors are treating nonfiction, it is not surprising that this literature is extremely popular with children and that it is experiencing a sort of renaissance.

II Linking Nonfiction to the Elementary Curriculum

The Voice of Learning: Teacher, Child, and Text

Bette Bosma
Calvin College

We hear a lot about author's voice in the study of literature today. On the book jacket of *The People Could Fly: American Black Folktales* (Knopf, 1985), we read that Newbery Medal winner Virginia Hamilton speaks with a "voice that echoes the slaves and fugitives from her own American black ancestry." Patricia MacLachlan, speaking at a 1987 conference, says she has the "voice of a child in a middle age package." Kathryn Lasky, in her reflections on writing, asserts that "I have always tried hard to listen, smell, and touch the place that I write about—especially if I am lucky enough to be there" (1985, 530).

The use of the term *voice* recognizes the complexity of written communication. It acknowledges the person behind the writing in a broader and deeper sense than the term *point of view*. Within the narrator's voice, the author chooses to speak from the perspective of the first, second, or third person and with either an omniscient or limited viewpoint. Voice embraces point of view, tone, humor, imagination, and bias. The identity of the author and his or her purpose for writing are revealed in the narrative voice.

Recognizing and understanding voice makes learning personal and real in social studies, science, mathematics, the fine arts, and other required curricula in school. The voice in subject areas offers an irresistible vitality that draws the learner to interact with the text and the context of the reading situation.

A common goal of teachers in all subject areas is to teach the content in such a way that students gain knowledge and interest and become independent learners. We know they need to develop a knowledge base of the content before they are able to make independent inquiries. However, this knowledge will not develop without the nurturing of curiosity, excitement, and appreciation for learning. Each subject has a unique identity that must be unfolded and revealed to students in order for them to know and appreciate that body of knowledge. From social studies we want pupils to see their place in history by hearing from people and places in the political/social world. Science classes can lead them to appreciate their physical/natural world and to be filled with wonder and excitement for discovery. Mathematics shows the order of the universe and the consistency of order. The fine arts open their lives to entertainment, appreciation, and creative involvement.

How do we guide our students to recognize this voice of learning? Their own personal voice is nurtured in a learning environment that links the students' prior knowledge with a curiosity to know more. In the following pages, let us consider the teacher, textbooks, and literature as communicators in the classroom. In addition, the students' voice of inquiry is addressed in relationship to encounters with informational books.

The Teacher as Communicator

First of all, teachers become the communicators. They tap the vast background they possess from studying the field and distill, synthesize, and select the information which fits the time, the class, and the occasion for study. The enthusiasm of the teacher for the subject is passed on to the students. Teachers may choose to relay information with an authoritarian voice with little or no enthusiasm, or with a voice of inquiry and wonder. If the former is chosen, students tend to be content with having learned all they need to know. Teachers will perceive themselves as information givers and the students as receivers. Students will study to pass the test, but not to learn beyond the classroom.

On the other hand, if the voice of inquiry is used, students are apt to be stimulated to learn more on their own. Teachers communicate the message that they do not know everything: there is a world of knowledge for the students and teacher to explore together. This is a more comfortable role for the teacher as well. The field of knowledge in each subject area increases at an amazing rate, and one cannot be expected to be an authority in every field. Students become actively involved with the teacher in turning to new sources for information and in analyzing and evaluating the information. The role of the teacher is to provide strategies and opportunities for learning and to project enthusiasm for wanting to learn. A variety of media and experiences should be utilized, but the topic in this chapter is confined to material in print.

The Textbook as Communicator

In subjects such as social studies, science, and mathematics, a textbook is available in most schools. For students to be able to construct meaning from text, reading strategies must be taught. Setting a purpose for reading, assuming and maintaining a questioning attitude toward print, recognizing the text organization, and selecting pertinent information are examples of strategies needed. Applying these strategies to textbooks poses a problem for some readers. The students in each classroom represent a wide range of reading ability. Some textbooks are poorly organized, or the concepts are presented with such great density that the selection of pertinent information is difficult, even for the skilled reader. In some textbooks, the narrator asks questions which involve the reader before introducing a new topic. But often the voice of the textbook narrator is distant, rational, and authoritarian, though not objective. Textbook editors and authors must make many choices from all the information available, and what they select is influenced by their beliefs and attitudes. The more distant the voice of the narrator, the less involved and less critical the reader becomes. The reader tends to accept textbook authority passively, without interacting with the text or recognizing the choices that were made in presenting the information.

Informational Trade Books as Communicators

The third source of information is children's literature. Poetry, historical fiction, realistic fiction, folk literature, and fantasy contribute to learning in each subject area. However, I confine my attention here to the genre of informational books and biography, two nonfiction categories. Well-written informational books are an essential tool for teachers who are setting out to accomplish the goal of communicating knowledge and interest in a subject. Informational books are available in each subject area taught in elementary and secondary schools. The primary reason that these books are effective is that they provide a personal voice. The author shares with the reader a delight in the subject, a questioning or credulous stance toward information discovery, and a unique style of imparting information. That has not always been true of this genre. School libraries still contain many older books in which the information is set forth as impersonally as in a textbook. The personal voice is lacking in the book written simply for the purpose of stating facts. It is the personal voice of the author of informational books that makes recent nonfiction books an important influence in the classroom. Teachers can assist students in identifying and understanding the author's voice so that they become more effective readers. One simple way is to refer to the author by name frequently. Readers do not think of the voice that they are hearing through the book if they do not associate the writing with a person. Recognizing the person invites a critical stance; the reader can be directed to look for evidence of the author's point of view, attitude, and degree of humor or curiosity toward the subject. Strategies for directing the reader's attention toward the author's identity are suggested in the rest of this chapter.

Informational Books in Social Studies

The wide range of reading ability in a typical classroom is a problem when using a textbook. This problem can become an exciting challenge when informational books are used. Having a variety of nonfiction trade books makes it possible to provide reading material for every reader in the classroom. The reader who has trouble with the density of concepts in a textbook about the Revolutionary War can gain the same concepts through the spritely, historically accurate writing of Jean Fritz. Fritz uses unusual factual details to bring events and people to life and only includes conversations when she has a documented source for them. This approach to history can be shared by reading one of Fritz's books aloud to the class. Begin by encouraging students to hear the author's voice in her writing, and ask students to look for evidence as you read. Stop frequently, modeling and asking questions that direct their attention to process. For example, when reading *And Then What Happened, Paul Revere?* (Coward-McCann, 1973), ask students what mental picture they envision when you read the following:

> In 1735, there were in Boston 42 streets, 36 lanes, 122 alleys, 1,000 brick houses, 2,000 wooden houses, 12 churches, 4 schools, 418 horses (at last count) and so many dogs that a law was passed prohibiting people from having dogs that were more than 10 inches high. (P. 5)

Discuss with students how the author effectively draws the reader into the scene. Compare this account with a social studies textbook, such as *America's History*, a fifth-grade text published by Ginn and Company (Armbruster, Mitsakos, and Rogers 1986). The book names Boston frequently, but describes it only as a growing city. Paul Revere's contribution to the Revolutionary War is stated in three sentences:

> As the British began their midnight march, the colonists flashed a signal from the steeple of Boston's Old North Church. Paul Revere and William Dawes were waiting in the night. They jumped onto their horses and rode to warn the colonists of the soldiers' approach. (P. 154)

The humor in Fritz's books shows her own delight in the subject, and her enthusiasm is contagious. After reading from one of Fritz's books, discuss with students how she uses humor. Such a modeling session should enable readers to read other books on their own and to reflect more skillfully on what they are reading. Have books available that vary in reading difficulty so that children can be challenged at their own ability level. Fritz becomes an objective observer in *Traitor: The Case of Benedict Arnold* (Putnam, 1981), a book for middle-school readers. Grade-five textbooks generally make no reference to Benedict Arnold, but his name does appear in grade-eight texts. *Let Freedom Ring*, a Silver Burdett textbook, begins a two-paragraph account with the heading *Arnold's Treason* and concludes that his actions made no difference in the outcome of the war (Brown, Robinson, and Cunningham 1980, 160).

Read aloud a textbook account of Benedict Arnold's role in the Revolutionary War and then an episode from Fritz's book. Ask students how the two accounts are similar and how they are different. Encourage them to compare which facts are included or omitted. How does that influence their understanding of Arnold's role? Ask them to consider whether the textbook account was neutral and to show evidence to support their answers. Does being objective mean being neutral? Such questions can stimulate lively discussions in a classroom. The degree of understanding and enthusiasm that children develop for reading on their own makes the amount of time spent in discussion worthwhile.

Numerous and attractive photographs or artwork in informational books allow readers to visualize the cities and countries that they study. *A Visit to Washington, D.C.* by Jill Krementz (Scholastic, 1987) takes the reader on an informative tour of the capital. The endpapers feature a clear map, labeling the places described in the text. A more complex sense of the city is received from Brent and Jennifer Ashabranner in *Always to Remember: The Story of the Vietnam Veterans Memorial* (Putnam, 1988). The memorial is presented through the eyes and emotions of the people who come to visit.

The social studies teacher can accommodate the wide range of reading ability in the class more easily with trade books than with a single textbook. The concepts become more relevant through the personal voice of the writers and therefore more comprehensible to the reader. Biographies and informational books can be used along with textbooks to engage the reader in critical thinking.

Informational Books in the Sciences

The author's voice comes through loud and clear in the field of ecology. In commenting on his nonfiction books on ecology, Laurence Pringle states, "My voice is not a bland, neutral one, with equal space and weight given to opposing interests, and I avoid any claims of strict objectivity" (1989, 378). His writing reflects his love and appreciation for the environment and an impatience with abusers of our planet.

In *The Only Earth We Have* (Macmillan, 1986), Pringle documents astounding generalizations with facts. Is his evidence adequate to support his statements? To answer that question, other books should be available so that students can compare sources. Ask them to find evidence that Pringle is trying to persuade the reader rather than relate facts. As students consider and explain their choices, they will verbalize what they are thinking.

Seymour Simon is an author of children's informational books who has a gift for explaining complex subjects clearly. The computer-illiterate of any age can learn from Simon's simply written books, such as *The BASIC Book, Bits and Bytes: A Computer Dictionary for Beginners, How to Talk to Your Computer,* and *Meet the Computer* (all Crowell, 1985). Keep these books near the computer center for children to consult. Simon uses facts to create vivid images for his readers so that they can understand and remember what they read. "I want books to excite kids about science, to get them enthusiastic about things that I am enthusiastic about," states Simon, "and I only use information as a means of exciting them" (quoted in Micklos 1990, 32). He has written over one hundred books on a variety of science topics, all meticulously researched.

Informational books in the sciences offer the teacher a forum for introducing controversial topics and for guiding readers to recognize the bias of the author. Complex scientific concepts are clarified by capable authors. Trade books, therefore, can help students recognize causal relationships and analyze their own attitudes and ideas.

Informational Books in Mathematics

Mitsumasa Anno invites young readers to share his fascination with numbers. In endnotes to *Anno's Counting Book* (Crowell, 1975), he claims that children are natural mathematicians and that they are performing basic mathematical feats when they try to bring sense and order into whatever they observe. Each one of his books is a mathematical adventure, from associating number concepts in *Anno's Counting Book* to puzzling over *Anno's Mysterious Multiplying Jar* (Philomel, 1988) or *Anno's Math Games* (Philomel, 1987). Each book includes notes that help adults understand Anno's world of imagination and that enhance their sharing of the book with children.

The imaginative illustrations by Steven Kellogg and the clear text of author David M. Schwartz in *How Much Is a Million?* (Lothrop, Lee and Shepard, 1985) and *If You Made a Million* (Lothrop, Lee and Shepard, 1989) offer a forceful and humorous presentation of number concepts and earning money. Detailed endnotes by the author make each picture book a valuable source for older children as well as primary-grade learners. Both Anno and Schwartz use a voice that is imaginative and playful, inviting a response from the reader.

Two important roles that trade books play in mathematics are to clarify abstract number concepts and terms and to show the reader the importance of mathematics in today's world. The books introduce children to people who use humor and a sense of wonder to make mathematical knowledge relevant. These books are appropriate for reading aloud at the beginning of a mathematics class or as a source for problem solving.

Informational Books in the Cultural Arts

Many children first encounter the cultural arts in literature. Books introduce them to songs and games, and the beautiful illustrations in picture books build a foundation for appreciating art. Tomie dePaola encourages the young artist in *The Art Lesson* (Putnam, 1989), which is a story of his own beginning as an artist. He writes with a humorous style, as does Karla Kuskin in her delightful *The Philharmonic Gets Dressed* (Harper and Row, 1982). In Kuskin's book, the young reader sees that stately musicians are ordinary people who get dressed to go to work. Before reading either of these books aloud, ask the listeners to think about how the author is sharing with the audience a love of art or music. After the book is read, chart the responses from the students. Reread parts of the book, if necessary, to elicit more response. Conclude with a statement about how authors write in different ways to share their feelings about a subject.

Theater Magic: Behind the Scenes at a Children's Theater by Cheryl W. Bellville (Carolrhoda, 1986) brings the reader right into the theater with this invitation: "When you leave the familiar world outside and enter a dimly lit theater, you can let your imagination go and become a part of a story from any time and place" (p. 6). This is a book that children can read on their own after they have been guided in using the strategies explained in this chapter, or they can use it as a model for their own productions.

A trip to Paris with Linnea offers a unique presentation of Monet's paintings and a childlike explanation of impressionism. *Linnea in Monet's Garden* by Christina Bjork (Farrar, Straus and Giroux, 1987) was translated from the Swedish language and includes information about museums and other places to visit in Paris, as well as interesting facts about Monet's life and family. The book could be used in an art class as a source of information about painting and impressionism and as a basis of discussion about appreciating art. Ask students how Linnea shows the readers that she loves Monet's paintings.

Informational books assist both teachers of the arts and classroom teachers by offering an appealing array of aesthetic presentations. Beauty, rhythm, humor, and clarity of expression invite readers to add their voices in appreciation of the arts.

The Students' Voice in Encountering Informational Books

Students are not consulted when textbooks are chosen for their school. However, when the classroom contains a variety of informational books, children become actively involved in the selection of books. This promotes students' ownership of learning and implies that the teacher trusts and respects their judgment. Teachers provide guidance in making judgments by involving the pupils in planning.

A teacher using informational books instead of a prescribed textbook constantly asks questions such as the following in a process of self-evaluation:

What did my students learn?

Where was extension or support needed?

What do interactions between students and their work on group and individual projects tell about the quality of learning?

Such questions can be asked directly of students as well. In responding to their own and their group members' work, students clarify for themselves what they know, what questions they still have, and what they need to have clarified in their reading. They exercise judgment on the materials they are using and the learning experiences in which they are participating.

One sixth-grade teacher defines with the children the expected learning outcomes during a unit-planning period. Students are involved in determining criteria for both the knowledge and the process components of learning. While they are working on the unit of study, students are responsible for weekly reports that assess the following areas:

1. Process—students make notations about understanding the material, vocabulary needs, and rate of progress toward self-developed goals.
2. Knowledge—students prepare a progress report on what is being learned.
3. Presentation—students state how they plan to present learnings to the class, or present a plan for evaluating the presentation when finished.

After completing one unit of study, students use the form in Figure 1 to evaluate the books that they have consulted. The teacher introduces the chart by modeling responses with a book that is familiar to most students. This evaluation makes students more aware of what a good informational source should contain and improves their ability to select sources in the next unit. The evaluation is usually done with partners, since in most cases more than one child uses the book. The activity produces lively discussions as children try to reach consensus on some of the questions, and leads to a sense of ownership. Students feel that their voices are heard in selecting books, in assessing their own progress, and in preparing an evaluation of informational books, which they share with their classmates.

Conclusion

Children who are excited about learning are the ones who have a voice in what and how they learn. They see that what they learn in school relates to the world around them.

Authors who bring excitement into the classroom are captivated by their subjects and are able to use vivid language and a vigorous style to kindle the curiosity of the reader. A variety of voices can be heard: humorous, cajoling, curious, delighted, respectful, hopeful. The artistry of the book comes in the communication of knowledge. Of course the book must be authentic and exact in its content, but research without personal artistry places the informational book close to the level of a textbook.

The reader responds to the active voice of the writer of informational books and, with the guidance of enthusiastic teachers, will be eager to read more and to communicate to others what has been learned.

Figure 1
Student evaluation of
information books.

Student Evaluation of Information Books

Author

Subject

+ Good   ✓ OK   − Poor

Format (What it looks like)

1. Is the print easy to read?

2. Are binding and paper of good quality?

3. Are the table of contents and index easy to use?

Quality of content (What's in it)

4. Is the information up-to-date for the time the book was published?

5. Are statements supported with facts?

6. Does the information given match what you expected to find in the book?

Author's style (How the book is written)

7. Does the author write in clear language?

8. Does the author explain with enough detail?

9. Is the information well organized?

Illustrations (drawings, charts, photographs)

10. Do they help your understanding of the text?

11. Do the pictures make you want to read the book?

Title

On the Road to Literacy: Pathways through Science Trade Books

Marjorie Slavick Frank
Manhattan College and Bronx College

Recently I had occasion to talk with several fourth and fifth graders about their science classes. The group included boys and girls from various ethnic backgrounds in New York City. During the conversation I learned that the children spent most of their class time engaged in hands-on experiences during which they asked questions and made observations, inferences, and measurements. I also learned that they kept science journals in which they recorded their work, their thinking, and their conclusions. For homework, the children periodically read from a textbook and answered teacher-prepared questions that tapped reasoning as well as recall skills. Overall, the children were enthusiastic about what they were learning in science class and about science in general.

The children's descriptions represented the incarnation of a model science program—a predominance of hands-on experiences, student-generated record keeping, and the textbook used as a resource, not a curriculum. At the very least, the descriptions compared favorably to the National Science Teachers Association position statement (1986) regarding science education for middle-school and junior high students and to the research-based viewpoints of leading science educators (Shymansky, Kyle, and Alport 1983; Yager 1987). In light of this seeming confluence of theory and practice, I was all the more surprised at the outcome of my conversation with the fourth and fifth graders.

Before the children and I parted, I asked them to draw pictures of a scientist at work. Because of their nontextbook-based experiences in science, I expected to see a rich diversity of drawings (Powell and Garcia 1988). However, their drawings were sufficiently consistent that the examples shown in Figures 2 and 3 can be taken as representative. The cause of my surprise was the wholly stereotypic

Figure 2
Child's drawing of a scientist.

Figure 3
Child's drawing of a scientist.

nature of the representations—a white male, complete with spectacles, woolly hair, lab coat, pocket pens, Bunsen burner, and test tubes, working alone in a laboratory. In present-day vernacular—a lonely nerd.

It seemed apparent to me that despite the children's generally superior experiences in science, they were missing out on at least one important dimension of scientific literacy: an understanding and appreciation of the real work of real scientists. While children themselves were encouraged to act and think as scientists, their concepts about scientists and scientific inquiry remained naive. Apparently they had not made the connection between the similarity of their school-based experiences and the work of real scientists.

One way to help the children make this connection would be to invite to the classroom a succession of scientists—men and women of color as well as white males—to describe their work and answer questions. However, such an approach is not usually feasible; nor is it necessarily the most effective strategy. Talks with scientists would likely be brief expositions that telescope the work of a lifetime into thirty to sixty minutes. While children may enjoy such talks, their value as a learning experience may depend upon the idiosyncrasies of the speakers, such as personality and speaking style, instead of the message. In the hands of an inexperienced speaker, even the most exciting work can seem obscure and pedestrian.

Nonfiction literature—real stories about real scientists doing the real work of science—is a viable alternative. Like other types of literacy, children can move toward scientific literacy on pathways that lead them to construct meaning actively through story.

In the next several pages, I will discuss what it means to be scientifically literate in the late twentieth and the twenty-first centuries and will explore how nonfiction can reveal aspects of scientific literacy that can be difficult to access through other instructional strategies.

Scientific Literacy— Definition and Exploration

While the notion of literacy has emerged as the instructional goal of various disciplines, the term itself has almost as many interpretations as it has users. Educators and other professionals in many fields continue to strive for a clear definition. Until the publication of *Science for All Americans* in 1989, the field of science education was no exception.

In 1985, the American Association for the Advancement of Science (AAAS) began a three-phased initiative called Project 2061. The purpose of the first phase of Project 2061 was to prepare a set of recommendations "on what understandings and habits of mind are essential for all citizens in a scientifically literate society" (AAAS 1989, 3). To that end, the AAAS appointed a group of distinguished scientists and educators to the National Council on Science and Technology Education. The outgrowth of their three-year effort was *Science for All Americans*, a fully articulated set of recommendations concerning the substance and character of science education in the United States. The text begins with a discussion of scientific literacy:

> Scientific literacy . . . has many facets. These include being familiar with the natural world and respecting its unity; being aware of some of the important ways in which mathematics, technology, and the sciences depend upon one another; understanding some of the key concepts and principles of science; having a capacity for scientific ways of thinking; knowing that science, mathematics, and technology are human enterprises, and knowing what that implies about their strengths and limitations; and being able to use scientific knowledge and ways of thinking for personal and social purposes. (P. 4)

Having read this definition of scientific literacy, readers might now be thinking: "Fine, it sounds good, but what does it really mean? How does it translate into classroom practice? And where do science trade books fit in?"

Perhaps the most appropriate response to these questions comes directly from nonfiction literature, specifically through the voice of Marian Calabro, author of *Operation Grizzly Bear* (Four Winds, 1989), the exciting story of a twelve-year study of grizzly bears in Yellowstone National Park. The study was carried out by Frank C. Craighead, Jr., and John Craighead (brothers of the award-winning author and naturalist Jean Craighead George) from 1959 to 1971 and has provided the basis for much of our current knowledge about these once-endangered animals.

In addition to being a rich source of information about grizzly bears, the book could help readers, such as the fourth and fifth graders that I visited, construct a more accurate concept of the work of scientists and the nature of scientific inquiry. What follows in Table 1 is a series of excerpts from *Operation Grizzly Bear*, with annotations highlighting the aspects of scientific literacy revealed in each excerpt.

While *Operation Grizzly Bear* is especially rich in insights into the nature of science, scientific habits of mind, the scientific endeavor, and the interaction of science, society, and technology, it is not unique. *Turtle Watch* by George Ancona (Macmillan, 1987) provides younger readers with the possibility of similar insights. *Turtle Watch* is the story of a team of Brazilian oceanographers—one woman and three men—working to save the endangered sea turtles off the northeast coast of Brazil. Their efforts, which include educating and enlisting the cooperation of the people in the surrounding community, gently but clearly illustrate the intersection of science and society. Two children in the town become particularly important to the scientists' work as they discover and help to save the eggs in a turtle nest overlooked by the professionals. Ancona's forthright text draws the reader into the narrative, while his remarkable black-and-white photographs lend a substantive and contextual reality to the events that might otherwise be difficult to attain.

Scientific literacy includes the understanding that science is neither static nor authoritarian (AAAS 1989). The relevance of this concept is illustrated regularly in newspaper reports of new insights into prevailing theories and revisions of accepted explanations. Patricia Lauber has captured this same dynamic view of science in *The News about Dinosaurs* (Bradbury, 1989). Of the many dinosaur books to choose from, this title is unique in revealing scientific reasoning processes as well as the tentative nature of much scientific knowledge. Beginning with the notion that dinosaurs were a kind of reptile, Lauber examines the standard conclusions about dinosaurs one by one, each time demonstrating how the conclusion has been revised in light of new evidence. Her sensitivity to the continuing tentativeness of our knowledge is even revealed in the verb structures she chooses. Compare the following paragraphs:

> Most of today's reptiles do not take care of their young. The young find their own food. No adult protects them from animals that want to eat them. Scientists used to think dinosaurs did not take care of their young, either.
> THE NEWS IS:
> At least some dinosaurs do seem to have cared for their young. They seem to have tended the young and guarded them. (P. 26)

In the first paragraph, when presenting conclusions that can be supported through direct observation, Lauber uses the simple present tense to suggest certainty. In the second paragraph, when

Table 1
Text Passages Promoting
Accurate Concept
of Scientists
and Scientific Inquiry

Excerpts	Annotations
Frank and John Craighead came to Yellowstone National Park in 1959 to study grizzly bears. . . . They knew that *Ursus arctos horribilis*, as the grizzly bear is classified scientifically, had been named an endangered species: one in danger of becoming extinct. But for the most part, the grizzly was a mystery. How did it live? Why did it die? There were plenty of stories but surprisingly few facts. Most people knew only that the great bear was in trouble. Together, the Craigheads formed the idea of a new, joint project. Its purpose was as bold as it was simple: to gather the kind of information that could help save the endangered, magnificent grizzly bear. (Pp. 1–2).	*The story and the study begin with a series of questions, modeling one of the most important aspects of scientific inquiry. The importance and processes of gathering evidence on which to base answers to questions is modeled through the remainder of the book.*
The study was headquartered in Canyon laboratory, a big, old, wooden building. No test tubes or jars of formaldehyde could be found there. The lab was filled with long wooden tables, maps, data form sheets, and files. Citizen band radios, headsets, speakers, antennas, and receivers were all around. Imprints of bear paws adorned the walls. (P. 13) Frank Craighead took up his large-caliber rifle and aimed. Bull's eye! Forty feet away, a grizzly bear whirled toward him. A dart hung from its neck. It had been shot with a hypodermic needle containing a drug that would keep it motionless for a short time. (P. 17)	*Descriptions like these, plus photographs of the lab and of the Craigheads at work, help children's concepts about the setting of scientific inquiry approximate those of the literate community. They also help break down stereotypes of the lone scientist at work.*
The first task was to weigh the grizzly. This one was easy to handle, because she was small and light. The men rolled her into a nylon net rope attached to a scale on their pickup truck. They hoisted her up and took the reading: 175 pounds. John nodded and smiled at his brother. When they first saw the bear, Frank had guessed that she weighed 180 pounds. The accuracy of his observation was very important, because the bear's body weight told the scientists how much drug to administer. (P. 19)	*This passage illustrates the interdependence of science, mathematics, and habits of mind associated with the application of thinking skills—in this case the appropriate use of mathematical estimates.*
Wes [one of the Craigheads' assistants] was busy measuring the bear. She was four feet, eight inches tall. . . . He quickly made some other notes: footpads eight inches, neck circumference twenty inches, . . . general condition excellent. And he made a plaster mold of her right front paw. Her five claws alone were almost as long as Wes's fingers. (P. 20)	*Passages like this one help reveal the importance of accurate measurement in science as well as the process of acquiring data.*
Radio-tracking, also known as telemetry, was the break-through the Craigheads needed. . . . So while John spent his winters analyzing biological data from the study, Frank turned his attention to telemetry. With the help of a friend and ham radio operator, Hoke Franciscus, he drew up some requirements for a transmitter-collar system that could be used to track grizzlies in mountainous country. (P. 27) With these specifications . . . , Frank contacted several electronics companies. . . . Eventually Frank found a sympathetic ear at the Philco Corporation, a famous maker of radios and televisions. (P. 28) And so began a year of tests. . . . The engineers worked on making the smallest transmitters feasible. The study team worked on attaching them to silvertips. Neither job was easy. The Craigheads made twenty-seven attachment tests in all. . . .	*Here the interdependence of science and technology is illustrated, with each field of endeavor drawing on and contributing to the other. In addition, the passage reveals the notion that science is a human endeavor where failure as well as success is possible.*

Only one prototype collar was a success. (P. 29)

Everyone knew that grizzly bears wandered far and wide in search of food and mates. But no one know how far.

And everyone knew that grizzlies denned up for the winter. But no one knew exactly when or where.

Now these mysteries could be solved. (P. 37)

By tracking silvertips to their dens each autumn and returning to explore in the spring, the Craigheads made many discoveries. They found that every grizzly den is . . . cleverly located and constructed. . . . They also learned that grizzlies almost always dig their own dens, instead of using ready-made caves, and that they seem to excavate new dens each year rather than reuse old ones.

But the brothers wanted to unlock more of the mysteries of hibernating grizzlies. How warm was a den? How deeply did a grizzly sleep?

Determined to find answers, winter after winter the team approached grizzly dens. Each time the growling inhabitants sent them on their way. . . .

The scientists had to face facts. The conditions were simply not in their favor. Yet they weren't about to give up. If they couldn't safely study *Ursus arctos horribilis* in winter, they'd study its cousin *Ursus americanus*—the American black bear, which hibernates in basically the same way. (P. 51)

So the Craigheads began to explore the idea of radio-monitoring bears in their dens from afar. It was a logical step beyond direct observation and radio-tracking.

By fall 1969, the experiment was under way. With help from NASA and the National Geographic Society, the weather satellite Nimbus became the team's newest research tool.

The satellite belonged to NASA. It circled the earth hourly, gathering data. Seven hundred miles above Yellowstone, it read the temperature of a hibernating black bear and the amount of light in its den.

The data was beamed to a dish in Fairbanks, Alaska, then transmitted to the Goddard Space Flight Center in Maryland. It came to the Craigheads in the form of computer printouts, to be studied in the comfort of their warm winter offices. (P. 56)

The year 1967 was a turning point for "Operation Grizzly Bear." (P. 81)

. . . Yellowstone had a new superintendent and head biologist. . . . They disagreed with Frank and John on many points—most of all on the closing of the dumps where grizzlies fed.

Park officials had been considering dump closures for a while. It was part of a plan to restore America's national parks to their original, primeval state. . . .

John and Frank foresaw disaster if the dumps were closed abruptly. They warned that such a move was almost guaranteed to force hungry grizzlies into campgrounds. (P. 82)

A battle had begun. At stake were the Craigheads' freedom of speech, the right to conduct independent research in America's national parks, and the survival of Yellowstone's grizzly bears. (P. 84)

Passages such as this one reveal how scientists work to develop and expand the knowledge base of science and how they provide windows onto science as a human enterprise.

The perseverance of the Craigheads in their attempt to learn more about the grizzlies models another important dimension of scientific inquiry.

Here, Calabro sheds light on the limitations of science as a human enterprise while focusing on the resiliency of scientists to solve problems by applying their understanding of the ultimate unity of nature.

Scientific inquiry, by nature, is a collaborative effort. Here, Calabro reveals how scientists and agencies from various disciplines work together toward a common end.

Calabro reveals the interaction between science and society by providing a detailed account of the conflict between the Craigheads and the National Parks Department over management of the grizzlies in Yellowstone.

presenting conclusions based on inference from fossil evidence (which is described in the next paragraph of text), she chooses a verb structure that suggests tentativeness. While many students may not be conscious of these subtle shifts in syntax, such changes reinforce the overarching message of the text and can themselves be a focus of discussion and a model reflecting the craft of science writing.

Toward Scientific Literacy

The three books described above share a common, but important, characteristic: a narrative, storylike approach to nonfiction, in which information, characters, setting, plot, and theme are all threads of a tightly woven tapestry. As such, these books, and others like them, can work surprisingly well as read-alouds for whole-class listening and discussion.

Shared learning experiences and regular read-aloud sessions have broad support as strategies to enhance learning and literacy (Trelease, 1985). Applying these strategies to carefully selected works of nonfiction can add depth and breadth to the learning experience. Using them within a larger pedagogy can further enhance their value.

Similar to a constructivist view of reading and writing acquisition (Graves 1978; Pearson and Tierney 1984; Rumelhart 1980), developing ownership of science concepts is a process of change (Anderson 1987). In the former, learners' concepts of print evolve until they match those of the literate environment. In the latter, the change is from naive or incomplete conceptions of natural phenomena, for example, to mature conceptions that reflect the current understandings of the scientific community (Anderson 1987). Explaining, experiencing, and evaluating—some of the processes scientists use in their exploration of the natural world—are also processes that can contribute to the development of scientific literacy in children.

Explaining consists of interacting with a phenomenon and then articulating an explanation for this phenomenon prior to participating in learning experiences related to the phenomenon. Asking learners to dress up like, to draw, or to describe a scientist, as I did, is a kind of explaining strategy. From the teacher's standpoint, the outcome of the explaining phase is a window onto students' naive conceptions (prior knowledge), thought processes, and knowledge base. The scene observed through the window can then be used to plan learning experiences that lead students from their current conceptions to those that more closely approximate accepted scientific theory. From the students' standpoint, the outcome is a record of their thinking to be preserved for later evaluation.

Experiencing consists of participating in learning experiences related to the phenomenon under study. Throughout this phase, nonfiction literature can play a pivotal role in the learning process. For example, reading *Operation Grizzly Bear* and then discussing the aspects of the story highlighted in the commentary could form the basis for a learning experience that helps children perceive the relationship between their own work in science class and the work of real scientists. From the standpoint of classroom management, the story could be read aloud in segments by the teacher, read in pairs by the learners, or used as reference material in cooperative groups.

Several characteristics of nonfiction literature make it particularly well suited for use in a cooperative group setting. One of the most important is its diversity. The three books already discussed in this chapter are among many that touch on a fairly narrow aspect of scientific literacy. When the focus of learning broadens to topics such as bears or dinosaurs, the diversity of titles is far greater. On a recent trip to the children's section of the library in my neighborhood in Brooklyn, New York, I counted forty-five books on dinosaurs alone. There were more than two dozen books on bears throughout the Brooklyn system and many more when the whole of New York City was taken into account. Even discounting the books that were outdated, inaccurate, or poorly written, the variety in approach, depth of treatment, targeted age level, and degree of difficulty was remarkable. In 1989 alone, Patricia Lauber's *The News about Dinosaurs* was one of at least six noteworthy books published on dinosaurs. With the exception of *Dinosaurs, Dinosaurs* by Byron Barton (Crowell, 1989), which is targeted for the very youngest learners, all the books could work well for heterogeneous groups of middle-school and junior high school students engaged in cooperative learning projects. And herein lies one of the most important strengths of their diversity.

In most cases, heterogeneous groups are made up of learners of varying abilities. Providing groups such as these with resource books at varying levels of difficulty can enable each group member to make a significant contribution to a cooperative effort. By themselves, the 1989 dinosaur books represent just such a diversity. *What Happened to the Dinosaurs?* by Franklyn M. Branley (Crowell, 1989) is a lightly written, profusely illustrated discussion of current theories related to dinosaur extinction. The small blocks of text and straightforward writing style make it an appropriate introduction to the topic for younger and less able readers. Patricia Lauber in *The News about Dinosaurs* uses a more elaborated writing style to explore this and other fundamental dinosaur questions in greater depth. In *Dinosaur Mountain: Graveyard of the Past*, Caroline Arnold (Clarion, 1989) focuses on the work and fossil discoveries of scientists at the Dinosaur National Monument in northeast Utah. The photographs of scientists at work provide a real-world context for the information conveyed in the text and go a long way toward dispelling stereotypes of men in pristine science labs and white lab coats. Woven throughout the history of Dinosaur National Monument is information about the specific dinosaurs and fossils found in the quarry. In *Tyrannosaurus Rex and Its Kin: The Mesozoic Monsters* (Lothrop, Lee and Shepard, 1989), Helen Roney Sattler focuses on a particular family of dinosaurs rather than on the dinosaurs discovered at a particular excavation site. While Sattler's repeated use of the term *monsters* to refer to dinosaurs is unfortunate, tyrannosaurus buffs will nonetheless enjoy the detailed descriptions and illustrations. Many readers will be surprised by the large number of family members. David Peters provides an even broader picture of prehistoric animal life in *A Gallery of Dinosaurs and Other Early Reptiles* (Knopf, 1989). The sheer size of the book (approximately 9½ by 13 inches) allows for larger illustrations, which contrast with the dense but informative text. Unlike the dinosaur books described previously, the encyclopedia-like format and highly compact prose of *A Gallery of Dinosaurs* are suggestive of a reference text rather than a resource book likely to be read from cover to cover. Even among these few books, there is a diversity that provides for learners who "can't get enough" facts about dinosaurs as well as for those who find it tedious to "get" any facts at all.

The diversity of books on a given topic not only enables many types of learners to participate meaningfully in learning experiences, but it also invites critical thinking through comparison, contrast, analysis, and evaluation:

> Which book is most likely to contain information needed to answer a particular question?
>
> How can the index, glossary, and table of contents help you find out?
>
> When the books present similar information, do the facts agree?
>
> Why might there be disparities?
>
> How can the information be verified?

Working together, children can use trade books to operate as scientists while simultaneously moving ever closer to constructing new concepts or restructuring existing concepts.

Evaluating, a third phase in the process of concept development, leads learners to reflect upon the path they have traveled. In this phase, learners review their initial explanations for the phenomenon under study and revise them in light of new understandings. Suppose those students with whom I talked had read and discussed *Operation Grizzly Bear*, *Turtle Watch*, or *Dinosaur Mountain*, and had read newspaper or magazine articles about scientists in other specialties. During the evaluation phase, they would critique their initial drawings, describing any changes that they would want to make and explaining why those changes seem appropriate. In asking these students to make new drawings, their teachers could expect to see images that reflect at least some of the diversity of real scientists in the real world, thus bringing them that much closer to an accurate view of the profession.

As we approach the twenty-first century, the road to scientific literacy is one on which we must travel if our nation is to maintain its leadership position in the world. But that roadway is broad and ribbed with many possible paths. At least one of them should be a pathway paved with science trade books.

Windows through Time: Literature of the Social Studies

Diane Goetz Person
Columbia University

Bernice E. Cullinan
New York University

Windows let us look upon our world in both a literal and symbolic sense. When we look through the window provided by the National Assessment of Educational Progress (Hammack 1990) over the past twenty years, we see a uniformly dismal picture. Students are not performing well on standardized tests used to measure their educational progress. Although we recognize the inadequacies of standardized tests as the sole indicator of achievement, we need to acknowledge what the tests reveal:

> July 29, 1990. *New York Times.* Only 2.6 percent of 17 year-olds could write a good letter to a high school principal about why a rule should be changed. Only 5 percent could grasp a paragraph as complicated as the kind you would find in a first-year college textbook. And only 6 percent could solve a multi-step math problem. (Shanker 1990).

> April 11, 1990. *Education Week.* Most fourth graders know why Thanksgiving and July 4 are celebrated—but only 36 percent know why Columbus sailed to America. More than three-fourths of eighth graders could identify the Rev. Martin Luther King's "I Have A Dream" speech—but fewer than half know he advocated non-violence. Only 38 percent of eighth graders know that Congress makes laws, less than half know the meaning of separation of powers—and just half know the United States is a representative democracy. (Rothman 1990).

When students' lack of knowledge is documented in headlines that proclaim "U.S. Kids Not Making the Grade in History!" "NAEP History, Civics Test Reveal Knowledge Gaps," and "What Happened to History in the Grade Schools?" we can be certain that something is wrong. Educators are charged with ineffective teaching practices by a chorus of critics who try to identify *what* students should know and the level at which they should perform. Even if we disagree with such critics as Diane Ravitch and Chester Finn (1987) in *What Do Our 17-Year-Olds Know? A Report on the First National Assessment of History and Literature* (1987) and E.D. Hirsch in *Cultural Literacy: What Every American Needs to Know* (1987), who specify their ideal content, we dare not ignore our own observations that children's learning about their heritage needs to be improved. This chapter reviews some of the criticisms, identifies the goals of social studies education, and proposes a new approach to presenting social studies concepts through literature that makes them more meaningful to young learners.

Purpose of Social Studies

Teaching and learning social studies is a complex process that involves major concepts about how social groups interact. Part of the process involves studying how groups interacted historically. By looking at the past, we draw implications for life today. Byron advised, "The best prophet of the future is the past" (1821, 462), and George Santayana warned, "Those who cannot remember the past are condemned to repeat it" (1905, 703). We need social studies education because our students are growing up in a complex world, one that requires active participation from every citizen. Literature provides a window on the past in terms that students can understand. The essence of Thomas Jefferson's statement that a democracy cannot succeed without an educated people is just as true today as it was two hundred years ago. Democracy depends upon informed citizens. All children will occupy the office of citizen; it is crucial that they are informed. Further, as new groups of immigrants come to America, we need to understand their various cultures and respect their contributions. Only through understanding and appreciating differences can our cultural mosaic be blended into any kind of unity or cohesive pattern.

A great deal of the background knowledge that most of us take for granted was learned in the early grades: who Pocahontas was; how George Washington became the father of our country; and why Abraham Lincoln saved the Union. Why did St. George slay the dragon; how did King Arthur and his Knights of the Round Table fight to uphold honor and virtue; how did Jason, with Medea's help, capture the Golden Fleece and sail away on the *Argo*; and why was Helen, the most beautiful woman in the world, abducted by Paris? Our students know Spider Man, but do they know that Spider Man is a twentieth-century cartoon incarnation of the West African trickster character, Anansi the Spider? (Yolen 1981). They have heard of the Apollo Space Program and Conan the Barbarian, but can they identify who Apollo and Conan were? Most adults know these things, but, we must ask, have we passed this information on to our students? According to the report of the National Assessment of Educational Progress (Hammack

1990) in its twenty-year overview, we have not. Social studies helps students develop a sense of history, a sense of existence in the past as well as in the present. Literature contains all the great stories of human-kind. Students, therefore, can develop an appreciation for their historical heritage through informational books, biographies of famous people, and carefully researched historical fiction.

Social studies also attempts to help students understand spatial relationships of their immediate environment as well as those of other areas of the world. Geography helps them to understand how physical environments influence the development of various cultures. Anthropology and sociology help them to understand how various cultures developed and how each culture contributes to society. This chapter shows how we can provide students with a window through time by using trade books to teach social studies.

Research on Using Trade Books

Critics' words have not fallen on deaf ears; educators continue to look for new ways to help students learn about their historical past. One promising new direction, using story as a framework for understanding, is proposed here. This line of research, promoted in England, arises from the work of Barbara Hardy, who sees narrative as a primary act of mind. According to Hardy, all of our mental constructs of reality are stories that we tell ourselves about how the world works:

> We dream in narrative, day-dream in narrative, remember, anticipate, hope, despair, believe, doubt, plan, revise, criticize, construct, gossip, learn, hate, love by narrative. In order really to live, we make up stories about ourselves and others, about the personal as well as the social past and future. (1978, 13)

In fact, we see our lives as narratives in which we are the central character. Thinking in the narrative mode is not only characteristic of adults; it is the primary mode for children. James Moffett says that "children must for a long time make narrative do for all" their thinking (1968, 49). He observes that children "utter themselves almost entirely through stories" (p. 49). We note that many current nonfiction books use narrative story grammar so familiar to young children.

Literature speaks to our elemental need for story. Jerome Bruner calls for using literature in the curriculum because it is most constitutive of human experience. Literature, he says, is an "instrument for entering possible worlds of human experience" that is the driving force in learning (1984, 200). Since social science contains the study of human experience, it bodes well for using nonfiction trade books with a narrative voice to convey those experiences.

Trade books provide windows (Cullinan 1989) on other worlds and other experiences, windows that become virtual experience as we read. Readers add these virtual experiences to their knowledge of the world, and the increase in knowledge, in turn, increases the possibilities for responding to the world. At the same time, readers add to their storehouse of experiences as they read trade books. Understanding in social studies is enhanced through literary experiences.

Using Trade Books in Social Studies

According to Charlotte Crabtree, students tend to lose interest in history rapidly because it is most often taught using only textbooks. She suggests that teachers learn how to integrate other resources, such as speeches and primary source documents, with the literature of historical periods. She proposes that elementary students read Greek mythology and literature as a foundation for learning about history and ethics. Crabtree emphasizes that history should not become a recitation of names, dates, places, and facts, noting that "literature would help make these things real" (1988, B10). This is achieved through the context and human-interest appeal provided in books. Crabtree's goal is to make history come alive for children; it should not be regarded as an elite, stuffy subject.

According to Diane Ravitch, "History as a good story is not a bad approach to take with children aged five, six, seven, and eight years. History, as an opportunity to exercise the imagination and live in another era, is also a good approach for very young children." They enjoy history, she writes, and "learn painlessly when their minds and sense of romance and adventure are engaged" (1987, 351). This prepares them, Ravitch contends, for studying history and literature in later grades.

Children who are introduced to the characters of history, folklore, and mythology discover the greatest stories of all time; the stories and characters that have endured come down to us as mnemonic codes for models of valor, bravery, and character. These stories provide children with dreams to enlarge their own lives, and offer them the knowledge that heroes are made—not born—and that if you fail the first time, you can pick yourself up and try again. They also serve as referents for art and literature and as models of clear writing—as a child who has read Jean Fritz's literate and honest biography *The Double Life of Pocahontas* (Putnam, 1983) will verify. Fritz's rousing story is full of accurate information that she researched scrupulously; as a result, Pocahontas becomes a believable person with real doubts and fears. If children hear and read stories from mythology and history, long-ago times become real to them. Later, during more formal study of world or Greek history, the stories serve as a starting point for a thorough exploration of other eras and other cultures.

Jane Yolen says in *Touch Magic* (1981) that children who read or listen to stories of Anansi, the trickster rogue who helps his community and its vulnerable creatures, as in Harold Courlander's *The Hat-Shaking*

Dance and Other Tales from the Gold Coast (Harcourt, Brace and World, 1957) or Eric A. Kimmel's *Anansi and the Moss-Covered Rock* (Holiday House, 1988), have a basis for studying West African culture and understanding the cultures and eras that produced Prometheus in Greece and Robin Hood in medieval England. Children who know about the Bionic Woman and Wonder Woman are excited to hear and read myths about Diana the huntress or the Amazon warrior women whose queen battled with Achilles during the Trojan War.

Children who watch hours of television each week are aware of international upheavals; books such as Jean Fritz's *Homesick: My Own Story* (Putnam, 1982) give a child's eye view of the early days of the Chinese Communist insurgency, the Chinese civil war, and the threatened Japanese invasion of China. In Fritz's *China Homecoming* (Putnam, 1985), which recounts her return to China more than fifty years later, she gives a rationale for studying history through literature:

> As a child, I'd always felt sorry for Chinese boys and girls with such a long history to learn—4,000 years of it—but when I began to read about those years, I stopped feeling sorry. With the kind of history they had, I didn't see why they'd need TV. So many ready-made heroes and villains! So many hair-raising adventures! (P. 22)

Fritz's books provide an enticing way to make sense out of what is happening in the world today between China and the United States. The social-historical and cultural content of Fritz's writing cannot be found in any textbook, nor can textbooks have the immediacy and spontaneity of the author's firsthand experiences.

The wealth of trade books becomes an endless resource for teachers and librarians who turn to them as a means of teaching about historical periods. As the school curriculum becomes more crowded, teachers are frustrated in their attempts to use trade books in the classroom. Too often, trade books are not given their place as a central part of the curriculum. If, however, they are used in an integrated social studies curriculum, then students have access to their literary heritage and learn social studies concepts in a memorable way. Below are two examples of social studies teaching units integrating the use of nonfiction and fiction trade books. The first is about the Vietnam War, a turbulent period in American history about which children are curious; the second is a more fully developed unit on the medieval era.

The Vietnam War in Literature

Youngsters whose parents were caught up in the Vietnam War years can make sense of that era by reading a novel by master storyteller Katherine Paterson. Her book *Park's Quest* (Dutton, 1988) tells about thirteen-year-old Park, who is looking for answers to what happened to his father in Vietnam and how and why the war affected his family. A picture book by Eve Bunting, *The Wall* (Clarion, 1990), shows a young child searching for his grandfather's name on the Vietnam Veterans Memorial and longing for the grandfather he never knew. Reading these books in tandem with Huynh Quang Nhuong's autobiography, *The Land I Lost: Adventures of a Boy in Vietnam* (Harper and Row, 1982), which recounts loving memories of family and friends left behind in the central highlands of Vietnam, makes that era and distant place believable for children. Theresa Nelson's novel *And One for All* (Orchard, 1989) shows how disagreement over the Vietnam War separated families and friends: Geraldine's brother goes to fight in Vietnam while his best friend goes to Washington, D.C., to march in peace demonstrations. For a clue to the culture and character of the Vietnamese, children can read Jeanne Lee's *Toad Is the Uncle of Heaven: A Vietnamese Folk Tale* (Holt, Rinehart and Winston, 1985). Brent Ashabranner's *Always to Remember: The Story of the Vietnam Veterans Memorial* (Putnam, 1988) puts the American experience in Vietnam in perspective. Black-and-white photos by Jennifer Ashabranner capture the spirit of our national effort to honor slain American servicemen from an unpopular war. Used together, these informational, fiction, and picture-book titles weave a seamless fabric giving children a cohesive picture of a volatile historic era. They convey emotion and imagery along with information, as no textbook could possibly do.

Medieval Times in Literature

The Middle Ages is another historical period that children have difficulty understanding. Trade books can help them make sense of this crucial period in world history. In this section, we propose an extensive social studies unit based on new and classic trade books about the medieval era. One title, *Illuminations* by Jonathan Hunt (Bradbury, 1989), serves as an excellent introduction to a study of the Middle Ages and is used here as a reference work to introduce related titles. This lavishly illustrated alphabet book provides a rich, comprehensive guide to aspects of medieval life using vocabulary appropriate for young readers. While tales of knights and tournaments excite middle-grade readers, they often do not have the background knowledge to be comfortable reading Arthurian legends. Even older elementary school students need a wide range of information concerning medieval costumes, symbols, customs, and architecture to comprehend the era. Each of these subjects provides entry to a study of the Middle Ages.

An interesting way to proceed is to explore *Illuminations* through its text and illustrations, which resemble medieval illuminated manuscripts. Encourage students to handle the book, examine what is special about its design, observe how it differs in appearance from other books today, and note the referent for the title, *Illuminations*. Turning to the letter *I*, students see the term *illuminated manuscript* and a famous historical example, the *Book of Kells*. This provides an introduction to Deborah Nourse Lattimore's *The Sailor Who Captured the Sea: A Story of the Book of Kells* (HarperCollins, 1991). The ornateness of the illuminated manuscript complements this ancient historic tale of Irish bravery. Once children have an appreciation of the craft of illumination, Lattimore's look back into history comes alive, and a single book can be appreciated as a historic treasure. Combining the Lattimore book with the letters *S* for *scribe* and *X* for *xylography,* woodcut engraving, provides enough material to begin a research project on methods of illumination and the subsequent development of the printing press. After reading Lattimore's book and Cynthia Harnett's biography *Caxton's Challenge* (World, 1960), students can put to use what they have learned and can try making their own illuminated manuscripts. By examining the detailed illustrations in the sidebars of each page in *Illuminations,* students learn about the labor and craft involved in illustrating and engraving techniques and gain an understanding of the nature of daily life in the Middle Ages.

Architecture is an important aspect of medieval life that can be studied in *Illuminations.* The letters *N* (*Normans*), *P* (*portcullis*), and *W* (*wattle and daub*) offer a starting point to learn about the history of the castle as an architectural form developed in response to the needs of its lordly inhabitants; *W* depicts the modest building style typical of most medieval construction and explains the terminology. These pages lead to further study of medieval architecture through the text and the main and sidebar illustrations, which depict events such as a construction project. Students can then go on to read such books as David Macaulay's *Castle* (Houghton Mifflin, 1977) and *Cathedral: The Story of Its Construction* (Houghton Mifflin, 1973), Sheila Sancha's *The Castle Story* (Crowell, 1982), and John S. Goodall's *The Story of an English Village* (Atheneum, 1979) and *The Story of a Castle* (Atheneum, 1986).

Let There Be Light: A Book about Windows by James Cross Giblin (Crowell, 1988) has several fascinating chapters about the development of windows for light and defense purposes in castles, as well as the use of stained-glass windows for religious purposes in medieval churches and cathedrals. The information is conveyed through stories and anecdotes about people and places that no textbook could possibly contain, nor would a textbook refer to flying buttresses and rose-colored windows as creating "dazzling panels" in an "enchanted room made of nothing but color and light." The author's voice is chatty and conversational; he lifts a prosaic topic above the mundane. He reveals that windows were considered such luxuries and signs of wealth in the Middle Ages that the nobility would take their windows along when they moved from one castle to another. This same attitude toward windows is seen in Cynthia Harnett's novel about the medieval wool trade in England, *The Merchant's Mark* (Lerner, 1984). Windows, "too great a luxury to be treated with such contempt" (p. 56), are referred to with awe.

Many activities coordinate with the subject of medieval architecture. Children enjoy the hands-on activity of constructing their own scale-model castles with sugar cubes or small blocks. They also enjoy making stained-glass windows with plastic or cellophane or by melting various colored hard candies.

The practices and customs of everyday life in the Middle Ages are largely unfamiliar to young readers. While *Illuminations* emphasizes life at court, the sidebar illustrations, especially for the letters *V* (*villein*) and *Y* (*yoke*), remind readers that daily life flourished to support courtly life. An informational picture book, *A Medieval Feast* by Aliki (Crowell, 1983), also illustrated in the style of an illuminated manuscript, lightheartedly describes the week of preparation by serfs and villeins for a visit from the king and queen. The hunting, cleaning, harvesting, roasting, and baking show the work involved in providing for basic needs in the Middle Ages. An excellent companion book with outstanding illustrations is Joe Lasker's *Merry Ever After: The Story of Two Medieval Weddings* (Viking Penguin, 1976). This book describes two marriages, one among the nobility and one among the lower classes. The contrast here between the two classes is unmistakable, and students can easily compare the differences in lifestyles between nobles and peasants. There is enough information for students to try preparing for themselves the foods for a medieval feast or wedding festival.

Children are also very interested in what people did for sports and recreation in the Middle Ages. According to Lasker's *A Tournament of Knights* (Crowell, 1986), "they played at war—in a 'tournament.' To the people of medieval times, the violent tournament was an important entertainment, as a big-league sports event is today." The lively text, the excellent glossary, and the elaborately labeled illustration of a mounted knight make *A Tournament of Knights* useful and enjoyable reading. The colorful illustrations are sprightly and engaging, helping students visualize the life of people in medieval times. After reading this book, students might enjoy planning and hosting a medieval tournament or training for knighthood.

Information about trade and commerce is woven throughout the text and illustrations of *Illuminations*. Explicit information is articulated in Sheila Sancha's *Walter Dragun's Town: Crafts and Trade in the Middle Ages* (Crowell, 1989), a thorough, informative book with a storylike setting. The portraits of the characters, based on sculpted heads adorning Lincoln Cathedral, are drawn from entries in the Hundred Rolls, parchment census documents compiled for Edward I in 1275. Sancha uses recorded responses from the Hundred Rolls to create a story of commercial and social life in the town of Stanford. This accurate re-creation of medieval life coincides with descriptions in Fernand Braudel's scholarly three-volume work, *The Structures of Everyday Life* (1981), yet it reads like an exciting story. Sancha re-creates the processes of preparing cloth—spinning, weaving, and dyeing; she describes the metalworking and leather trades in detail and explores women's roles in commerce and social life. There is a glossary of terms and the origins of family names, as well as an explanation of the Hundred Rolls. Enough detail is given to help students construct an authentic scale-model medieval village, an activity that students enjoy.

At this point, students may ask if King Arthur was a real figure or just a heroic legend as portrayed in such classics as Sidney Lanier's *King Arthur and His Knights of the Round Table* (Grosset and Dunlap, 1950) or Rosemary Sutcliff's *The Sword and the Circle: King Arthur and the Knights of the Round Table* (Dutton, 1981). Catherine M. Andronik's *Quest for a King: Searching for the Real King Arthur* (Atheneum, 1989) is a scholarly attempt to discuss the evidence in a way young readers will understand. Using documents, original sources, and geographical artifacts, Andronik builds a case for Arthur's existence and shows how he and his knights became the subject of legend. Her painstaking research shows, for example, how the transformation of one letter in a Latin document may have given rise to the legend of "the sword in the stone." Plausible explanations are offered for the growth of the Arthurian legend. Students will want to explore some of the research efforts that Andronik describes to discover if new leads can be found or confirmed. They would also enjoy writing and performing dramatic scenes based on Arthurian legends.

The medieval era can be defined by the music and poetry that have survived. "Greensleeves," a popular ballad from the Middle Ages, is still a popular folksong today. Looking at the letters *T* for *troubadour* and *Z* for *zither* in *Illuminations*, students can imagine how people were entertained before the days of radio and cassette players. As the text suggests, troubadours wandered through western Europe at the time when madrigals, short lyric love poems sometimes set to music, were first introduced in England and France. Many nursery rhymes also originated in the Middle Ages: students can look at "The Lion and the Unicorn" in Kathleen Lines's *Lavender's Blue: A Book of Nursery Rhymes* (Oxford University Press, 1954) and the letter *U* for *unicorn* in *Illuminations*; then they can try to interpret the symbolic meaning of the nursery rhyme.

Next, students can look at Naomi Lewis's *Proud Knight, Fair Lady: The Twelve Lais of Marie de France* (Viking Penguin, 1989), a book of twelve lyric poems, called *lays,* written by Marie de France in the twelfth century. Based on tales of chivalry and love, the lays or songs were spread by troubadours through England and France. Some of the lays can be traced to familiar fairy tales, such as "The Honeysuckle," which retells a French version of the Arthurian legend *Tristan und Isolde.* The language of these lays, or short tales, retains the lyric quality of their original rhymed couplet form, just as the haunting essence of the fairy tale is apparent in the magical transformation of princes, knights, and wild creatures. Compare Angela Barrett's illustrations in this beautiful edition with the illuminated style of illustrations in Hunt's *Illuminations*.

More than six centuries ago, troubadours sang the romantic lay of *Valentine and Orson*, royal twins separated at birth. Now Nancy Ekholm Burkert (Farrar, Straus and Giroux, 1989) has written and illustrated, in medieval style, a rollicking tale, in rhymed couplets, of the escapades of the knightly Valentine and the "wild man" Orson. This book invites comparison with two recent editions of Chaucer's *The Canterbury Tales*, one by Barbara Cohen (Lothrop, Lee and Shepard, 1988) and the second by Selina Hastings (Henry Holt, 1988). After being immersed in the music and poetry of the Middle Ages, students will want to try writing their own nursery rhymes, lays, folksongs, and tales of chivalry and courtly love. The epic language used invests the poetic tales with a near mythic quality that students can try to capture in their own writing.

The above teaching unit shows how the use of nonfiction titles, picture books, and historical fiction can give young readers more than isolated collections of facts, and it shows how to integrate various sources to develop a coherent picture of the era. Children discover how little daily life has changed, regardless of how much technology has changed. The integrated approach is consistent with current research on how children learn.

The accompanying web (see Figure 4) is a visual schemata listing books and subject areas through which students can gain a rich understanding of medieval times. The web illustrates how reading, research, writing, drama, construction, science, math, social studies, literature, art, and music cut across traditional disciplinary lines. It demonstrates the use of literature in a truly integrated curriculum.

Conclusion

The goals of social studies education demand an understanding of the past as a guide to the future. Students can read factual presentations of history, biographies of famous people, and historical fiction to understand the past and use it as a guide to the future. Trade books provide students with a window on other worlds and other experiences by adding to their virtual experience. Trade books add virtual experiences to students' firsthand knowledge of the world and increase their ability to respond.

Figure 4
Web of medieval times.

Social Life and Customs

- *A Medieval Feast* by Aliki

- *Merry Ever After* by Joe Lasker

Printing and Books

- *Caxton's Challenge* by Cynthia Harnett

- *The Sailor Who Captured the Sea* by Deborah Nourse Lattimore

Music and Literature

- *Valentine and Orson* by Nancy Ekholm Burkert

- *The Canterbury Tales* by Geoffrey Chaucer; Barbara Cohen, adapter

- *The Canterbury Tales* by Geoffrey Chaucer; Selina Hastings, adapter

- *Proud Knight, Fair Lady*, Naomi Lewis, trans.

- *Lavender's Blue*, Kathleen Lines, ed.

Knighthood

- *Quest for a King* by Catherine Andronik

- *King Arthur and His Knights of the Round Table* by Sidney Lanier

- *A Tournament of Knights* by Joe Lasker

- *The Sword and the Circle* by Rosemary Sutcliff

Illuminations by Jonathan Hunt

Trade and Commerce

- *The Merchant's Mark* by Cynthia Harnett

- *Walter Dragun's Town* by Sheila Sancha

Architecture

- *Let There Be Light* by James Giblin

- *The Story of a Castle*

- *The Story of an English Village* by John Goodall

- *Castle and Cathedral* by David Macaulay

- *The Castle Story* by Sheila Sancha

Graphic design by Adam Frank, age 10

Reading Aloud and Responding to Nonfiction: Let's Talk about It

Sylvia M. Vardell
University of Texas at Arlington

Kathleen A. Copeland
University of Illinois at Urbana-Champaign

Have you seen the editorial about the school board?

Did you read that article about the state of emergency medical care?

Dolphins really are amazing creatures.

Our everyday lives are filled with comments and observations about the world around us. We scan newspapers, flip through magazines, turn on the evening news—feeding our need for information and understanding. We talk about our interests and concerns with friends, spouses, colleagues. Yet we seldom connect the natural engagement of information with the teaching of our children. We introduce our children to great storybooks and novels, forgetting the fascination of facts. We discount the benefits of our daily talk, relying mostly upon written exercises to muster learning experiences.

The linking of nonfiction and oral language has been a slow arrival to our classrooms. A bit of reflection upon tradition helps clarify why. We have assumed that fiction will be a source of pleasure, easily fostering talk from our students. Nonfiction, on the other hand, often has served a utilitarian role. We have assumed that nonfiction is akin to the textbook and is fine for school reports, but that it is not the basis of genuine talk among students. Besides, serious learning is supposed to be connected with written work. Current insights, however, can help change all of that, providing a strong rationale for bringing nonfiction and oral language together.

We are beginning to realize that today's nonfiction attracts even the most reluctant readers. And when students are tuning in to nonfiction, they want to talk about it, just as we do when we are captivated. In an era in which television and video games dominate children's leisure time, the hunger for information may yet lead children to books as entertainment—to hearing, reading, and talking about nonfiction books.

Current insights from researchers and theorists (Vygotsky 1962; Britton 1970; Moffett and Wagner 1983; Wells 1986) point out that talking and listening can also play an important role in our classroom, offering support for linking nonfiction and oral language. Talking is not only valuable as a means of communication, but also as a tool for thinking and learning. When students transform their thoughts into words, they are better able to shape, organize, and understand experience. In other words, oral language experiences are valuable in their own right, and we need not apologize for time devoted to speaking and listening. Furthermore, the talking and listening that surrounds nonfiction can promote children's oral language development in special ways. Through nonfiction, students encounter new vocabulary and information that they would not meet through daily conversations or through reading only fiction. And because good nonfiction engages students, a great potential exists for these new concepts to become a part of students' repertoires of experiences that can be talked about with others, without the "forced feeding" that often surrounds subject-matter learning. Perhaps the most marvelous is that good nonfiction captivates students so that students ask their own questions, a sure sign of learning and a way of using oral language that students are often denied in the classroom.

Additionally, oral language experiences can complement written language experiences, fostering success in reading and writing. Talking and listening make it possible for students to be exposed to reading materials that they may not encounter on their own. When students exchange responses to ideas read or heard, they are exposed to viewpoints that could reaffirm, challenge, or extend their own understanding. Talking and listening also can make it easier for students to move into writing experiences, helping them garner their thoughts and realize that they have ideas to share.

Reading Nonfiction Aloud

One of the easiest, yet one of the most important, ways to bring nonfiction and oral language together is through reading aloud. The first step is to recognize nonfiction as a viable genre for reading aloud. Typically, we think of picture books and novels as most appropriate for read-aloud time. Memories of the nonfiction of our childhoods consist of dry and solemn prose, sprinkled with a few charts or murky photographs—hardly sufficient to hold the interests of thirty wiggly third graders. It may help, however, to reexamine the genre and to note the dramatic changes that have taken place recently in the writing and illustrating of informational books for children. Nonfiction books today are available on an incredible array of subjects, often with full-color drawings or photographs and in a variety of formats useful across the grade levels. Informational literature for children can now be found in the forms of photographic essays, journals, and autobiographies, or even specialized books for those with very specific interests. Very young children also can encounter informational literature through concept books, picture books, and identification books.

Quality works currently available not only inform or instruct; in addition, these works capture emotions, entertaining or fascinating their readers. Russell Freedman, noted writer of nonfiction for children, suggests that nonfiction writers, in fact, strive to keep their readers reading:

> Most writers want a wide and willing audience. . . . What could be more dismal than to write a book—any kind of book—and have your intended reader hang up on you? If I'm excited enough about a subject to spend months researching and writing about it, I want my reader to be excited, too. I want to convey something about that subject as clearly and accurately and honestly as I can. But just as important, I want to hold the reader's attention from the first page to last. (1986, 27–28)

We know students' engaging encounters with nonfiction will afford them the benefits that we associate with reading fiction aloud: expanding knowledge of vocabulary and sentence patterns, extending background experiences, exposing them to books too difficult to read on their own. We also know that reading aloud is an invaluable way to help students become familiar with authors and types of reading that they may not have discovered through their independent choices. Some students already know that informational literature may be rewarding, but many students have had little or no exposure to the world of good nonfiction. For these students, hearing nonfiction is especially important so that they can discover the pleasure that informational literature holds. However, even if students have encountered much good nonfiction in their classrooms, reading aloud remains important. Telling students about the latest addition to the class library may not convince them to give the book a chance if they are not already interested in an author or topic. If we think a book will appeal to students, reading aloud, even just an excerpt, can be a more effective introduction. Students who choose informational books for their leisure reading may also enjoy participating in read-aloud times by sharing their favorite parts of books. As well, children often respond quite spontaneously to the interesting details included in good nonfiction so that reading aloud becomes particularly interactive and dynamic.

Like good fiction, quality nonfiction has much to offer. Reading aloud is a key way to help students reap the rewards. But where do we start? As we will discuss next, teachers can capitalize upon nonfiction in a number of ways as they read aloud to their students.

Visual Appeal   Readers of all ages are often stunned when they encounter the new beautiful *look* of nonfiction. The full-color, full-scale paintings of animals by Kenneth Lily in *Large as Life: Daytime Animals Life Size* (Knopf, 1985) and *Large as Life: Nighttime Animals Life Size* (Knopf, 1985) by Joanna Cole are two outstanding examples. Though a book does not have to be "pretty" to be powerful nonfiction, publishers today are taking greater care in the design and illustration of informational books. Advances in technology have made such production more feasible; attracting a media-savvy audience has probably made it more necessary. The Eyewitness series from Great Britain (distributed by Alfred A. Knopf) features numerous books on a variety of topics (such as *Shell* by Alex Arthur, *Music* by Neil Ardley, *Dinosaur* by David Norman and Angela Miller, *Plant* by David Burnie, and *Flag* by William Crampton [all Knopf, 1989]), with essentially a caption approach accompanying bold, colorful photographs. Barbara Bash combines vivid paintings with artful calligraphy in *Desert Giant: The World of the Saguaro Cactus* (Little, Brown, 1989), while Seymour Simon has practically cornered the market on the photographic essay in his series of books on such topics as planets, volcanoes, and whales, in which he utilizes photographs from scientific sources. Though just looking at and discussing the artwork in all of these books is informative, each book also includes a clear and well-written text to be sampled as needed—a good introduction to what the genre can offer.

Relevance   A second entry point into the genre is to choose nonfiction books of particular relevance to the interests of your students. Are they constructing illicit paper airplanes? Encourage them to dip into Seymour Simon's now-classic *The Paper Airplane Book* (Viking Press, 1971) to understand properties of lift, thrust, and drag, and to try and build variant models. Are students concerned about environmental issues? Refer to the terminology in *Trash!* by Charlotte Wilcox (Carolrhoda, 1989) to explain the processes of waste disposal and to raise the issue of recycling. *Wild Turkey, Tame Turkey* by Dorothy Hinshaw Patent (Clarion, 1989) offers excellent read-aloud chapters which discuss both the wild animal as well as the tame Thanksgiving bird. Patent also considers the issue of animal rights, which is on the minds of many students today. Are holiday preparations making the classroom crazy? Share the chapters about St. Nicholas in *The Truth about Santa Claus* by James Cross Giblin (Crowell, 1985). As suggested previously, informational books stimulate students' questions. Read-aloud time could provide a forum for students to share their questioning and subsequent research, using a "Did you know?" approach. As timely tidbits are shared during read-aloud time, students could be encouraged to participate by investigating their own individual interests and then by reading aloud what they have discovered.

Personal Growth   Nonfiction books also offer support for children asking questions about feelings, families, and friends. Share the sections entitled "Living with Stepparents" and "Having Stepsisters and Stepbrothers" from *Dinosaurs Divorce* by Laurene Krasny Brown and Marc Brown (Knopf, 1986). Students can discuss their own experiences and feelings about the increasingly common phenomenon of stepfamilies while gaining information and insight from an objective outside source. Jill Krementz's How It Feels series explores the serious topics of death, divorce, disability, adoption, and illness through interviews with real children who share their stories. Any one of the entries is powerful read-aloud material bound to stimulate questions and discussion. Whether the issues are personal or general, the vehicle of an informational book can help provide facts as well as a forum for airing concerns.

Storylike Nonfiction   A growing number of nonfiction books successfully incorporate a story frame into the nonfiction format. These are books whose informational integrity is not compromised by having a "beginning, middle, and end" and which lend themselves particularly well to being read aloud. One outstanding and popular example is *Koko's Kitten* by Francine Patterson (Scholastic, 1985), which tells the story of a gorilla's relationship with its pet cat. The simple descriptions of gorilla behavior combine with vivid closeup photographs to make an excellent cover-to-cover read-aloud book. Such storylike nonfiction is an excellent contribution to read-aloud literature, especially for the primary grades. Beware, however, of books in which the story frame sentimentalizes the content; readers come to nonfiction for accurate information, not for "cute" or condescending caricatures.

Facts and Features   Few students can resist the appeal of the odd tidbit of fact to be found in the *Guinness Book of World Records* by Donald McFarlan (Bantam, 1991) or *The Kids' World Almanac of Records and Facts* by Alice Siegel and Margo McLoone (Pharos Books, 1986). Learning about the fifty-two-hour joke-telling record or the origin of the name M & M candies fascinates readers of all ages. Books of trivia, lists of statistics, and collections of facts all provide an excellent entry point into the genre of nonfiction. Though not meant to be read from cover to cover, these works are excellent for sharing in those extra minutes which occur here and there throughout the school day. Children will enjoy sharing their own favorite facts, reading aloud excerpts for all to marvel over, question, discuss, and even double-check, or verify, new information. Often the most reluctant reader is drawn into browsing through a fat book of facts, although this same reader is intimidated by a very slim novel.

Here, also, newspapers and magazines offer excellent sources of up-to-the-minute information reported in usually brief and readable prose. In fact, many contemporary magazines for children go beyond trivia to include well-researched pieces on subjects of current interest to children, often including appropriate drawings and photographs. Because of their timeliness and brevity, these articles also can be excellent read-aloud material.

Familiar Formats

Nonfiction sometimes appears in the most unlikely places. More and more alphabet, counting, and concept books use a familiar and predictable format to convey information. These formats provide a comfortable and unifying theme or focus in which to introduce new and often unfamiliar information and terminology. Hope Ryden's alphabet books, *Wild Animals of Africa ABC* (Dutton, 1989) and *Wild Animals of America ABC* (Dutton, 1988), for example, introduce wild animals indigenous to Africa or the Americas with large, closeup photographs followed by three concluding pages of information about each animal. *ABCedar: An Alphabet of Trees* by George Ella Lyon (Orchard, 1989) introduces a tree for each letter of the alphabet, providing pictures of each tree's leaf drawn to scale as well as the tree's silhouette. After presenting this book orally, let children try to identity the trees by their leaves as the book is poured over in repeated sharing. Lois Ehlert provides a similar introduction to the recognition of new and familiar fruits and vegetables in *Eating the Alphabet* (Harcourt Brace Jovanovich, 1989). Share the glossary of names, pronunciations, and origins provided at the end of the text with the class. As you hold the book and display each letter, have students read or tell what the glossary says about the fruit or vegetable. With twenty-six letters to cover, almost every student will participate in the oral sharing of the book.

Because these books introduce new information of interest to a variety of age levels, the ABC format can extend beyond the traditional primary grades. In fact, some alphabet books contain enough text to challenge even older students, such as Margaret Musgrove's *Ashanti to Zulu—African Traditions* (Dial, 1976) or Ted Harrison's *A Northern Alphabet* (Tundra, 1982) about northern Canada and Alaska. A cover-to-cover oral reading, however, could become tedious. Instead, students can participate by taking individual letters or pages to present. Or they could choose to skim and skip by guessing what might be pictured for *A* or *Q* or *X*, for example, and then check and discuss their findings.

Biography

Although some argue that biographies written for children are more fictionalized than factual, the best biographies paint a realistic portrait based on careful research. These books also make excellent read-aloud nonfiction because the act of reading aloud gives the subject a very real voice. Probably the best introduction to this type of book is the work of Jean Fritz. Her briefer biographies (48–78 pages) of American Revolutionary figures (such as Ben Franklin, Paul Revere, Sam Adams, and Patrick Henry) and other historical personalities (Columbus and

Pocahontas, among others) capture the spirit of the individual, as well as the times, with humor and humanity. Her longer biographies (such as those of Sam Houston, Benedict Arnold, and Stonewall Jackson) offer the same careful documentation crafted into an engrossing narrative. Even individual chapters can stand alone as read-aloud material. For instance, chapter six of *Make Way for Sam Houston* (Putnam, 1986) presents an excellent description of the onset of the Civil War from a very human perspective and the struggle to preserve the Union.

The first-person voice of autobiographies makes them especially powerful when read aloud. Sally Ride's account of space shuttle travel in *To Space and Back* (Lothrop, Lee and Shepard, 1986) has a conversational style and abundant details that come to life in an oral reading. Fans of Bill Peet's books will enjoy the drawings and anecdotes in *Bill Peet: An Autobiography* (Houghton Mifflin, 1989), especially the story behind the tale of Chester the pig.

Curriculum Connections

Probably the most obvious avenue for using nonfiction is as supplementary content for math, science, social studies, and other subjects. And now, more than ever, an abundance of quality nonfiction on a multitude of subjects makes this a practical idea. What may not be quite as obvious is that many new books (or excerpts from them) lend themselves to being read aloud. Consider a math lesson that integrates David M. Schwartz's *How Much Is a Million?* (Lothrop, Lee and Shepard, 1985), in which the reader learns, "If you wanted to count from one to one million . . . it would take you about 23 days." *The Way Things Work* by David Macaulay (Houghton Mifflin, 1988) offers concise one-page and two-page accounts combining descriptions and drawings that could enrich many a science lesson, such as how a photocopier reproduces documents or how a toilet tank works. For enhancing social studies, Rhoda Blumberg's book *The Great American Gold Rush* (Bradbury, 1989), offers a chapter about the role of women, which begins, "Miners suffered from loneliness and lack of love." Many books on a variety of "teachable" topics are available. Such books need not be limited to the content areas, however, as good writing makes entertaining reading any time of the day.

In fact, the connections that nonfiction can offer to reading and language arts instruction are often overlooked. Ruth Heller's colorfully illustrated *The Reason for a Flower* (Putnam, 1983), very scientific in its premise and content, is written largely in rhyme. What an interesting extension to a poetry study this could be. And many popular authors of fiction also have written nonfiction works which students may enjoy discovering. Peter Spier's *People* (Doubleday, 1980) and Tomie dePaola's *The Popcorn Book* (Holiday House, 1978), for example, make excellent nonfiction read-aloud material.

Dramatic Potential

One final consideration in choosing nonfiction for reading aloud is the dramatic potential that the genre offers. Surprised? Factual books offer new information which comes alive in pantomime, performance, or readers theatre. For instance, as a leader reads aloud "Building the West" in Russell Freedman's *Children of the Wild West* (Clarion, 1983), students enact the events described. In fact, several of Freedman's books, including *Cowboys of the Wild West* (Clarion, 1985) and *Immigrant Kids* (Dutton, 1980), offer vivid details of time, place, and character which lend themselves to dramatic interpretation.

Some texts, in fact, have a built-in format ideal for multiple voices or for readers theatre. Joanna Cole's Magic School Bus books, for example, offer three levels of text: one presents the story line; a second features the children's dialogue; and a third shares simple reports that the children in the story have composed. Each level offers opportunities for children to participate in an oral reading or multiple oral readings of the same book. Aliki's "day in the life of" biography of Louis XIV, *The King's Day: Louis XIV of France* (Crown, 1989), also contains two parallel texts. With such detailed description of a life of luxury, students will surely enjoy an audience participation role. Sharing informational literature need not be a dry experience. With a bit of imagination, description becomes narration, and facts can be transformed into action.

From Students' Reading to Talking

In addition to the talking and listening that can come about through reading aloud, students' individual reading experiences can be a springboard for oral language. When students are enthusiastic about a topic or genuinely concerned, they often want to share aloud their responses to ideas they have encountered.

Small-Group Conferences

Increasingly, teachers are interested in incorporating trade books as the basis, or as a strong component, of their reading programs. Once students are exposed to good nonfiction, many will choose nonfiction when they self-select literature. One way to ensure that students have a forum for sharing their responses is to set aside time for conferences with individual students or small groups on a regular basis. Some teachers, for instance, assign a day of the week to a group, changing each group's membership periodically. Students who are reluctant to talk before the whole class often feel more comfortable with a smaller audience. Yet even in a small-group situation, some students may have little to say because they are unsure about what is expected or because they seldom have talked with peers as part of a classroom learning experience. One way that teachers can foster more student talk is to participate as group members themselves and to provide modeling, such as presenting a brief overview of a book that they are reading and sharing their thoughts and reactions to the book or to a favorite part.

Additionally, if teachers actively participate as group members, students are more apt to respond to each other's comments and not just take turns talking to the teacher in the small-group conference.

Whole-Class Sharing

The procedures used for small-group conferences also could be used for whole-class sharing on a daily basis. As well, teachers can set aside a special time each week during which students can share their responses through art, drama, and book talks. Students might sign up for a particular date, ensuring that each student gets a turn. Some students will choose to talk about a book or read aloud favorite sections. Others, however, may wish to share fiction or nonfiction through mobiles, posters, games, dioramas or models, or informal drama presentations that they have worked on during the previous week.

Collaborative Research and Learning

Units of study based upon students' nonfiction reading can offer an exciting way to explore a topic. Many topics about which students want to learn more are not presented in their textbooks, but can be encountered through informational literature. Additionally, nonfiction can offer a more in-depth look at a topic or some aspects of it. Third-grade teachers Diane Dutton and Sandy Issacs have found that oral language experiences help ensure that students enjoy learning through nonfiction, rather than viewing nonfiction as the source of another school assignment.

One way these teachers have approached units of study is to provide an overview of a topic through a trade book read aloud. After students talk about what they have learned thus far, they brainstorm questions for further study, which are recorded on a chart. Each student then selects a question to research in independent reading. On a designated day, students meet again as a group, sharing what they have learned as well as posing new questions that have arisen.

Students also collaborate by working in small groups to research an aspect of a topic. Observations of these groups in progress have revealed that although the groups vary in the approach that they take, the children find ways for all in the group to contribute. For example, students help one another to find an appropriate book or show a friend how to use the index. They take turns reading and recording the ideas that they encounter. Completed research could be shared with the class through student writings that classmates read, or it also could be presented through oral language activities, such as whole-class sharing of art, drama, games, and writing, which reflect information gathered.

Final Thoughts and Suggestions

Nonfiction can provide both a literary and a learning experience. Oral language experiences have the potential to let our students share the pleasure of nonfiction. Yet even well-intentioned talking and listening experiences can undermine nonfiction if we force student participation or if a testlike atmosphere looms. We do not want to "kill" nonfiction in the name of learning.

Just as we choose good fiction to intrigue and excite children, we want to select nonfiction books that have a contagious effect upon the students. When reading aloud, start with a book *you* like. Rather than relying solely upon a recommendation, read any book yourself before sharing it with children.

Because works of nonfiction can contain content that is unfamiliar to students and can provide a vast amount of information, it might be helpful to provide background information before launching into the text. Some works will lend themselves to being read aloud from cover to cover. Others will best be shared through a "browsing" approach, reading aloud selected excerpts while showing illustrations.

Read-aloud time with nonfiction often becomes spontaneously interactive. Questions arise, experiences are remembered, responses are shared, discussion occurs. Half the reading time may be spent talking about this new information. But this is a great gift of the genre—to develop critical thinking so that students become more active in their processing of information and less accepting of text as the final word. As Patricia Lauber has so eloquently demonstrated in her book *The News about Dinosaurs* (Bradbury, 1989), the news is that information changes as new discoveries are made. Informational books for children have changed, too. They are not just for research reports any more; they offer literary quality, variety, and appeal. They are something to talk about.

10 Reading and Writing Connection: Supporting Content-Area Literacy through Nonfiction Trade Books

Rosemary A. Salesi
University of Maine at Orono

T hat author ended his story just like I did," announced a third grader in Carol Ustach's class. Carol had expanded her writers' large-group sharing session to include discussions of the stories that the children had read in their basal readers. Even though the author of the basal story was not present to confer about the story, the children conferred using the same procedures that they used with their own stories. As a result, children began to "read like writers" (Smith 1983, 562), making those important connections between the texts that they read and the texts that they wrote. The dynamics of engaging in writing had caused them to read and think about reading in a unique way (Cambourne 1988). As writers, they could not write without being readers. Reading and writing were no longer separate domains. These children were learning that "writing encapsulates reading" (p. 184) and that through the act of reading we learn about the complexities of writing (Cambourne 1988; Smith 1983; Rosenblatt 1989).

We observed that these young writers employ two types of reading: they were reading and rereading their own written texts as they wrote, and they were also using the information that they had acquired from reading other texts, which was stored in their "linguistic data pool" (Cambourne 1988, 186). This residual of their past experiences with language, both spoken and written, provides the ideas from which writers construct new text. Even new ideas are reconceptualizations or extensions of the linguistic pool. When we write, we do more than recall past experiences; we also interact or have a transaction with our stored experiences (Rosenblatt 1989). This transaction occurs whenever we are creating language and thought. Thus, it is reasonable to expect that when we provide instruction in either reading or writing, it can affect the student's ability in the other. The effectiveness of the transaction or reading-writing connection will be dependent on the nature of instruction and the educational environment. When we take all of this into consideration, it is easy to understand why language learners need a variety of encounters with all aspects of language—reading, writing, speaking, and listening—to develop an interconnected linguistic data pool (Cambourne 1988).

Where Reading and Writing Meet

Several studies have investigated how prior reading experiences affect the narrative writing of students, and have found that writers do borrow language and literary structures (Jaggar, Carrara, and Weiss 1986; Graves 1983; Tierney and Leys 1984; Cairney 1990). Graves found that first-grade students internalized story grammars and used them to create narrative texts. Jaggar, Carrara, and Weiss's study of fourth graders showed that children will gradually incorporate words, content, and structure from the literature that they encounter.

Trevor Cairney (1990), in his research on intertextuality (the tying of prior texts read with written text composed at a later time), asked children if they ever thought about previous stories that they had read as they were writing a story and if there was any similarity between their stories and the ones that they recalled. He found that 90 percent of sixth graders, irrespective of reading ability, were aware of the connections between texts that they had previously read and the ones that they wrote. The majority of the borrowing was at the level of ideas and plot, with a few borrowings at the level of specific ideas, characterizations, and even linking the subject of one text with a completely different genre. This evidence suggests that when we provide a variety of rich literary experiences with various genres, students do draw upon previously read texts as they compose new texts.

Researchers interested in improving students' ability to read and write expository text have turned their attention to researching instructional strategies to encourage the reading and writing connection (Shanahan 1988; Cox, Shanahan, and Sulzby 1990; Englert and Hiebert 1984; Berkowitz 1986; McGee 1982). As with narrative text, reading plays an important role in children's learning to write expository text. Instructional strategies for improving reading comprehension, retention of written text, and connections to the children's composing have created interest in the potential use of nonfiction trade books as models. Several strategies are emerging which allow the teacher to organize instruction to encourage the use of certain linguistic forms, structures, concepts, and conventions (linguistic spillover) from reading to writing.

Strategies That Build Connections

Hazel Brown and Brian Cambourne, in their book *Read and Retell* (1987), advocate the common strategy of retelling found in many whole language classrooms. They have systematized their procedures and offer a ready-made set of sessions appropriate for large or small groups. I believe teachers can easily use and expand on this model to develop their own lessons to meet specific needs of students.

Retelling uses the natural form of everyday language behavior that we have all experienced from our early childhood—the need to tell someone about the events in our life. In the process of retelling, children are more aware of the language associated with the topic and the structure of the text, while experiencing minimal anxiety. This exchange of ideas and dialogue in the classroom is a key element in encouraging cross-fertilization in both the reading and writing processes. Favorable educational environments, where verbal transactions are encouraged, aid children in developing metalinguistic insights which improve performance and understanding of skills, conventions, and the deep structures of language. This is particularly true for reading and writing expository text.

Retelling and Nonfiction

Expository text requires additional considerations because it places different demands on the reader than narrative text does (Brown and Cambourne 1987). In expository text, the reader attempts to abstract meaning in order to retain, use, or act upon the information, which requires a closer adherence to the author's intent; while in narrative text, the reader savors or experiences the events, which allows for considerable latitude in interpreting (Rosenblatt 1989). Retelling activities using expository text need to be preceded by first immersing the child in the details of the subject matter. Immersion will help the child build concepts and vocabulary about the subject prior to retelling activities. In the elementary program, we use nonfiction that describes, persuades, argues, explains, or instructs. Retellings also include opportunities to describe illustrations, diagrams, and maps found in nonfiction text. Usually, the children are encouraged to look at the diagrams and maps during the process of retelling.

Brown and Cambourne observed student growth using this classroom strategy. The children demonstrated increased incidental, unconscious learning of text structure, vocabulary, and conventions that have proved to be pervasive, durable, and intense. They also internalized linguistic features, were more confident when engaged in literary activities, and demonstrated increased ability to adjust reading behaviors to the demands of different texts.

Enriching the Knowledge Pool: Data-Gathering Strategy

Another strategy for connecting reading and writing is suggested by Donald Graves in *Investigate Nonfiction* (1989). Crucial to writing expository text is a skill at data gathering. When children are ready to write, it is essential that they have ample information about their topics. Skill at data gathering has its roots in the home in the structures that children use to learn language and interact with family members. These structures have their equivalent in the rhetorical structures found in writing. Our early encounters of talking and listening feed into the linguistic pool of language and its structure, and overall knowledge. When children engage in complex transactional communications, they also engage in reason and negotiation. Some examples of preschool data-gathering transactions are recounting what has happened, interpreting shared events, inventing data to embellish accounts and interpretations, explaining or demonstrating skills of how to do things, planning for the future, providing directions for others, and understanding the logic behind differing points of view. Children also encounter these structures and narratives dealing with dual points of view in literature that is read aloud to them.

To prepare children effectively to be successful expository writers, Graves suggests that teachers help children become capable data gatherers. Using preschool language transactions, teachers should encourage children to tell stories about themselves, to assist in collecting such daily classroom information as the lunch count, and to interview and poll classmates and experts in the community. These experiences can nurture children's skills at identifying what they know and what they want to know, organizing their questions, seeking information, taking notes, and preparing information to share with others. Through letter writing and learning logs, children will gradually build the skills to write essays based on their need to express their own opinions. In the course of letter and essay writing, children will encounter differing points of view and the need to attend to audience. As children mature and view themselves as knowledgeable individuals, they will learn to gather data from a variety of sources and will be better able to engage in more formal report writing.

Using Informational Books as Models

Informational books offer children models of the many organizational structures, language styles, and techniques used by writers to describe, instruct, persuade, generalize, demonstrate solutions, and trace events. Using the National Council of Teachers of English (NCTE) 1990 Orbis Pictus Outstanding Nonfiction Books for Children, I will discuss the opportunities that exist to help children further the reading and writing connections of expository text. It is important to note that authors of recent children's nonfiction often include many features long associated only with adult nonfiction. The majority of the NCTE outstanding books include tables of contents, indexes, authors' notes, and bibliographies of sources. All of these features can be used by students to acquire additional information on the topic or as models for their own expository writing. To avoid redundancy, I will focus on the unique aspects of each book.

Picture books offer all readers, no matter what their age, a global introduction to a topic. Authors of informational picture books limit and focus their topics, emphasizing basic information about the subject. When I want to explore a new topic, I often turn to picture books for an introduction to broad general information. As my overall schema for the topic develops, I move on to increasingly more sophisticated presentations. This is a strategy that all students need to have modeled for them. As initial questions are answered, new questions will arise, leading students to seek more advanced information.

Another factor to consider in encouraging children to begin their research of a topic with picture books is the superb illustrations, photographs, and graphic arts that accompany the text. Children can learn as much from the visual as the written, including both knowledge about the topic and how to present information.

So many of today's ABC books are information books organized around the alphabet. *Illuminations* by Jonathan Hunt (Bradbury, 1989) is an exquisite, meticulous presentation of the art of illumination and a tantalizing view of medieval times. Each page presents a brief essay on a medieval term, such as *A* for *alchemist*. The illuminated letters and illustrations are both entertaining and enlightening and will inspire interest in the Middle Ages. By using the alphabet to focus on specific subtopics, abundant information becomes manageable. I would use *Illuminations* to help children address the issue of sufficient prior knowledge, whether reading or writing this type of material.

Several of the NCTE outstanding nonfiction picture books are devoted to animals, such as Seymour Simon's *Whales* (Crowell, 1989). Written from general to specific, it is an excellent model of an all-about book similar to what children begin to write in the primary grades. Simon's introduction uses a quote from Herman Melville's *Moby Dick*—an excellent opportunity to model the use of quotes to introduce a story or report. I think this is a perfect moment to show children how to use *Bartlett's Familiar Quotations*.

Simon's discussion shifts from general characteristics of all whales to a specific description of the two main groups (toothed whales and baleen whales), ending with a discussion of specific whales. Comparisons with fish and other mammals, terms and definitions, and numerical data are expertly woven within the body of the text, giving it a narrative quality. Devoting his last page to reinforcing concerns about the potential extinction of whales, Simon leaves the reader with a problem: "Will whales be allowed to remain to share the world with us? The choice is ours." This demonstrates that a writer does not have to answer all the questions. Why not leave the reader with some?

In contrast to the all-about book which attempts to be comprehensive in its examination of a topic, a more focused approach is preferred by Downs Matthews in his book *Polar Bear Cubs* (Simon and Schuster, 1989). He successfully narrows his topic to the first two years of life for the cubs and in doing so is able to discuss the significant characteristics of the species from gestation to independence. I especially like Matthews's lead paragraph. The reader is invited into the experiences of the cubs by being asked to imagine "a place so cold that oceans freeze . . . a place where tall trees can't grow . . . a place where the sun never shines in the winter nor sets in the summer." In a few sentences he captures the polar bears' environment and introduces the readers to the subject. Dan Guravich's photographs of polar bears are an excellent example of a well-planned photographic essay.

In Dorothy Hinshaw Patent's *Wild Turkey, Tame Turkey* (Clarion, 1989), the photographs by William Muñoz were planned in collaboration with the author. Clearly, a decision was made to develop the text through comparison and contrast, with the majority of the book devoted to the wild turkey, an endangered species, and the last few chapters to the turkey industry. Knowing readers are more familiar with the domestic turkey, Patent uses them as her jumping-off point in making comparisons. New vocabulary words are printed in italics, with definitions integrated into the sentence.

Through the use of an introduction and afterword, an author can discuss similarities and differences. Joan Anderson, who wrote the text to accompany George Ancona's *The American Family Farm: A Photo Essay* (Harcourt Brace Jovanovich, 1989), uses her introduction and afterword to present in brief the common experiences of three farm families in their struggle, despite adversity, to continue to maintain their own farms. Through description, explanation, use of data, and direct quotes from family members, the reader learns about their lives and values. Quotations are successfully integrated into the narrative and serve as a model for students.

Ideally, biographers prefer to interview their subjects, but when the individuals are deceased, it is necessary to turn to other sources. Leslie Sills was fortunate enough to interview one of her subjects for her short collection of biographies of four women artists, *Inspirations: Stories about Women Artists* (Whitman, 1989). Although Sills could not interview the other three artists, we discover from her bibliography that she consulted a variety of sources on the artists, including their artwork. Like Sills, students could also engage in observational writing by describing the art of their favorite illustrator. This type of writing enhances a student's ability to write precise descriptions of objects and events.

After reviewing several exhibition catalogs, children could create a catalog of their own artwork.

Donald H. Graves (1989) states that students should write after having gathered an ample amount of information about their topics. It is after examining collected data that a clear direction for the writing may become evident. Thus, revision can begin in the prewriting stage. When Aliki was ready to write *The King's Day: Louis XIV of France* (Crowell, 1989), she found, after several years of research, that she had gathered volumes of information and needed to limit her topic to present it in picture-book format. She noted the constancy of the king's days and solved her organizational problem by selecting a typical day as the vehicle for presenting in brief an abundant amount of information about how Louis XIV conducted both his personal and royal life as a ruler. Additional information is presented through captions, illustrations, and diagrams. By using the definition or synonym in apposition, she cleverly introduces correct French terms. Aliki also uses the dash extensively to set off parenthetical words, phrases, and clauses. I would not be surprised to find children experimenting with the dash and Aliki's layout techniques after a single reading of *The King's Day*.

Currently, most writers of biography for children avoid fictionalizing any portion of their subjects' lives. Possibly, it is Jean Fritz who is most responsible for this shift. In her Orbis Pictus Award–winning book, *The Great Little Madison* (Putnam, 1989), Fritz captures the integrity and values that guided James Madison's life, creating a highly accurate and authentic biography. Fritz draws the reader into the intrigues of the times—the conflicts, the personalities, and many issues facing the Colonies. Her extensive research on both the personalities and politics of our early history allows her to describe, elaborate, and clearly explain the conflicting points of view that existed during the Continental Congress. I found that her exploration of personal relationships and her use of details, anecdotes, and quotations helped me to clarify the complex events and to see how Madison, though small in stature, was great in influence.

Bill Peet's Caldecott Honor Book, *Bill Peet: An Autobiography* (Houghton Mifflin, 1989), a collection of personal anecdotes, is chronologically organized from his early childhood to recent years. Peet's interest in art began as a young child and eventually led to his being hired by Walt Disney Studios, where he worked for over twenty-seven years. Peet started writing children's books before he left Disney and now has written and illustrated over thirty picture books. For me, the striking quality of this autobiography is Peet's ability to find humor in the world around him and in himself. I think this book will help children to answer the question "What kind of stories should I tell about myself?" Through self-interviews and being interviewed by classmates, children can learn what they did not realize they knew about themselves, recalling experiences, ideas, thoughts, and feelings.

Memories of historical times of crisis can be obtained through interviews and such primary sources as diaries, letters, government records, newspapers, ballads, speeches, memoirs, and artifacts. In Milton Meltzer's *Voices from the Civil War* (Crowell, 1989) the decisive events and issues are traced from the 1850s to today through the use of excerpts from personal statements found in these primary sources. Before each excerpt, Meltzer provides a brief note about the person speaking and the events concerned. History is not just about dates and famous people; it is about *all* people and what happened to them. Whether about a war, the first streetcar, the new school, or just a typical day, family journals and primary sources found in many libraries or historical societies open the door to new understandings of previous eras.

In a style similar to Meltzer, David A. Adler focuses on the Holocaust in *We Remember the Holocaust* (Henry Holt, 1989), but he limits his book to the personal remembrances of survivors and to original photographs from private collections. He uses two organizational structures to present information: by topics suggested by the quotes of those interviewed and in chronological order. Transitions, descriptions, and narrative neatly bridge the quotations, creating a continuous history. Like Adler, children can also interview neighbors and members of the community to discover the history around us.

When Christopher Columbus anchored off the Atlantic coast of Panama, he thought he was in Southeast Asia. It was over four hundred years later that the Panama Canal was finished and westerly seabound traffic could move across Panama to the Pacific Ocean in relative safety. Judith St. George's *Panama Canal: Gateway to the World* (Putnam, 1989) is written like a suspenseful adventure story. She does not simply present the history of the canal, but tells the story of some individuals who devoted many years of their lives to bring about this amazing engineering feat. St. George weaves information from a variety of sources to trace the canal from its early inception to the recent agreements returning the canal to Panama in 1999. The statistics, detailed descriptions of the building procedures, and terminology do not intrude upon the flow of the "story." Instead, they allow teachers to link the book with current events, science, and mathematics. This is an excellent example of an author's having an abundance of information and still maintaining control over the text.

The days of writing children's books from encyclopedias is disappearing, and so may be the days of children doing most of their research from encyclopedias. *The Great American Gold Rush* by Rhoda Blumberg (Bradbury, 1989), an Orbis Pictus Honor Book, does with its opening what no encyclopedia can do. "Streams Paved With Gold!

Glittering nuggets loose on the ground, scattered everywhere!" How can children help but wonder, What was the Gold Rush really like? The inclusion of personal anecdotes and quotations from diaries and newspapers results in a vibrant style. Blumberg also skillfully models several approaches: comparison and contrast, use of details, and cause and effect.

History is not limited just to wars, major events, or even people. Suzanne Jurmain explores the history of an animal in her *Once upon a Horse: A History of Horses—And How They Shaped Our History* (Lothrop, Lee and Shepard, 1989). She researched the role of horses in the evolving civilizations of the world. Rather than present information by place or time, each chapter discusses a specific role of horses. Since literature has also included horses, Jurmain introduces each chapter with a literary selection. Illustrations using every form of art—from cave paintings to portraits in oils, from illuminated manuscripts to postage stamps—complement the text. I was left with a profound sense of the close relationship of horses and humans over the course of centuries. This book will supplement both social studies and science units.

Conclusion

As we create a learning environment which supports connections between reading and writing, we have available several teaching strategies. Reading aloud, retelling, and data gathering are only a few of the highly successful strategies being employed to guide children's conscious awareness of text and language structures, conventions, and format. Nonfiction books provide many fine models of these structures while at the same time supporting and extending information on content-area topics. Because their quality far exceeds the typical stilted language and formats of content-area textbooks, I urge teachers to use more nonfiction books in the classroom.

Invite Children to Respond Using the Fine Arts

Patricia Grasty Gaines
West Chester University

The little *Santa Maria* is crowded with thirty sailors, although we understand from Milton Meltzer's *Columbus and the World around Him* (Watts, 1990) that Columbus had forty men on his flagship. There are sailors sleeping in steerage, cramped and very close together. Columbus is in his cabin writing in his log. Other sailors are barefoot and working on deck, under order of the ship's master. The sailors who are not working or resting are talking to each other about conditions aboard ship—how they are pleased with the fresh fish for dinner caught that day and how uncomfortable it is to sleep so close to each other. The sailors are fourth graders who have read excerpts from Columbus's log in Peter and Connie Roop's *I, Columbus: My Journal, 1492–3* (Walker, 1990). They have heard facts read to them from Meltzer's book and have contrasted the information with additional details provided in Nancy Smiler Levinson's *Christopher Columbus, Voyager to the Unknown* (Dutton, 1990).

The students are in a classroom where the teacher has provided several examples of information in the form of nonfiction books. The teacher has used these books in different ways by reading aloud to the class, giving the children opportunities to read independently, and reading to answer questions raised by the class. Additionally, the classroom teacher has used her knowledge of a specific kind of drama, Dorothy Heathcote's unique role-play (Wagner 1976). Here, the students are listening, exchanging information with one another, suggesting answers to questions posed during role-playing, and demonstrating what they understand by participating in the improvisation.

The scene that is enacted might be replayed another time with different actions and changed dialogue, but that will be because the teacher guides these learners to reflect on how they feel—physically and emotionally—as crew on this particular ship in Columbus's fleet. In other words, each child's own life experiences, sophistication in spontaneous language use, and comprehension of the information provided in the literature selections will affect the individual response.

Inviting children to respond to the literature that we share with them is giving learners a chance to do something. The invitation takes into account the child as an individual and as part of a cooperating group. The kind of responses suggested by a teacher reflects that teacher's knowledge of the children, the books read, and a variety of ways to guide children to react thoughtfully to literature.

The idea that teachers should invite young people to respond to literature is not new in the language arts field. Illustrations of classroom activities, where teachers accept and encourage varied response to trade books, are widely available (Glazer and Williams 1979; Purves, Rogers, and Soter 1990). Children's responses are personalized. Guidance in response can converge on a thematic unit, a book, a motif, or contrastive ideas. Generally, we are offered examples of children's trade books that are fiction; far less often do suggestions of nonfiction books appear as related to aesthetic responses.

The literature provides descriptions of why response is worthwhile. Glazer and Williams develop several major proponents, including expanding understanding and communications skills. In addition to these goals, we can consider the encouragement of creative abilities.

In this chapter, I first examine the importance of response activities to creative thinking and creative production and then explore the importance of inviting aesthetic responses. Finally, four kinds of responses are presented: art, music, movement/dance, and drama, with suggestions based on current nonfiction books for children.

Response Activities Encourage Creative Abilities

When we invite children to participate in response activities, we also encourage them to use their creative abilities. The creative traits reported in the literature cover cognitive and affective abilities. E.R. Holman reports that "fluent thinking, flexible thinking, original thinking, and elaborative thinking abilities are all considered to be divergent" (1988, 6). Holman describes and illustrates these thinking abilities. He also names affective creative abilities as preference for complexity, curiosity, imagination, and risk taking.

Here is how these creative abilities relate to children's responses to books. Fluent thinking occurs when a child is able to generate many suggestions in response to, for example, the problem of "all the ways we could use art materials" to express feelings about an animal. Flexible thinking can be encouraged when learners are invited to consider different ways of enacting a scene based on a description in the text. When children respond to the invitation to suggest a quantity of various ideas in relation to a passage in a book, the possibility of thinking of unique and original ideas is increased. Finally, as is often the case, when we encourage the production of ideas, one idea suggests another related idea, and then elaborative thinking can be practiced. A poem can be set to original music, but we can also "borrow" a familiar tune like "Happy Birthday" for our melody.

Another author in the field of creativity, John S. Dacey, suggests that the trait of tolerating ambiguity is important because it "fosters ability to react creatively" (1988, 19). When we work with children to develop new ways of responding, we are in ambiguous situations. We do not know if the enactment or the depiction drawn will really work. When we join the children in what can be seen as an adventure into unexplored and untested areas, we may encourage this creative ability of "tolerance for ambiguity." Responses to text assist children in self-expression. It is good to know that we can also enhance the abilities that are important to creative thinking and problem solving.

The Value of Integrating Aesthetic Responses

Assisting children in using aesthetic response activities to nonfiction books may appear both simplistic and complex. The idea of drawing a quick depiction to explain a concept seems easy. Yet, how do you encourage drama, music, or dance in response to nonfiction material? The literature suggests that it is important to assist children in exploring the artistic elements of the environment. Stephanie Feeney and Eva Moravcik suggest numerous ways to help children perceive the artistic qualities of the classroom itself, the children's own products, and specific objects which display artistic qualities. "Children's literature," they state, "provides examples of the aesthetic use of language and fine art" (1988, 46), and they suggest that "aesthetic enjoyment provides an avenue through which people can find focus and achieve balance in an increasingly fast-moving world" (p. 47).

Howard Gardner (1983), highly regarded as a current leader in creativity, has proposed a theory of seven intelligences: linguistic, musical, logical-mathematical, spatial, bodily-kinesthetic, intrapersonal, and interpersonal. In view of his work, it seems essential to encourage practice of these abilities. When children are encouraged to dance or construct as responses, bodily-kinesthetic intelligence is further developed. Spatial ability is encouraged when children find and create their own space, understand arrangement, and find a pleasing pattern.

Particularly interesting is Gardner's view that there is a connection between linguistic intelligence and musical intelligence. This connection supports the value of moving from reading material that provides information to producing a musical response or simply enjoying the musical patterns and rhythms of language, as in a poem.

David Perkins, a colleague of Gardner's, reminds us that the arts are also mental processes (Fowler 1985). Once again we have confirmation that this is the right direction: teachers designing activities that assist aesthetic appreciation. These experiences can lead children to produce artistic responses related to the beautiful, well-researched nonfiction books available today.

Suggested Applications

It seems appropriate to share some background for the book selection and the proposed approaches. First, the books chosen include recent award-winning books—books by authors who are consistently producing significant nonfiction for young people—and books which I have purchased to use in my work as a teacher-educator.

Secondly, it is evident, when the books are read, that responses can be planned in all the arts for each of the selected titles. The focus here, however, is to suggest applications that may be overlooked by busy practitioners.

Thirdly, you will find specific poems and poetry books included. It is not possible for me to discuss any one genre of literature without making a few connections to poetry. Just as the writer of informational books and biographies provides facts and descriptions of events, so can the poet. A poem is an art form that is easy to follow because of its brevity. Our children recognize the sound of poetry as a literature form that they have known since the first Mother Goose rhyme was recited to them. I feel that the poetry written for children today is interesting and appealing, and hope that teachers will consider using poetry related to the nonfiction books recommended here.

Finally, these response ideas reflect a lifelong belief that the elementary school learning environment is where children have varied experiences and have time to explore—everything.

The responses here pertaining to the arts are deliberately focused on process and not the production of a polished product. Respect must be given to each of the fine arts, yet the arts can be used as an educational tool in the classroom. It is all right, then, for young people to display their paintings one day and to add a new color or object the next day; to develop a dance step and to share it only with their team members; and to develop a dramatic improvisation that is performed just once because the next time there are different ideas portrayed and new players have added more roles. Children will participate in aesthetic responses to nonfiction trade books as long as teachers extend the invitation.

Suggested Sources of Nonfiction Books

L.N. Gerhardt, who presents more than fifty publishers' previews of nonfiction books, states, "Nonfiction for children and adolescents is the hot topic in book selection for the young" (1989, 34). It is hoped that the tradition of sharing forthcoming books in this way will be maintained by publishers and will continue to be reported in professional journals.

There are several key resources for teachers. Beverly Kobrin's *Eyeopeners! How to Choose and Use Children's Books about Real People, Places, and Things* (1988) is efficiently organized and offers books categorized in topic areas that teachers use. Booklists that should be on our desks include Mary Jett-Simpson's *Adventuring with Books: A Booklist for*

Pre-K–Grade 6 (1989), an annotated booklist published periodically by the National Council of Teachers of English, and the annual listing of *Teachers' Choices,* published by the International Reading Association. Of course, there are many other collections that we can utilize.

The nonfiction trade books that we share with children will change according to the needs and interests of the learners. The teacher-leader will, however, need to engage in metaphorical thinking to design responses to these books. New connections will encourage innovative uses of the books in this genre.

Nonfiction Books and Art

Artistic responses afford children the chance to explore, enjoy, compare, and contrast what is provided visually. The literature reports that children grow in their ability to give their impressions of the artwork that they see in books (Kiefer 1988; Sebesta 1987). Time should be provided for children to reflect on the techniques, texture, composition, and so forth of the artwork presented. Barbara Kiefer's observations of how children respond to picture books lead her to report:

> These variations in response to picture books helped me to see that as children communicate with and about picture books they seem to develop a growing awareness of aesthetic factors and of the artist's role in choosing these factors to express meaning. (1988, 264)

This notion of using the art in books is a fine way to build sensitivity and appreciation.

Equally workable as a response is to help children identify objects and inventions that they can construct or produce using paint, chalk, and other media available. Sam L. Sebesta suggests that "the array of children's books to instruct the child artist is limitless" (1987, 81).

For a study of an artist's techniques, including use of space, color, and line, *Anno's U.S.A.* (Philomel, 1983) provides an excellent vehicle. Distinguished artist Mitsumasa Anno provides a visual portrait of the United States without text. The sequence portrays travel across the country from west to east and depicts people and activities of the past and present.

Another book, *Dancing Tepees: Poems of American Indian Youth* by Virginia Driving Hawk Sneve (Holiday House, 1989), allows us to call attention to the way artist Stephen Gammell has carefully duplicated the traditional art of North American Indians. *Dancing Tepees* is a wonderful addition to poetry collections; it provides an interaction with nonfiction text about Native Americans. The artistic response to this book might be to design other visuals, which could include the construction of collages and posters to illustrate poems read. Or, consider encouraging children to produce drawings for animation—a chance to see the butterflies and eagles fly.

Some books are so rich in concepts that may be new to children that they may need to see the ideas in another form. Gail Gibbons's *Catch the Wind! All about Kites* (Little, Brown, 1989) illustrates many different kinds of kites—box kite, compound kite, delta kite—and tells us exactly how to construct a flat kite. The straightforward text makes us feel confident that we can make a kite and fly it, which is what we should do immediately after collecting the materials that Gibbons lists. Huynh Quang Nhuong's *The Land I Lost: Adventures of a Boy in Vietnam* (Harper and Row, 1982) asks for quite a different response. The reader moves to the central highlands of Vietnam and finds social customs, the jungle environment, and childhood activities in great contrast to life on the mainland of the United States. Children might respond to this book by finding parts that they think need illustration, and by creating scenes that the book's illustrator, Vo-Dinh Mai, did not select to depict.

Nonfiction Books and Music

Musical responses to books can include composition and performance. There is a natural connection when the text contains words that are carefully selected to describe and explain such elements of music as rhythm, tone, and melody. Sebesta advocates: "Music and movement form a bridge to poetry, for, after all, poetry probably began as a song. For most children, it's easier to sing a lyric than read it aloud" (1987, 85). We can let children see this relationship for themselves by relating music and poetry.

Marilyn Singer's *Turtle in July* (Macmillan, 1989) collection is a natural source. The birds in "Myrtle Warblers" really sing "me me me." You hear the music because of the word patterns. Children can try changing the pitch of their voices from high to low until they have used their singing voices. My favorite selection is "Beavers in November," in which the rhythm established for the beavers as they work at building the dam is so realistic. The poem invites listeners to pick up rhythm instruments that are handy and to give a musical performance to accompany the reading of the poem. The poems housed here offer grand connections to informational texts about animals at work, such as the bustling beaver.

Peter Spier's *People* (Doubleday, 1980) might not readily conjure up a connection to music. The illustrations are sumptuous as we look at similarities and differences in people around the world. Here, for example, we might look at the different feasts and holidays celebrated and find examples of music that is authentic to these events. Elsewhere in the book, Spier says, "People everywhere love to play. But not the same games everywhere." The sounds of a Western rodeo have rhythms that differ from the sounds of darts falling on an English dart board, which in turn contrasts with the sounds of pebbles falling on a mahogany Wari board in Africa. Music can be composed based on the repetitive patterns heard; songs to instruct can be created.

Nonfiction Books and Movement/ Dance

Using the body to express a concept or to demonstrate an activity is both liberating and disciplining. Moving in space and creating an individual place in a designated area requires coordination.

Children can practice designing their own dance interpretations of the text in nonfiction books. Yvonne Mersereau, Mary Glover, and Meredith Cherland report experiments in third-grade and fourth-grade classrooms in which the children interact with literature, responding in various ways including drama and dance. These teachers, as experimenters, first show that they see value in using the expressive arts, reporting, "In working with the children, and through dialogue with others interested in holistic education, Mary and Yvonne [two of the authors] came to see the potential for using dance to enrich and extend the study of literature" (1989, 111). They describe one experience in which the children hear seasonal poetry to assist their imaginations and then express themselves in dance. Additionally, the teachers find creative connections. They use terms and activities from the writing process in their dance training with the youngsters. There is a direct relationship between written expression and dance when the children move from ideation to drafting. The authors reveal, "We came to see that learning in one mode can serve as a metaphor for learning in another. Choreographing dances can help children understand composing as both readers and writers" (p. 115).

Dance depiction is a possibility after reading Seymour Simon's *Whales* (Crowell, 1989). This author has once more combined scientific information with beautiful visuals and a commanding text. Once students understand the features and importance of the whale's flippers, comparisons can be made to humans. They can design dance steps to balance themselves much like whales do. The "music" of the humpback might serve as background for the creation of a dance of swimming whales like those Simon introduces: the fin whale, the blue whale, the humpback, and the minke.

Diane Siebert's *Mojave* (Crowell, 1988) presents, in rhyme, the climate, the birds, and the animals who live on this North American desert. What is unique is that the desert is speaking. And since everything is not still, there is much movement to demonstrate. At a signal, sleeping tortoises can begin to creep home, and the black raven can fly off screaming. The many animals glide, hop, and gallop. It seems that even the Joshua trees are in motion. Children can use their bodies to show that this great desert is alive with activity.

Older children can do further research related to the four main North American deserts to find out how climate affects the inhabitants and how these birds, small and large desert animals, and plants exist from season to season. They might also move differently at the hottest point of the day contrasted with the evening hours.

Nonfiction Books and Drama

Drama responses are opportunities for children to portray what they understand and to include their own impressions of how characters, animate or inanimate, might move in their own environments. In particular, the informal or improvised drama forms are closely tied to children's play and originate there. The drama activities initiated can include pantomime, improvisation, puppetry, role-playing, and story dramatization for all ages.

Christine San Jose depicts the use of story drama as related to subject matter in the content areas. She sees "story drama" as direct work with material that is read, and reports two major aspects of this kind of drama. Her second characteristic affords clear application in use with nonfiction books: "the teacher and students who work with story drama are guided and supported throughout by the text they have chosen, with all the clarity, or force or beauty or humor that it has to offer" (1988, 28). The literature continues to remind us that with informed guidance, children can demonstrate creative and critical thinking in dramatic portrayals that move beyond the natural spontaneity of dramatic play.

Vicki Cobb's *Writing It Down* (Lippincott, 1989) provides information on the invention of paper, ballpoint pens, pencils, and crayons. Young children can be invited to dramatize the story of paper inventor Ts'al Lun. Older children can develop scenes that portray many different methods for making paper, all presented in Cobb's book.

Jean Craighead George's *One Day in the Woods* (Crowell, 1988) is a treasure for child and adult lovers of the forests of the Northeast. The information reads like a narrative, with Rebecca, the adventurer, getting to know the woods in one day. Children can engage in story dramatization, easily identifying the characters, such as a flying squirrel or a raccoon. The book gives appealing descriptions of plants, birds, and animals to which children can continually refer in the text to ascertain if their depictions are accurate. Another book, Patricia Lauber's *The News about Dinosaurs* (Bradbury, 1989), offers children opportunities to build improvisations in which they pantomime dinosaur actions or create puppets that use dialogue to talk about contrasts between the most recent information about dinosaurs and prior information. There is a great deal of material here for dramatic expression.

Rhoda Blumberg's *The Great American Gold Rush* (Bradbury, 1989) takes us along the many routes that prospectors followed to California. This was a diverse group of people, and we learn about where and how they lived. I would like to see young people envision and then portray shipboard life on the Cape Horn route to California. Blumberg informs us about the conditions, with descriptions of climate, space, and provisions, providing usable materials to investigate and then dramatize.

Milton Meltzer's biography *Mary McLeod Bethune: Voice of Black Hope* (Viking Penguin, 1987), the story of the distinguished black educator, is a readable source in which students can find scenes to dramatize that lead to understanding the goals and achievements of Bethune. The description of how she began her "dream" of a school (chapter 3) could be the source of many scenes to be enacted in order to compare and contrast the schooling and culture of the South during the early part of the twentieth century with that of today.

Conclusion

Albert Cullum's proposition that we "push back the desks in a classroom to allow the natural creative and intellectual drives in children to flow" (1967, 15) remains a valid pursuit. He describes classroom activities in which subject-matter content is integrated with the expressive arts. The classroom lessons become genuine learning experiences— actual events in the lives of these children. Cullum is a master host for response.

Trade books in the nonfiction category are enticing. The information presented in these books should persuade teachers to summon readers to action. Response to books encourages many behaviors, including creative thinking abilities. Aesthetic responses support appreciation of the arts and give children the chance to feel, reflect, and reply with their own interpretations.

There is a multitude of books and ideas for aesthetic responses. So extend an invitation to children to paint, compose, dance, or become members of the cast.

III Finding a Place for Nonfiction in the Elementary Classroom

Nonfiction Books in the Primary Classroom: Soaring with the Swans

Peter Roop
McKinley Elementary School, Appleton, Wisconsin

Once upon a time nonfiction was the ugly duckling of children's books. Appealing picture books, fascinating folktales, and enchanting fairy tales dominated the literature pond in primary classrooms. Hardworking nonfiction was the neglected ugly duckling, used by teachers in preparing lessons or by the highly motivated student eager to search through comparatively unattractive books to find information.

Now, however, thanks to a new wave of engaging books, nonfiction is finally being accepted for its own artistry and integrity. On the way out are the many dull-looking information books, accurate but with little aesthetic appeal. In their place are books exploding with color and exciting to read, books that are as inviting as they are informative. Nonfiction authors such as Seymour Simon, Joanna Cole, Patricia Lauber, Dorothy Hinshaw Patent, Milton Meltzer, and James Cross Giblin are becoming as well known as established fiction storytellers and illustrators. The ugly duckling has grown into a swan of surprising beauty.

Young children's natural curiosity about the world is a most powerful learning strength. In one evening at the seashore, I fielded these questions from my two children, aged five and eight:

Where do itches come from?

Why is only half the moon shining tonight?

Where do sea gulls go at night?

Does anyone eat sea urchins?

Will rock burn?

Why is the sea salty?

What makes the waves go all one direction?

Why does the sun burn us and not the seals?

When will mackerel run?

Why can you see things on the bottom of shallow water, but not where it's deep?

Do lizards live in the ocean?

Multiply these inquiries by the thirty students in a class, and you get a sense of children's fascination with their world. (We raided the village library the following day for the answers that we were unable to figure out or that I did not know.)

When school starts each year, my classroom is awash in books. I want my students to see, hold, look at, and read as many books as possible beyond their regular checkouts. I have been building up my classroom library for years, buying books at rummage sales and secondhand stores, ordering through book clubs and book fairs, browbeating my school librarian for discards. Until recently, however, I skimmed over most nonfiction books because so few seemed to have any appeal to my young readers. That is not the case now. Nonfiction books, exploring everything from ants to zeppelins, are increasingly available in both hardback and paper, a crucial element in promoting access to quality informational books. My nonfiction shelf is bulging, forcing me to weed my collection for the first time in years.

Now that my choices have increased, I am much more selective about the nonfiction that I choose for my library. First, in making a decision, I skim the book, reading a page or two to assess reading level. Then I study the illustrations or photographs. Will the book appeal to children? Will the kids pick this book up on their own? Will I have a hard time selling this book, or will they argue about who gets it (usually a good sign)? I read through the entire index, checking to see if my knowledge of the topic finds any loopholes in the book. Then I read the entire book, confirming the accuracy of the information as well as pictorial content. All the while I am seeking ways to involve my students with the book, either individually or as a group. With their natural curiosity as the hook, nonfiction books can be the line and pole to reel children into broadening their reading experiences.

Over the past several years, as I have incorporated more nonfiction into my classroom, I have found that many of the approaches used with fiction work as well with nonfiction. Reading aloud, creative dramatics, art projects, poetry, and creative writing are all effective means of introducing nonfiction to children and encouraging them to interact with the books. Every teacher has his or her own best methods for using fiction books. I hope that the following unit, Digging Dinosaurs, will serve as a model for using nonfiction books with primary-aged children.

Digging Dinosaurs

Sometimes I think that if dinosaurs had not existed, children would have invented them, so strong is their interest in these long-vanished animals. Everything from the tongue-twisting names to their mysterious disappearance has fascination for children, especially primary-aged students.

There are so many dinosaur books currently available that I limit my teaching focus to a few selected favorites, although I also use sections of other books. As an introduction, I first read *Fossils Tell of Long Ago* by Aliki (Harper and Row, 1972), followed by her *Digging Up Dinosaurs* (Harper and Row, 1981). As we delve deeper into dinosaurs and their world, we explore the size differences with Seymour Simon's two books, *The Largest Dinosaurs* (Macmillan, 1986) and *The Smallest Dinosaurs* (Crown, 1982). Franklyn M. Branley's *What Happened to the Dinosaurs?* (Crowell, 1989) helps us look for answers to that fascinating question, and our culminating activities revolve around *Tyrannosaurus Was a Beast: Dinosaur Poems* by Jack Prelutsky (Greenwillow, 1988) and *Tyrannosaurus Wrecks* by Noelle Sterne (Harper and Row, 1979).

I set the scene for our dinosaur study by asking the children to bring in rocks, any rocks that they might have collected from near and far. Soon our activity table is sagging beneath a mountain of rocks of various sizes, shapes, colors, and geologic history. I have the children sort the rocks according to size, color, and texture. All the while I want them to be on the lookout for fossils. (I include samples from my own collection in the event that no one brings in a fossil.) We then examine whatever fossils we have.

"What are fossils?" I ask, leading students to understand that fossils are the imprints of the remains of plants or animals. We next discuss what usually happens when an animal or plant dies. What happens to the skin, muscles, feathers, bones, leaves, stems? After I have collected this information on chart paper and the children are focused on fossils, we turn our attention to Aliki's *Fossils Tell of Long Ago*.

Sitting in my fat old armchair with the students grouped around me, I share nonfiction books just as I would read a picture book. As I read, we pause to discuss the text and illustrations. Is this something that we knew before? Do the pictures show us things that we had not mentioned earlier? Is there new information that we might add to our list?

After we have finished the book, we begin our first project, a sequence picture of the steps of fossilization, based on a section of the book. The children fold their papers into four boxes and color a fish swimming, dying and rotting, being buried, and finally being discovered.

At the end of class, I ask the children to bring in something hard and something soft for tomorrow's activity because we are going to make our own "fossils." We fill another table with every-thing from feathers to paper clips. We discuss which items might make a real fossil and why: a feather would because it was living, but a bottle cap would not because it was never alive.

I give each child a ball of clay in a plastic bag. After selecting an object from the table, he or she flattens the clay and impresses the chosen object into the clay. The "fossils" are shared, and we try to guess what each impression is. We finish the day by reading and discussing *My Visit to the Dinosaurs* by Aliki (Crowell, 1985) as review and in preparation for further dinosaur activities the follow-ing day. I ask the children to bring an old toothbrush, a request that brings more than a few puzzled looks. (Once someone offered to bring toothpaste—I wonder if he thought we might be brushing dinosaur teeth!)

In preparation for reading *Digging Up Dinosaurs,* we review what we already know about fossils by boning up on the facts. Instead of listing this information on chart paper, I write down each fact on a cutout bone. To solicit information from the children, I ask the following types of questions:

How big were dinosaurs?

Were they all the same size?

What kinds of environments did they inhabit?

What are some names of dinosaurs?

Where can we see dinosaurs today?

Then, as we read, we pause for discussion and add more bones to our chart as we uncover more information.

Next we turn into fossil hunters. We divide into fossil-hunting teams, and armed with our toothbrushes, we discover and uncover "fossils." In preparation for this activity, I have buried the students' objects in several boxes of sand. Their job is to carefully uncover the "fossils" and bring them to our museum, where they will be dis-played.

Our museum is a counter on which we display our exhibits: fossil impressions, our best real fossils, and some of the fossilization pictures that we have drawn. The children label the exhibits, which change as we progress with the dinosaur study.

In one of the boxes, I have buried a cutup cardboard skeleton of a triceratops. When this dinosaur is unearthed and brought to the museum, the children reassemble its skeleton just as a paleontologist does. As a follow-up activity, I hand out copies of other dinosaur skeletons, which we mount on cardboard, cut up, and keep in plastic bags for other young scientists to reassemble.

We finish the day by reading the chapter "Dinosaurs Walked Here" from Patricia Lauber's excellent book *Dinosaurs Walked Here and Other Stories Fossils Tell* (Bradbury, 1987). This chapter links new information with what we have already learned. *Dinosaurs Walked Here* quickly becomes a silent reading favorite because children love to browse through the book, enjoying the outstanding color photographs. Caroline Arnold's *Dinosaur Mountain: Graveyard of the Past* (Clarion, 1989) and Kathryn Lasky's *Dinosaur Dig* (Morrow, 1990) are other favorites for "reading the pictures."

We get "plastered" in the next project when we make plaster casts of a real dinosaur footprint. Several years ago I made a plaster cast of a dinosaur footprint at Dinosaur State Park near Hartford, Connecticut. The oohs and ahs accompanying the exhibit of this cast heighten the anticipation for this project. This is a messy, hands-on time in which everyone gets involved over the next few days. First, we smear the cast with petroleum jelly. Then we mix the plaster, pour it into the mold, and allow it to set. When we remove the plaster, we have a life-sized footprint. After I demonstrate the process, I assign fossil teams that work cooperatively to produce a footprint for each student to take home. This project is ongoing for the next week or so. You would be surprised at how many kids give up recess to make their dinosaur footprints!

While the plastering is going on, we have other projects underway as well. We look again at the books that we have read, this time focusing on the dinosaurs' environments. We make collages of land, ocean, desert, and forest environments to link our time period with the days of the dinosaurs. We invent new dinosaurs by mixing up the parts of real dinosaurs (putting a tyrannosaurus head on an apatosaurus body, for example).

The next books we read are by Seymour Simon, *The Largest Dinosaurs* and *The Smallest Dinosaurs*. In preparation, I ask each child to bring in a stuffed dinosaur, a toy dinosaur, or a picture of a dinosaur and to be prepared to tell us one thing about that dinosaur. We record these facts on the cutout dinosaur bones and add them to our expanding bone collection.

Beforehand, on chart paper, I list the dinosaurs discussed in these books. As we read about each dinosaur, we add appropriate information to the list: weight, size, food, environment, enemies, prey. We discuss each dinosaur name and why the dinosaur was given that name (for example, *saltpous* means "leaping foot"). As a follow-up, each child picks a dinosaur, draws it, cuts it out, colors it, and lists appropriate information on the back.

We expand this activity to focus on modern animals—their sizes, habits, and habitats. As we discuss modern animals, we make connections with dinosaurs and their world. I purposely have selected books here that provide links to the dinosaurs: Joanna Cole's *Hungry, Hungry Sharks* (Random House, 1986), Carol and Donald Carrick's *The Crocodiles Still Wait* (Houghton Mifflin, 1980), and *Never Kiss an Alligator!* by Colleen Stanley Bare (Dutton, 1989).

Throughout this unit, one of my goals is to introduce children to the importance of an index. Whenever the chance arises, either due to a student question or my own, I look things up in the index. For example, before we read Patricia Lauber's *The News about Dinosaurs*, Camey asks, "Did volcanoes kill the dinosaurs?" I ask her to tell me the most important word in her question. She hesitates and then says, "Volcanoes." I pick up Lauber's book, turn to the index, and explain that by using the index, we can find specific information in a book very quickly. I find volcanoes, turn immediately to the correct page, and read the information that answers her question.

At first the students are puzzled by my doing this, but when they see how quickly I can find something, as opposed to the time it takes to page through a book, some of them begin using the index on their own during silent reading time. Although the skill of consulting an index is important, I purposely do not drill this skill; instead, I demonstrate it so that those ready to learn this skill can use it on their own.

As our work on dinosaurs proceeds, I also bring in dinosaur fiction stories for additional reading experiences. *Patrick's Dinosaurs* (Clarion, 1983) and *What Happened to Patrick's Dinosaurs?* (Clarion, 1986) by Carol and Donald Carrick are highlighted as we discuss the difference between fiction and nonfiction in each book.

As a lead-in to the death of the dinosaurs, we discuss extinction: what does it mean, how does it happen? *As Dead as a Dodo* by Peter Mayle (Godine, 1982) is an excellent beginning book for this topic. As we read the book, we talk about each animal and how it became extinct. Then we brainstorm all the causes that students already know for the extinction of the dinosaurs.

Our next reading experience is *What Happened to the Dinosaurs?* by Franklyn M. Branley. We talk about each theory and why or why not it might have led to the disappearance of the dinosaurs, adding new theories to our list and crossing off ones which we feel do not belong. I want students to begin making the connection that scientists' theories are like our brainstorming list and must constantly undergo change as new evidence is examined.

For a hands-on activity, we make shoe-box dioramas and group murals depicting the theories. The fossil-hunting teams regroup to create and act out one of the theories. We invite other classrooms to watch our meteorites, plant-eaters, meat-eaters, small mammals, and rodents explain the various extinction theories.

We have fun with dinosaurs throughout the unit, but we really enjoy ourselves with our culminating activities. Using Jack Prelutsky's *Tyrannosaurus Was a Beast,* we write dinosaur poems as a large-group activity. I then copy the poems, which we put together to make our own "big book." Each child picks a favorite poem, copies it, and mounts the poem on a piece of paper cut in the shape of that dinosaur. We then tape-record the poems for our own listening as well as for sharing with other classes. We even form a "Stega-chorus" for choral readings of several of the poems. Noelle Sterne's *Tyrannosaurus Wrecks* provides us with many laughs as we puzzle our way through these jokes and riddles. I say *puzzle* because we look at each joke and talk about why it is funny. I feel this activity is especially important because so many young children laugh at a joke without realizing just why it is supposed to be funny. Exclamations of "Now I get it!" pepper this activity. Favorites are chosen and illustrated for sharing at home.

On the last day of our formal study of dinosaurs, I bring a layered cake to school for a treat. Unbeknown to the children, I have planted "fossil" nuts in the cake, burying them at different layers. Before I slice into the cake, I ask them to study it first. Does it remind them of anything to do with dinosaurs? After several guesses, Michael says, "That looks like one of those layery rocks in our museum," running to get the rock. As the rock is passed around and the connection is made, other theories about the cake come up.

"Maybe there are bones hidden in it."

"Bones, in a cake. Yuk. Not even Mr. Roop would do that."

"Yeah, we'd all become extinct."

As soon as I cut the cake, Amanda shouts, "There are fossils in it. We get to dig them out!" As they dig into their cake, discovering their "fossil" nuts, I overhear Bryan, an avid fiction fan, say, "You know, I really like reading these true books." An even bigger reward is the next trip to the library, when almost half the class chooses their books from the nonfiction section.

Conclusion   Nonfiction books provide many opportunities for both learning and fun for young readers. And like any worthwhile learning experience it takes time, effort, and planning to make it successful. Now that we have so many appealing, interesting, and kid-catching nonfiction books, let's soar with the swans.

13 Get Real, Teacher! What Happens When At-Risk Middle-School Readers Become Involved with Nonfiction

Nancy DeVries Guth
Fred Lynn Middle School, Woodbridge, Virginia

D.J. stood out among the class as they bustled into the library. Wherever he went, a slight flurry surrounded him. He was tiny and wiry, with huge dark eyes that widened with humor whenever anyone spoke to him. I walked over to him and his bevy of buddies and said, "Okay, D.J., you're supposed to be choosing a book for free reading. What would you like to read?"

"Get real, Miz Guth. I don't wanna read nothin'!"

"Oh, come on, D.J. There must be something you'd like to read about!"

"No, I don't read no books unless I have to read it for class. Then I just kinda pretend . . . you know, look at the page and think about somethin' else."

"Why don't you read it?" I questioned.

"Cause readin' ain't no fun. It's boring to me. I like real stuff."

For D.J. and so many others at my middle school, "readin ain't no fun." Over 40 percent of our students fall in the bottom quartile on standardized tests of reading ability. Many of these students come from homes where English is a second language. They do not have personal reservoirs of "book language" and literacy schema built into their everyday experiences. For them, reading is not real. It is something imposed upon them by the school, something unrelated to their daily life or expectations. In my position as reading consultant at a middle school, I strive to make reading "real" for all the students. I assist teachers with "at-risk" readers (those reading two or more grade levels behind), and provide reading incentives and lessons for all teachers and students.

"Get real!" That's often the comment I hear when I ask my at-risk readers if they have read any good books lately. As I "student-watched" throughout my eighteen years of experience as a language arts educator, I noted that many below-level readers gravitate to factual material when allowed to make a choice. Newspapers, magazines, journals, biographies, cookbooks—these were the materials selected by most of my students, whether they were young adults or children.

When presented with the opportunity to design a classroom research question for my study with the Northern Virginia Writing Project, I decided to observe what happens when at-risk middle-school readers interact with nonfiction reading material. Is nonfiction their "preferred" genre? Does their motivation to read change? Does free-choice reading in the nonfiction mode affect their writing? Three examples of students' learning experiences with nonfiction books will be discussed to provide answers to these questions.

Biography: Choosing Heroes from the Past

Tuning into conversations around me, I often heard students discussing their heroes, usually modern-day stars and sports figures. By capitalizing on their interests and prior knowledge, a sixth-grade teacher and I designed a Biography/Autobiography unit. Excerpts from several biographies were included in the students' literature book. From this introduction, we moved to encounters with "real books." We structured the assignments to require students first to read and then to write their responses to the section read. We incorporated cooperative learning groups as a strategy for brainstorming writing ideas and also for peer editing.

The teacher, librarian, and I had collected over thirty different biographies at all reading levels. I watched with fascination as students chose from the selection. Length was a factor for some reluctant readers; however, interest seemed to be the deciding factor as students scanned books, paged through them, and grabbed the ones that looked interesting. An aspiring dancer chose the biography of Isadora Duncan, although she had never heard of Duncan. When asked why, she responded, "I want to be a dancer, so I want to read about all dancers I can for ideas."

A basketball player chose a biography of his hero, Michael Jordan; an amateur filmmaker chose a biography about Steven Spielberg. A girl who had recently moved to Virginia from Texas chuckled often over *Annie, Get Your Gun* by Robert Quackenbush (Prentice-Hall, 1980). I noted that neither race nor gender seemed to influence students' decisions over which person to study. Interest was above all the deciding factor. Anglo-Americans were reading about black sport stars and entertainers. Black Americans were reading about Anglo film stars and political figures.

Students were allowed to choose what activity they would pursue during each of the two daily language arts class periods. Their only restriction was that they could not bother others, and they had to be doing *something*. Students wrote notes in their writing journals, which were collected every two or three days. The teacher and I held conferences with individuals throughout the class periods. The teacher commented after a week of this unit: "I cannot believe how well they are all working! I have not had any problem with discipline at all."

When I asked the students how they were enjoying this language arts unit, one student who had told me the previous week, "Language arts is my most boring subject!" now responded with, "I like reading this stuff because it's real, not made up. And it gives me ideas what life was like in those times."

"Yeah," agreed his buddy. "I wish I could go back to the Civil War time. I wouldn't have to go to school anymore!"

"Remember," another boy reminded him, "it wouldn't be so great if you got sick. You know what we read about the hospitals and doctors." (The day before, I had read aloud from the book *War Nurses* by Sharon Cosner [Walker, 1988], and the students had been fascinated with the story of Clara Barton's work in Virginia.)

"Yeah, and no T.V. and radio or tape players."

"Wow! I'd really have to change if I lived then. They didn't have skateboards either!"

Every day I was asked to read aloud by the students from one or more of the books they "found." Often we think only of fiction as a vehicle for oral reading, but the students demonstrated a desire for expressive oral reading in the nonfiction genre as well. One student commented: "When you read out loud to us, I can 'see' what you are reading in front of my eyes. I want to draw it. It helps me understand."

All students in the class were "on-task," reading or discussing the subjects of their biographies. This previously nonmotivated class was devouring these books, and asking if they could trade when they were finished! They sat in groups of four, using these friends as peer editors for their writing. In this way, many developed interest in others' choices, and the unit was extended for free-choice reading. We structured the unit so that reading and writing would complement each other in terms of topic and idea. The students seemed to move easily back and forth between each mode. Most preferred writing and discussing the assignments with their groups during the second daily class session and focused on silent reading during their first session. The students who were more comfortable with solitary learning pulled their desks off to one side of the room by themselves, while others formed a discussion circle.

The discussion circle is student-directed and student-evaluated, with the teacher observing the interaction and serving as facilitator as needed. Students are encouraged to choose a leader, who reads aloud the question (or statement) to be discussed and then encourages all members to state their opinions and share their writing. The leader ends the session with a summary after each student has taken a turn.

After the discussion circle, most students returned to their desks to write or revise something that they had previously written. Most students kept the biography that they were reading close at hand to refer to as they were writing. When I asked them why, one girl replied, "It gives me ideas for how to write about my facts," adding, "Yeah, is it all right, you think, if I have some of the same goals like she did?"

I explained that one of the reasons for studying about the past is to help us with the present. "Oh, is *that* why we study social studies?" one skeptical learner replied, nodding his head as he finally could see some reason behind school requirements.

One of our below-reading-level students chose a biography about Christa McAuliffe, *Reaching for the Stars* by Patricia Stone Martin (Rourke Enterprises, 1987). I was intrigued by the choice of this large, nonathletic sixth grader who had never before seemed interested in space, science, or athletics. His only comments previously had been regarding television shows. When I asked him why he chose this book, he commented, "I admired her. I saw her on T.V. a lot. I saw when the space capsule blew up. I felt really bad." Then he continued, "I felt bad for her family too. My grandfather just died and I was very sad too."

This student expressed strong feelings in his writing journal in response to the book:

> About McAuliffe's death: "I was angry because it seems to me if people can build a space capsule they should be able to make it safe. I don't think it's fair to ask people to go up in space and then they get killed."

> About setting goals: "Christa McAuliffe went to college to get a degree to be teacher. She taught her students to dream."

> About his own life: "I was born in Mississippi. I was happy there living near all my relatives. My Grandfather lived near us. He taught me lots of things. He taught me to always dream and that I could do whatever I really wanted if I tried."

> About his grandfather's death: "The worst things in my life were moving from Mississippi and when my grandfather died. I was angry at the hospital at first because they didn't save him."

About his own goals: "I dream about going to college, getting a degree, and moving back to Mississippi. Just like Christa McAuliffe and my Grandpa said, if you dream and try, you can make things come true!"

This student illustrates how motivation and prior knowledge affect the final product. He remarked, "I have never read a whole biography before!"

"Why did you finish this one?" I questioned.

"Because it was interesting. I wanted to read about her 'cause I saw about her on T.V. and I wanted to know more." He found a hero by reading a biography that I would never have thought to suggest to him. He was using the past to make sense out of the present and set goals for the future.

By observing this student and his classmates, I realized for myself once again the *art* of teaching language arts, whether it be factual material or fictional. The teacher must provide the support and conditions necessary for students to derive their own meaning from reading and writing, such as using biographies of the students' heroes, and applying the hero's life to that of the student. Then one must provide the time, guidance, and language so that students can clarify their "knowing" for themselves within their own writing. By becoming attuned to students' prior knowledge, their interests, and their strengths, we as teachers can "tune in" to the "real" world of our students. Nonfiction provides a natural link to this real world.

Time Travel to the Past

While working with the sixth graders on the biography unit, the teacher, the library staff, and I were struck by their lack of knowledge about the past. Ken Goodman (1989) urges educators to unite our learners with content, to find out where our students are, and to assist them in finding their place in history.

This was the impetus for a unit planned by my seventh-grade teachers and students on decade research, built around reading and writing about a decade of their choice and culminating in the preparation of a brochure to "advertise" their decade. (See Figure 5 for a sample brochure.)

We were amazed at some of the questions students asked as they engaged in their research:

"What's a 'vac-cin'?" After looking at the word, I realized it was *vaccine.*

"Was that a cure for disease?"

"When was popcorn invented?"

"Guess when the first T.V. dinner was sold?"

Figure 5
Example of a
decade brochure.

> Visit the Fifties and Enjoy
>
> If you have decided to visit the Fifties, you will want to know the fashions. If you are a man, you will be wearing gray flanel suits, thigh length car coats, Bermuda shorts, Eishenhower jackets, Hawaiian shirts, cardigan sweaters, plaid wool shirts, and slacks.
> If you are a woman, you should wear hooded tube dresses, and the sack, chammies, and the western look. You can also wear a wasp waist, wide belts, lots of make-up, costume jewelry, and an elaborate hair style. Teenage boys wear jeans, slicked hair in duck tails, and black leather pants and jackets. Teenage girls wear caprie pants, hot pink sweaters, high heels, and sprayed hair.
> You will probably want to know what to do for fun in the Fifties. Well, you can watch TV, go to drive-in movies, see 3-D movies, and much more. Some of the TV shows you can watch are: I Love Lucy, The Untouchables, Twilight Zone, The Mickey Mouse Club, Davy Crocket, Ozzie and Harriet, Rin Tin Tin, Lassie, The Lone Ranger, and many more.

As students researched their decade, they gravitated to the events that helped to put their own world in perspective and to understand themselves and their parents and teachers a little better. The project culminated on Decade Day, when everyone came dressed in appropriate attire from their decade, and we took over the library as a display gallery for the afternoon. The students set up displays of memorabilia that they had gathered—photographs, magazines, fashions, music, and foods. We partied and performed, as students presented their decade in oral reports, highlighting what they had chosen as typical of the decade. Even sewing or pattern books (borrowed from the home economics room) and radio plays were poured over by students searching for information. They were learning alternate sources for finding information. As they read about decades in the past, I often heard the comment, "I wonder how students will present the nineties ten years from now?" They were using literature from the past to think about the present, and to form speculations about the future.

The strategy of cooperative learning groups also worked well with this assignment. Students individually signed up for the decade of their choice and then were grouped with others who had also chosen the same era. They could collaborate on a report, each focusing on an aspect of the decade, or independent learners could opt to research and write alone on a self-selected area. The students' finished products were varied, creative, and interesting.

In addition, my students' social studies teachers remarked, "They were so much more interested when we started studying World War I and II! I brought in newspapers from that time period, and they read and discussed them, and told all about their decade and what had happened. It really added to their understanding and interest."

Time Travel to the Future

After the students commented about being interested in how future students would view the 1990s, we decided to use their knowledge of the past to predict the future. The beginning of a new decade seemed like the perfect time. However, no one would have thought anything could spark interest on a cold, rainy Thursday during the first week of January. The students were still mentally on vacation, after only one day back at school since their holiday break. They sat at the library tables looking bored, lethargic, and uninterested in anything but gazing out on the bleak landscape, or looking in their purses for their latest beauty fix.

I asked them to think about the year 2000. "Think about yourselves in the year 2000. What do you think you will be doing?" I noticed a slight spark of interest; students began to think about a future career and to volunteer information: pro football players, policewoman, detective, anthropologist . . . I wrote all their suggestions on the board.

I asked the students to figure out how old they would be in 2000. Most were twelve now, so they would be twenty-two in ten years. "Will you already *be* an anthropologist, or will you be studying to become one? Will you *be* a detective? a jet flyer? a doctor?"

We focused on what they would be doing, and discovered that most would be studying to prepare for the future. I then inquired, "What will you be reading in the year 2000?"

One nonenthusiastic boy muttered, *"Nothin'*—I won't be reading nothing after I get out of school!"

Another student turned on him. "What do you mean?" he asked. "What are you going to do?"

"I'm going to be a pro football player. I won't have to read!"

"Oh yes, you will!" the students resoundingly retorted. "Think about it! How about play books, rule books?"

As we continued to brainstorm together, we developed quite a list of what they predicted they would be reading in ten years. I then asked what they noticed about the list. With guidance, they realized that the entire list was comprised of nonfiction materials.

I asked, "What is the purpose of going to school? Is it to prepare you to meet the challenges of the future?"

"Yes." No argument there.

"Then today's lesson is going to do just that. We are going to find a book most like that of the type you will be reading in the future."

The previous lethargy had flown. Excitement reverberated throughout the library as twenty-six seventh graders "let loose" and explored the card catalog with their own definite subject area of interest directing their search. After all were satisfied with their book choices, which ranged from Victorian architecture to computers, I explained the steps of the assignment:

1. Students skim the books and find the section in which they are most interested.

2. We review the strategy of Note Take/Note Make (Vaughan and Estes 1986). Students divide their papers in half. In the lefthand column, the note-take column, they record pertinent information that they gather as they read. They respond with their comments, feelings, and criticisms in the note-make column. (See Figure 6 for a sample note-take/note-make assignment.)

3. Students write a short report about the contents of their books, working from both columns of notes.

4. Students "advertise" their books in a brochure of their own design.

Students have developed fascinating, colorful, thoughtful brochures promoting their books for this assignment. The library staff and other teachers have used these brochures as advertisements for nonfiction books that previously sat untouched on library shelves. Students became interested in each other's books, although they still preferred reading in the subject area that they had originally chosen. Once they discovered the "numbers" (referring to the Dewey decimal classification numbers) of their subject interests, they

Figure 6
Example of note-take/
note-make assignment.

Education Careers	
Note-Take	Note-Make
Kindergarten	
Almost all are women	That would be helpful to me
4 years of training, 2 years liberal arts	Makes no difference
Prepares and motivates more than teaching	I would prefer teaching higher grades
Must like children and parents a lot!	That would be fine since I like both
Elementary	
More specialized each year	I prefer around middle school
Teach several subjects	
Requirements are the same for kindergarten basically but more academic	Fine with me
Low pay but many employed	Teaching would still be rewarding to me
Secondary school	
Instruct in Middle or High School	I'd like to teach middle school

returned to these shelves for other checkouts. At-risk readers who had never previously checked out books unless required came to the library voluntarily as they discovered that they could use these nonfiction books for silent reading, and also as entries on their reading log. When I asked one student why he had never before checked out these books for pleasure reading, he responded, "I thought I could only use those books like we have in the classroom library, or stories; you know, those made-up ones."

Another student interjected, "I never knew these books were here!"

I observed one student hiding a book behind her worksheet in class. I had *never* seen her with a book thus far in her school career, only occasionally with a magazine. When I asked about her book, she proudly shared with me *The Mode in Costume* by R. Turner Wilcox (Scribner's, 1958), and then she shyly pulled out her portfolio. She had carefully copied in detail many of the costumes and had included descriptive characteristics for each fashion. She confided, "I never knew they had books like these. I thought you could only find these things in magazines."

"What do you prefer?" I asked curiously.

"Oh, this book!" she exclaimed. "There's a lot more stuff in it than a magazine." And the clincher: "Besides, it's free!"

She revealed that her goal was to become a fashion designer. She was already focusing on the future, but had not considered books as having anything "real" to offer pertaining to her choice of career.

Conclusion

D.J. is visiting me in the library often nowadays. He comes in to tell me about another book he has "discovered." He is not a poor reader when reading material of which he has previous knowledge. But his knowledge is not from book experiences. His knowledge comes from the media in his life: television, radio, videos, advertisements. When reading about real things in his life, he told me, "It's fun to read. It's easy when I know about the stuff already!"

By observing and listening to D.J. and many other at-risk readers, I learned that *my* choices for pleasurable, meaningful reading material are often not the same as their choices. In reflection, I realized that we who become teachers are usually "good" readers who enjoy curling up with a book. Most of us "good" readers were raised in a literate environment. We were infused with a sense of story structure and vocabulary from the time we were very young. For a good reader, reading an interesting book is a relaxing, enjoyable activity. We can anticipate, predict, and "get into the story" because of prior story experience. For a poor reader who is lacking in story experience, reading the same book may be perceived as punishment.

At-risk readers become more "at-risk" each of their school years because of lack of practice. Nonfiction can provide interesting subject matter to generate positive experiences with real books for "real" below-grade-level readers. Authentic reading encounters with real books can give at-risk readers the confidence and enjoyment to "come back for more," and their reading experiences will become less of a punishment and more of a reward.

Using a Nonfiction Author Study in the Classroom

Judith W. Keck
Licking County Schools, Newark, Ohio

I n an author study, students examine all available books written by a single author, read widely from this collection of books, and explore the author's themes, topics, writing style, and format of published books. This chapter describes a process for selecting an author, gathering materials, preparing for the study, involving students in reading, extending students' reading, and grading and evaluating students' work.

Why a Nonfiction Author Study?

Real people write books. An author study helps disclose the person behind the name printed on a book's cover and helps reveal that person's interests. To explore the work of an author gives students an inside look at this person and his or her work. This exploration might one day lead the student to a similar career.

A number of readers, both children and adults, prefer nonfiction to fiction. A school curriculum that focuses only on writers of fiction excludes both readers and writers of nonfiction.

Each year it seems that the topics to be covered in classroom instruction increase. Teaching each of these topics in isolation is a luxurious use of time that we can ill-afford. A nonfiction author study provides opportunities to cover a variety of topics and to meet several curriculum objectives by integrating science, social studies, language arts, and reading.

Finally, and most importantly, a nonfiction author study is fun. You and your students will become familiar with an author and his or her work, and in the process you will encourage students' reading, writing, and critical thinking, and their active involvement in their own learning process.

Selecting an Author

The most important factor in selecting an author for study is to choose an author who writes about topics that are interesting to the students and who writes at a level at which most students will be able to read independently. The classroom teacher might test some materials with the class by reading one or two of the author's books aloud, asking students to read aloud from one or two books to determine students' fluency with the text, and placing a few books around the classroom to see if students are drawn to them.

For students to study the works of one author, it is important to select an author who has a variety of titles in print which are available to the classroom teacher. Books may be gathered from public libraries, school libraries, and classroom libraries. Some titles may be available as inexpensive paperbacks, while others may be out of print and can be located only in library collections.

Teachers may be able to gather multiple copies of some titles but only one of others; both multiple and single copies will be useful since it is important that students have many choices for reading selections. Russell Freedman has more than fifteen titles in print and has published more than twenty books. Jean Fritz has more than twenty titles in print and has published more than thirty books. Joanna Cole has more than forty titles in print and has published more than fifty books. These are just a few of the authors who would be good choices for a classroom author study. (A list of suggested authors appears at the end of the chapter.)

When determining the number of books needed for an author study, the minimum number should include at least one book per student plus several extras. The maximum number of books in an author study is determined by how many books can realistically be gathered and housed in the classroom.

Preparing for the Study

One of the best parts of an author study is getting to know the author as a person and not just a name printed on the book cover. The reference series *Something about the Author* (Commire 1990) provides biographical information, a complete list of published works at the time the article was printed, and, frequently, a photograph. Some articles in the series are quite lengthy and include interviews and illustrations from a variety of published works. For example, Leonard Everett Fisher's entry is ten pages long.

Publishers will often send promotional materials for classroom use, including photographs and biographical information. When writing for publishers' materials, indicate the number of students in the class and write well in advance of the author study to allow adequate time for shipping; school librarians can help locate publishers' current addresses.

Gather as many books by the author as you can locate from your public library, the school library, and your classroom library. Other teachers in the building may be willing to loan books by the particular author. If students are likely to own books written by the author, you might send home a letter to parents asking that students share their books at school. When special projects of this nature are about to occur in your classroom, it is a good idea to let parents, the school librarian, and school administrators know your intentions. The following is a sample letter from an Ohio teacher, Hazel Almendinger, notifying parents about an author study in her classroom:

Dear Parents:

On Monday, January 11, we will begin a special unit of study in our reading class. For three weeks, we will be reading and studying the books of Jean Fritz, a well-known author of books appropriate for fifth graders. The purpose of this project is to encourage more student reading.

During that time, students will be participating in the following activities:

1. Sustained silent reading.

2. Listening to the teacher read aloud.

3. Writing in a reading journal in which students record what they read and respond to such statements as "I wonder why the author . . ."

4. Small-group discussions in which students discuss questions that they have composed about their reading.

5. Extension activities—to be selected from a list of possibilities and completed after several books are read.

Students' grades for this special project will be determined by accumulating points for participating in these class activities.

If you have any questions or comments about this special project, please call or send a note to school. Plan some special sharing and reading time with your child on several occasions during the next few weeks. If you would like to visit our classroom during this time, please let me know as we would love to have you visit.

It is also important to consider grade-level curriculum requirements for your district and grade level. Textbooks are only one source from which students might read about designated grade-level topics. In an author study, students may read about topics that are also required for instruction in science and social studies. Books about the planets written by Seymour Simon may help meet curriculum requirements for studies of space. Jean Fritz has authored many titles about the Founding Fathers and the writing of the U.S. Constitution. Students may also use a variety of skills required in both the reading and language arts curriculum. Do identify the topics and skills that students will incorporate during the author study. It is good public relations to include this information in communications with parents and administrators.

As the time for beginning the author study draws near, create a classroom display featuring the author and his or her books. On the first few days of the project, read aloud selections from the author's biographical information and introduce the books to students. Select a few books at a time and talk about them, read selections from them, and show some of the illustrations. Creating student interest in the author and the books will pay off with student enthusiasm for the author study.

Student Involvement in Reading

For several days at the beginning of the author study, students should have plenty of classroom time to read. Rather than requiring students to read a certain number of books or a specific number of pages, I recommend that students record the amount of time that they spend reading both at school and at home. This approach does not penalize students who read longer books or books with fewer illustrations. Once students have had considerable time to read, teachers may want to organize discussion groups around titles or specific topics so that students can share information that they have acquired in their reading, their thoughts about the books, and any questions that they have.

Once students have read more of the author's books, they might want to:

Arrange and rearrange book categories (students may see connections among books of which you are unaware).

Arrange books in the order of their publication.

Determine the author's style by exploring related titles (such as reading other titles in Joanna Cole's Magic School Bus series).

Compare information in the author's book with the information in a textbook.

Compare and contrast two nonfiction books on the same topic.

At this point in the author study, the focus needs to be on students' reading, including listening to selections read aloud by the teacher and discussions among students about the books and the author.

Student Response to Reading

Following several days of involvement with reading, students should have the same opportunities to extend their nonfiction reading as they commonly would during a study of fiction books. Students should have choices in their extension activities which include projects focusing on art, drama, oral language, music, and writing. Yet another choice for students should include a decision about working independently, in pairs, or in a small group.

Projects for students might include the following:

Create a board game for a book. For example, a student might create a Seymour Simon board game, including titles and information about various books by the author.

Reenact a scene from *Shh! We're Writing the Constitution* by Jean Fritz (Putnam, 1987).

Design a new book jacket for Russell Freedman's *Franklin Delano Roosevelt* (Clarion, 1990), including jacket flap information about the book and the author.

Create a web of the more than thirty books written by Leonard Everett Fisher, including categorizing the books and preparing illustrations.

Write a new book for the Magic School Bus series by Joanna Cole in which Ms. Frizzell and her class visit an attraction in your area. (In a central Ohio classroom, students wrote a book about visiting the mounds, part of Ohio's system of Native American earthworks.)

Create an author song in which you include as many of the author's titles as you can.

Design a record album and paraphrase the author's titles and topics to become the "songs" on the album.

Write a dialogue between the frog in Joanna Cole's *A Frog's Body* (Morrow, 1980) and the cat in *A Cat's Body* (Morrow, 1982) in which each describes how they are similar and how they are different.

As the author study draws to a close, allow time for an exhibition in which students share what they have learned and their extension activities with each other, with students in other classrooms, and with parents and administrators.

Once students have thoroughly researched an author's life and work, they may wish to correspond with the author in care of the publisher's address or to arrange a telephone conference call. Students should be prepared for those experiences so they do not ask questions that could easily be researched in advance. If some students choose to correspond with the author, be sure to include a stamped, self-addressed envelope, which might expedite a response from the author.

Teacher Grading and Evaluation

The classroom atmosphere during a nonfiction author study should be open and supportive of student involvement in reading. Students should expect to be rewarded with good grades when they are appropriately involved with assigned classroom tasks. Students who are behaving in required ways can be rewarded with points. You might assign points on a daily basis for participation in sustained silent reading, attentive listening to the teacher reading aloud, and participation in book discussions. Daily points earned can easily be recorded on a class list with a grid for activities and days of the week, or you might prefer to convert this to a wall chart. I have adapted an analytic scale used for writing to create an instrument for evaluating student projects and book discussion (see Figures 7 and 8).

No predetermined criterion for evaluating student work is as significant as students' being involved in establishing classroom criteria. Do identify and discuss evaluation criteria with students before they begin their special extension projects. Students will then know how they will be evaluated, and their completed projects should be of higher quality.

Students might evaluate their own extension activities by answering the following questions:

1. How much time did you spend on this project?
2. Why did you choose this project?
3. What was the most difficult part of the project?
4. On a scale of zero to twenty, how many points would you give yourself?

Following this self-evaluation, the student and teacher confer to determine together the number of points they would assign to the project.

At the conclusion of the author study, student grades can easily be determined by balancing the number of points each student has earned against the maximum number of possible points. These figures can then be converted to the number-grade or letter-grade system required by your school district.

When the author study is completed, give students opportunities to discuss and write about their favorite parts of the study or the best book they read, and to make suggestions for improving the project. When students know that their comments are being heard, they are more apt to be honest, open, and constructive in their criticisms.

Conclusion

It is not the day-to-day worksheets and textbook chapters that make the school lives of students memorable, but the special projects that engage them both in and out of school. An in-depth author study can create a touchstone in the lives of students to "remember when we . . ." and to spark the recognition of an author's name. "Oh, yes, I've read several books by that author, and did you know . . . ?" That's the stuff of which real readers are made.

Figure 7
Evaluation form for student-created book jacket, bookmark, bumper sticker, record album cover.

1. Generates interest in the book	4	3	2	1	0
2. Displays three key features of the book	4	3	2	1	0
3. Communicates clearly	4	3	2	1	0
4. Demonstrates visual appeal	4	3	2	1	0
TOTAL POINTS					

Figure 8
Evaluation form for student participation in book discussions.

1. Participates in book discussions	4	3	2	1	0
2. Attends to the comments of others	4	3	2	1	0
3. Locates information in the book to present evidence in discussion	4	3	2	1	0
4. Relates personal experiences and feelings to those described in the book	4	3	2	1	0
TOTAL POINTS					

Potential Authors for Nonfiction Author Studies

Aliki—For readers of all ages; topics include dinosaurs, mummies, medieval times.

Arnosky, Jim—For readers of all ages; topics focus on experiences in the woods, including sketching outdoors, animals, and fishing.

Ashabranner, Brent—For middle-school and older readers, topics focus on other cultures, including Native American, Middle Eastern, and Mexican cultures.

Cole, Joanna—For readers of all ages; a variety of science and health topics, including human and animal development.

Fisher, Leonard Everett—For intermediate readers and older; topics about historic people, occupations, and locations.

Freedman, Russell—For middle-school readers and older; topics include the Western frontier in the 1800s and biographies; animal books appropriate for readers of all ages.

Fritz, Jean—For readers of all ages; topics include the American Revolution, China in the twentieth century, and biographies of historic American personalities.

Gibbons, Gail—For primary readers; topics include construction, transportation, holidays, and behind-the-scenes job information.

Giblin, James Cross—For intermediate readers and older; topics include building construction and holidays.

Lauber, Patricia—For primary and intermediate readers; science topics include animals, dinosaurs, earthquakes, and volcanoes.

Meltzer, Milton—For junior high readers and older; social studies topics include American history, politics, minorities, and biographies.

Patent, Dorothy Hinshaw—For primary through middle-school readers; nature topics, including plants and animals.

Sattler, Helen Roney—For intermediate readers and older; topics include dinosaurs and other animals.

Simon, Seymour—For intermediate readers and older; science topics include animals, astronomy, computers, and features of planet earth.

15 Using Informational Books to Develop Reference Skills

M. Jean Greenlaw
University of North Texas

When students are asked to locate information on a topic in order to write a report or to expand discussion in a classroom, the first and often only reference tool that they use is the encyclopedia. A standard dictionary is also used in the classroom when students are told to check their spelling. These two reference sources are certainly valuable, but they are only the tip of the iceberg of reference tools that are available to students.

The teaching of reference skills has often fallen into the realm of the rote and pedantic. As students would be quick to tell you, "This is *boring!*" and they are usually right. The reason for this response is that the teaching of these skills is often isolated from any meaningful context and is presented as a package of skills taught with boring exercises.

I would like to suggest an alternative. Reference skills should be taught in conjunction with course content as a means for extending and expanding content. These skills should be woven throughout the semester or year and should be aimed at a specific goal. This can be done for any grade level and for any content area. I will provide a specific example taken from a class that I taught recently.

In the state of Texas, we have mandated skills called Essential Elements. Many states have similar requirements, and it is necessary to target teaching to ensure that mandates are met. The required reference skills for fourth grade were found under the library skills mandate. I chose, however, to teach these skills through the science content at the fourth-grade level. I could have chosen any grade or

A condensed version of this chapter was published in the "Books in the Classroom" column in *The Horn Book Magazine* 65 (March/April 1989): 250–53. © M. Jean Greenlaw. Used by permission of the author.

content, but the state had just adopted new science books, and it seemed logical to incorporate an innovative approach with the new textbooks. I created activity sheets for teaching and practicing reference skills as we progressed through the school year. Teaching new skills took place from September through December; the implementation extended through the entire year and, one hopes, will continue for life. I was in the classroom one day a week; the teacher and librarian worked with me so there was continuity for the days I was not present.

The activity sheets that I developed are shown throughout this chapter as a means of illustrating how to teach reference skills using informational books. Of course, you will need to modify any you select to fit your grade level and content, and you may wish to create new ones that work better for you.

I believe that curiosity is a primary need of all students. As we began each new unit in science, the students were given a handout that was headed "Curiosity" (see Figure 9). They were to record the topic of study, things that they were curious to learn about the topic, and possible sources to consult to find the answers. The only reference tool mentioned by students at the beginning of the year was the encyclopedia. That response changed drastically by January. I emphasized to students that the textbook was only a framework for learning and that there were many other interesting ideas to pursue in relationship to each topic. Students were encouraged to follow their own lines of interest and to contribute their new knowledge to the class. They, therefore, became interactive rather than passive learners.

The first research topic that we worked on together was animals. The beginning paragraph in the textbook mentioned that groups of animals often have specific names. An activity sheet was created (see Figure 10), and class discussion led to the understanding that a group name often describes a characteristic of the animal. Students were asked to use reference books to locate information about several collective nouns: *gaggle, pride, pack, swarm,* and *covey.* Students were to identify the animal group and to hypothesize about the characteristic of the group that led to the names. They were then to do research on two animals that interested them and to create a group name for each animal. My favorites were a *curl* of cats, a *slither* of snakes, a *laughter* of hyenas, and a *taco* of kangaroos.

The curiosity sheets revealed that students were interested in a wide variety of topics that were not covered in the textbook. We used the text as a core, but since the object was to learn about animals, we expanded our study to incorporate the interests of the students. Several students expressed an interest in dinosaurs; why did they die, what colors were they, how did they live? These were

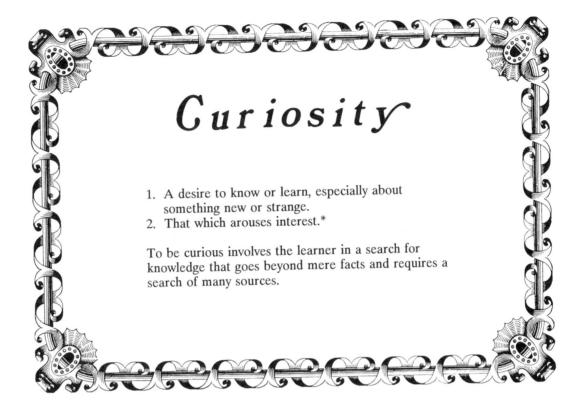

Curiosity

1. A desire to know or learn, especially about something new or strange.
2. That which arouses interest.*

To be curious involves the learner in a search for knowledge that goes beyond mere facts and requires a search of many sources.

TOPIC:

Things I am curious about:

Possibilities for research:

*The American Heritage Dictionary of the English Language. Boston: Houghton Mifflin, 1981, p. 324.

Figure 9. "Curiosity" activity sheet.

What's in a Name?

Specific names are given to groups of animals that live together. For instance, a group of fish is called a school and a group of elephants is called a herd. Often, the name describes some characteristic of the animals. Locate the animal group that matches each name below. Speculate on what characteristic of the animal caused the name to be used.

1. gaggle:

2. pride:

3. pack:

4. swarm:

5. covey:

Choose two animals that interest you and create a name for the group. Tell what characteristic caused you to choose the name.

Figure 10. "What's in a Name?" activity sheet.

questions that scientists are interested in answering! I read several poems to the class from Lee Bennett Hopkins's *Dinosaurs* (Harcourt Brace Jovanovich, 1987), which stimulated varied responses and a desire to learn more about dinosaurs. One student read Patricia Lauber's *Dinosaurs Walked Here and Other Stories Fossils Tell* (Bradbury, 1987), and the class discussed the brontosaurus tracks that have been found in Texas.

Students were interested in a wide assortment of animals. One student who wanted to know how a dog could tell by smelling that cats were around consulted Joanna Cole's *A Dog's Body* (Morrow, 1986). As I always encourage learners to be aware of the world around them, one student, after hearing on the news that many seals were being washed up on beaches, read Susan Meyers's *Pearson: A Harbor Seal Pup* (Dutton, 1980). Another remembered the news story about the moose that had fallen in love with a cow and read Pat Wakefield and Larry Carrara's *A Moose for Jessica* (Dutton, 1987). Two students went to a natural history museum, which led to interest in Judy Cutchins and Ginny Johnston's *Are These Animals Real? How Museums Prepare Wildlife Exhibits* (Morrow, 1984) and Peggy Thompson's *Auks, Rocks and the Odd Dinosaur* (Crowell, 1985), both of which deal with natural history museums. These are only a few of the informational books about dinosaurs read by my class members; further, there have been other informational books published since the time of this project that could be part of class research today. Students pursued different interests around a core topic and shared their knowledge with class members in various ways.

The dictionary was the first reference book to be studied, and an activity sheet listed four very different dictionaries: *The American Heritage Dictionary of the English Language,* Peter Bowler's *The Superior Person's Book of Words,* Arthur Cotterell's *A Dictionary of World Mythology,* and Helen Roney Sattler's *The Illustrated Dinosaur Dictionary.* Each dictionary was chosen for a specific purpose so that students could see that there are many kinds of dictionaries available for their use. I believe that good teaching reviews what has been learned and looks ahead to what will be studied. The dinosaur dictionary was chosen because it was illustrated, but also because we had been studying about dinosaurs. The dictionary about mythology was chosen because I planned to incorporate mythology when we studied about the solar system in several months.

Many activity sheets that were devised for this project featured tasks that were done as a class to teach the particular reference skill, and then a section for individual application of the skill. The first task on the "Dictionary Delight" sheet (see Figure 11) was completed as a class—determining the purpose and audience for

Dictionary Delight

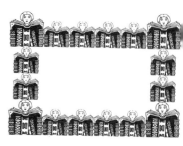

Each of these books is a dictionary and each has a different purpose. Hypothesize what the purpose of each might be and who the audience for the book might be.

The American Heritage Dictionary of the English Language. Houghton Mifflin, 1981.

Peter Bowler. The Superior Person's Book of Words. Godine, 1985.

Arthur Cotterell. A Dictionary of World Mythology. Putnam, 1980.

Helen Roney Sattler. The Illustrated Dinosaur Dictionary. Lothrop, 1983.

Locate four other types of dictionaries. Record their titles and purposes.

Figure 11. "Dictionary Delight" activity sheet.

each dictionary. For example, the class decided that the purpose of *The Superior Person's Book of Words* was to find words with which to show off and that the audience was a very smart person. During the next two weeks, students gathered numerous dictionaries for the room and were astonished at the variety that they were able to find. There were dictionaries of opera, biography, soccer, medicine, skateboarding, and computers. The students became aware that dictionaries were designed for more than checking the spelling of a word and that they could look further than one source when using a dictionary. My greatest sense of accomplishment came when several students announced that they had persuaded their parents to purchase dictionaries for them.

Gail Gibbons was going to be a guest speaker at the school later in the year, so I used her book *Check It Out! The Book about Libraries* (Harcourt Brace Jovanovich, 1985) both as a reference book and as a way to introduce the students to the skills of interviewing. We used one activity sheet, "Introducing" (see Figure 12), to learn about polite and interesting questions—as opposed to rude and dull ones. Another activity sheet, "Meet the Author" (see Figure 13), formed the basis for doing research about an author, using the many reference tools that can provide such information. Since Gibbons has written books that fall in various categories, many of them science-related, we also used this activity sheet to work on main ideas and categorization. The students conducted research to find out about Gibbons, created polite and interesting questions using the categories they had established, and organized the interview in an interesting and sequential fashion. A trial run enabled the students to practice their interview skills and to attain a natural conversational tone so that when Gibbons visited the school, the students were well prepared. The interview was videotaped so that other classes will be able to benefit from the interview in the future.

The encyclopedia, the first and only reference source for many students doing a report, was the subject of our next study. We discussed the strengths and weaknesses of an encyclopedia and learned to use it as a starting point only. By this time, the topic in our science books was how living things survive, so each student chose one living thing to research. The students were to begin with the encyclopedia, but were to use at least three other informational books to expand their knowledge. They recorded these additional references on their activity sheets, "Expanding the Encyclopedia" (see Figure 14). They soon learned that there was much information that could not "fit" in an encyclopedia. I knew that the message was getting across and that this was more than just rote response to a required activity when I discovered that most of the students had checked out the three books that they had used for research. The

INTRODUCING

Participating in an interview means asking questions that will give you interesting information. These questions should be polite and should be designed to give you information that is new.

Rude questions: How old are you? How much money do you make?

Polite questions: How old were you when you began writing? How much money can a beginning author expect to make on a book?

Boring question: How long did it take you to write . . .

Interesting question: Why did you decide to write informational (or any type of) books?

Practice writing polite and interesting questions.

Figure 12. "Introducing" activity sheet.

Meet the Author

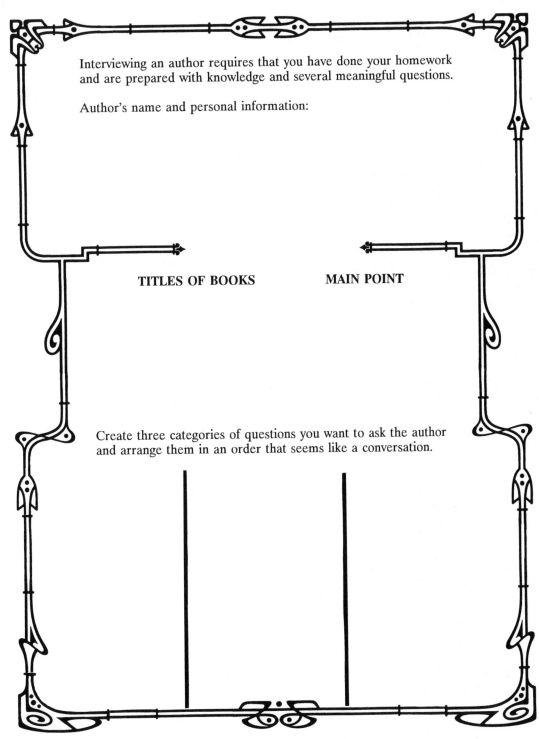

Interviewing an author requires that you have done your homework and are prepared with knowledge and several meaningful questions.

Author's name and personal information:

TITLES OF BOOKS   **MAIN POINT**

Create three categories of questions you want to ask the author and arrange them in an order that seems like a conversation.

Figure 13. "Meet the Author" activity sheet.

Expanding the Encyclopedia

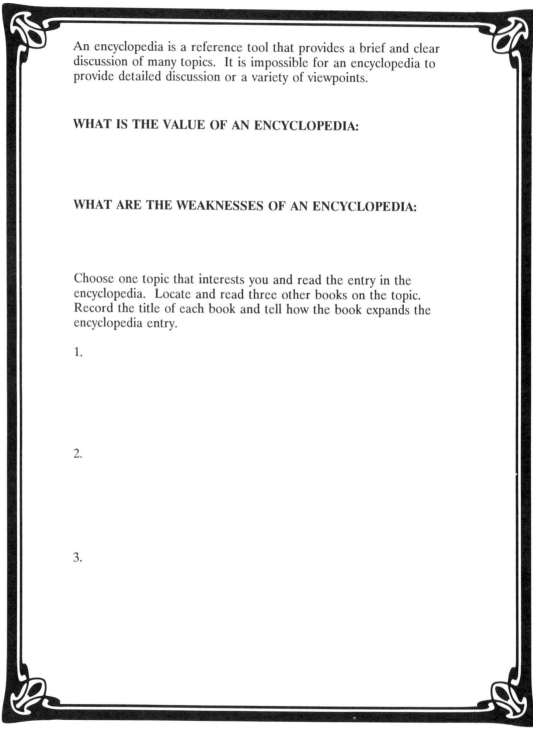

An encyclopedia is a reference tool that provides a brief and clear discussion of many topics. It is impossible for an encyclopedia to provide detailed discussion or a variety of viewpoints.

WHAT IS THE VALUE OF AN ENCYCLOPEDIA:

WHAT ARE THE WEAKNESSES OF AN ENCYCLOPEDIA:

Choose one topic that interests you and read the entry in the encyclopedia. Locate and read three other books on the topic. Record the title of each book and tell how the book expands the encyclopedia entry.

1.

2.

3.

Figure 14. "Expanding the Encyclopedia" activity sheet.

books were sitting on their desks, ready for consultation during in-depth discussion.

An activity sheet on reference books (see Figure 15) served as a means to review information about the science chapters that we had already studied as well as to gain knowledge about our current chapter, measurement in science. In addition, several of the reference books that students were to locate would be used in a culminating activity that I had planned to evaluate their knowledge and use of informational books.

The solar system was our next science topic. The students completed a "Search for the Source" activity (see Figure 16) that called for a hunt through the school library for such information as the names of the planets in order from the sun, the name of a famous comet, and the name of a magazine that publishes articles about the solar system. In each case, students were to provide the information and to record the source that they used. They were also to locate myths about the Roman gods or goddesses for whom the planets are named, or their Greek counterparts. The students had to hypothesize how the planet got its name and to tell one of the myths to the class. Books such as Leonard Everett Fisher's *The Olympians* (Holiday House, 1984) and Alice Low's *The Macmillan Book of Greek Gods and Heroes* (1985) were good sources and thus were checked out immediately. Storytelling was interspersed throughout our study of the solar system. Students also discovered Seymour Simon's excellent books on the planets and learned on the first page of *Mars* (Morrow, 1987) that the Romans named the planet for their god of war. Of course, the solar system leads to space exploration, and several students read Sally Ride's *To Space and Back* (Lothrop, Lee and Shepard, 1986).

Also on the "Search for the Source" activity sheet was a question for which I had no answer. I believe that it is important for students to bring knowledge to the classroom that even the teacher does not know. In this case, it was the time of year when Nobel Prizes were being announced, so I included the following questions: "What is a Nobel Prize? Who has won a Nobel Prize related to the study of the solar system?" I did not even know for sure if anyone had won such a prize, but the students located several winners. They felt very proud to be able to add to my store of knowledge as well as their classmates'. We then took a brief time to study several Nobel winners.

We next made arrangements to visit the local public library, at which the children's librarian gave a thorough tour and urged students to obtain library cards. They then completed a second "Search for the Source" activity sheet (see Figure 17), this time one that focused on energy, our science text chapter, and on details that would allow them to complete the culminating activity.

A reference book is any book to which we refer for help or information. Some examples are: dictionary, encyclopedia, atlas, almanac, thesaurus, and any book on a specialized topic.

Name a specific reference book that would provide specialized information on each topic listed below.

1. words about music:

2. birds of North America:

3. symbols of countries of the world:

4. size and location of countries of the world:

5. synonyms for "read":

6. books by Gail Gibbons:

7. information about Gail Gibbons:

8. why dinosaurs did not survive:

9. who holds the record for being the world's tallest person:

10. who discovered the theory of relativity:

Figure 15. "Reference" activity sheet.

Search for the Source

Search in the library for answers to these questions. Provide the answer and the name of the source you used.

1. Locate three books about the solar system. Give their titles and call numbers. Use them to supplement your textbook.

2. Name the planets in order from the sun.

3. Name a famous comet and tell how frequently it appears.

4. Locate myths about three Greek or Roman gods or goddesses for whom the planets are named and specify your sources. Why do you think they were named for these gods or goddesses? Share one myth with your class.

5. Locate a book about the solar system that is at least 15 years old and a book with a new copyright. What is one fact that is different?

6. What is the Nobel Prize? Who has won a Nobel Prize related to the study of the solar system?

7. Locate a magazine that publishes articles about the solar system.

Figure 16. "Search for the Source" activity sheet 1.

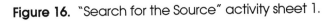

Search for the Source

Search in the library for answers to these questions. Provide the answer and the source you used.

1. What is a Jabberwock? Who wrote the poem in which you find it?

2. How many meanings does the word "iron" have? List five.

3. What is the distance from the earth to the sun?

4. Which element has the greatest density?

5. Locate and name at least five alphabets.

6. Give the birth date and death date of Albert Einstein. What is he famous for?

7. Where would you find a Jacob's ladder?

8. During what period of history were jousts popular?

9. Why doesn't an igloo melt inside?

10. What is an oystercatcher? What is its adaptation?

Figure 17. "Search for the Source" activity sheet 2.

For a culminating activity, we made color copies (after obtaining permission from the publisher) of the *J* page in Mike Wilks's *The Ultimate Alphabet* (Henry Holt, 1986) and the workbook page for that letter. This book is a marvelous series of paintings, one for each letter of the alphabet. It is a test of dedication and ingenuity to locate in the paintings each of the nearly eight thousand objects that are named in the workbook. The students had four weeks in which to make use of all the reference skills that they had learned and to locate the appropriate 102 *J* objects in the picture. They were to keep a record of the name of each reference book that they consulted in solving the puzzle. Diligent work produced two winners, who each received a copy of the book. When the reference and informational books were tallied, more than one hundred books were used by the students for this activity.

Conclusion

The most important outcome of this project was that the students continued to use their skills in other content areas and retained them in the next school year. They clearly know that there are reference books in addition to the encyclopedia. Learning reference skills does not have to be dull. If we coordinate learning them with specific curriculum areas and if we make the learning meaningful rather than abstract, students not only will learn the skills, but they will put these skills to use.

Putting It All Together: Theme Teaching with Nonfiction Books

Evelyn B. Freeman
The Ohio State University at Newark

As I entered the classroom, I heard "Music of Iran" softly playing on the record player. The first and second graders were enthusiastically writing their own folktales with a desert setting. Illustrated word cards with such desert words as *pyramid, cactus,* and *lizard* covered one bulletin board, while another displayed the children's own version of Jim Haskins's *Count Your Way through the Arab World* (Carolrhoda, 1987), which depicted ten tents, five camels, and so on. Photographs of the Arizona desert adorned another wall, and desert books of all kinds were everywhere. The teacher explained to me that her class had just begun a new theme of study on the desert.

A theme of study provides children with an opportunity to explore a topic in an integrated manner. "Thematic units," according to Christine C. Pappas, Barbara Z. Kiefer, and Linda S. Levstik, "reflect patterns of thinking, goals, and concepts common to bodies of knowledge. They link together content from many areas of the curriculum and depict the connections that exist across disciplines" (1990, 49).

A theme of study has several characteristics. It is sufficiently long in duration for children to have time to study a topic in depth and also to make choices among various types of learning experiences. Diverse resources are used as children engage in individual, small-group, and whole-class activities. This chapter discusses how one type of resource, nonfiction books, can support theme studies in the elementary classroom.

Before a theme study can begin, preplanning must occur. Teachers select a theme based on the interests of the children, the guidelines of the curriculum, and their own knowledge and interests. In order to begin planning a theme, teachers brainstorm the possible concepts to be developed and the myriad learning experiences which involve children in thinking, reading, writing, oral language, and creative expression. These experiences will include the content areas of math, science, social studies, the arts, and language arts.

As part of the brainstorming process, teachers web their thoughts. A web visually represents the learning possibilities associated with a theme. A web is fluid; teachers can modify it with additions, deletions, or extensions as the theme evolves. A web is not meant to serve as a lesson plan, but rather it provides an overall structure of how the theme is conceptualized and how aspects of the theme are interrelated. As specific concepts are developed or learning experiences implemented, teachers engage in more detailed and specific planning.

Using the theme of houses, I will describe the ways in which nonfiction books support theme studies. The discussion will focus on learning experiences appropriate for grades three to five, but these ideas may be adapted to other grades as well. I designed the web on the topic of houses with ideas borrowed from house webs created by two of my students, Carolyn Parrott and James Buehler (see Figure 18). I will highlight various aspects of the web to describe the role of informational books in the theme. Patricia R. Crook and Barbara A. Lehman (1991) advocate the use of nonfiction as well as fiction in developing themes of study.

In general, teachers can share nonfiction books in many ways, reading them aloud to the class, highlighting portions of books that relate to a specific fact or area under discussion, giving book talks on various books, and including them in the classroom library. Students may read the books independently, consult them for specific information or projects, or use them for research. Several concepts from the theme will be described to illustrate the specific uses of the books.

The first concept to explore within the house theme is that of architecture. *To Grandfather's House We Go: A Roadside Tour of American Homes* by Harry Devlin (Parents Magazine, 1967) provides students with a fine introduction to architecture and the distinct styles used in American homes. Illustrated with paintings of actual houses, it provides examples of the Georgian and Greek revival styles and of the Octagon house, to name a few. This book may be read aloud, or the pictures may be discussed by the children and used as a guide for a walking tour of their own community in which they observe various architectural styles. Perhaps an architect might visit the classroom to share drawings and to describe how houses are designed. The children can create a bulletin board of pictures of houses taken from magazines or old real estate books, with the styles labeled. They can begin to generate a vocabulary list dealing with architecture, perhaps culminating in the writing of their own "ABC

Figure 18. Web for the theme of houses.

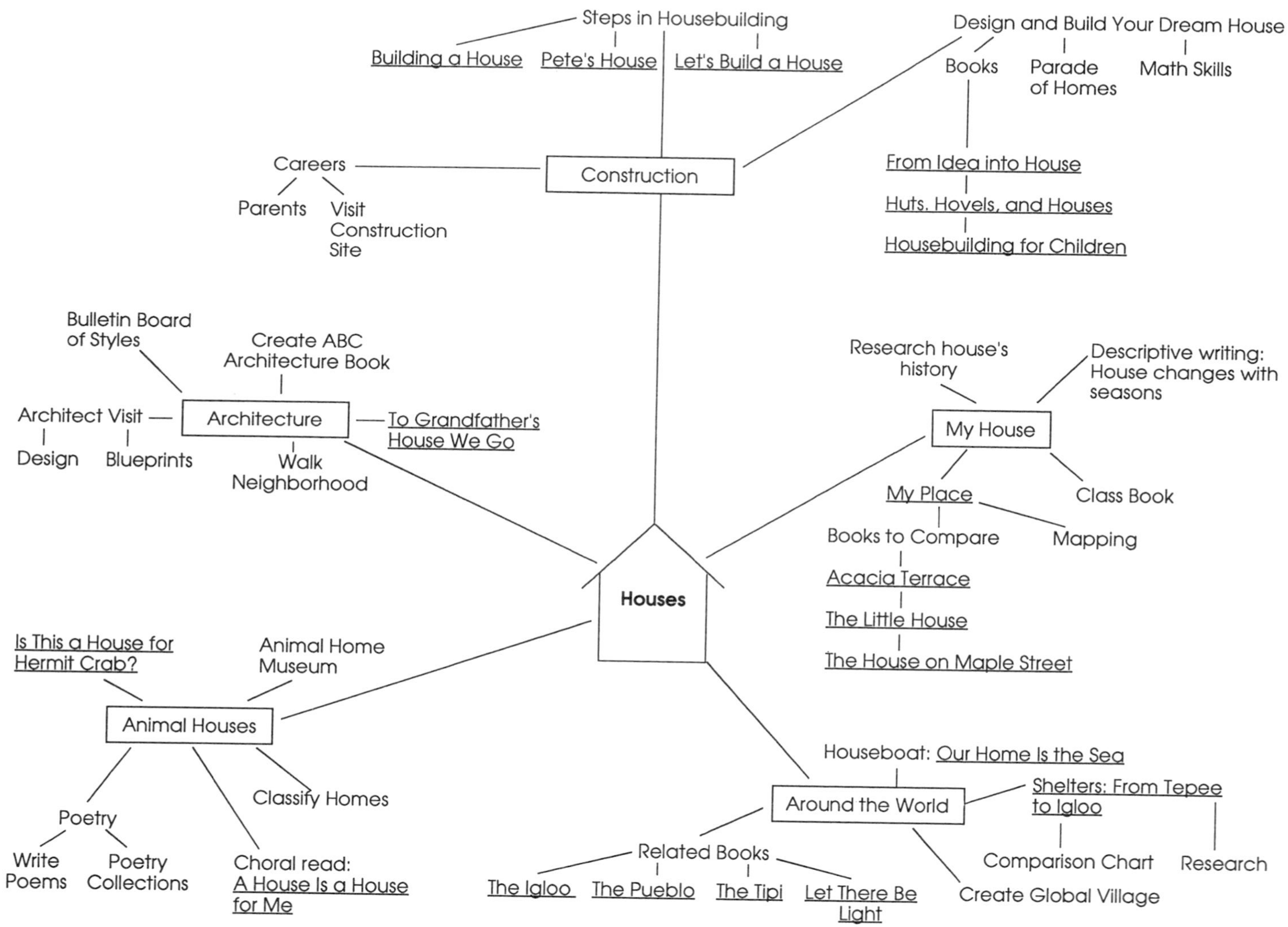

Construction
- Building a House
- Pete's House — Steps in Housebuilding
- Let's Build a House
- Design and Build Your Dream House
  - Books — Parade of Homes — Math Skills
  - From Idea into House
  - Huts, Hovels, and Houses
  - Housebuilding for Children

Architecture — To Grandfather's House We Go
- Careers — Visit Construction Site
- Parents
- Create ABC Architecture Book
- Walk Neighborhood
- Bulletin Board of Styles
- Architect Visit — Blueprints
- Design

My House
- Research house's history
- Descriptive writing: House changes with seasons
- Class Book
- My Place — Books to Compare — Mapping
- Acacia Terrace
- The Little House
- The House on Maple Street

Around the World
- Houseboat: Our Home Is the Sea
- Shelters: From Tepee to Igloo — Research
- Comparison Chart
- Create Global Village
- Let There Be Light
- The Tipi
- Related Books — The Pueblo
- The Igloo

Animal Houses
- Animal Home Museum
- Classify Homes
- Choral read: A House Is a House for Me
- Is This a House for Hermit Crab?
- Poetry — Poetry Collections
- Write Poems

Houses

of Architecture book, with each letter of the alphabet representing a vocabulary word.

A second concept focuses on the child's own home. A wonderful nonfiction book to introduce this concept is *My Place* by Nadia Wheatley and Donna Rawlins (Australia in Print, 1989). This Australian book traces the history of a house, starting in 1988 and moving back in time by ten-year intervals to 1788. Each page of the book includes a map showing the house in that decade in relationship to its neighborhood. A natural integration of map skills develops as students construct their own neighborhood maps. Other books of fiction and nonfiction have followed a similar format, such as Barbara Ker Wilson's *Acacia Terrace* (Scholastic, 1988), which features a house in Sydney, Australia, built in the 1860s, and the picture books *The Little House* by Virginia Lee Burton (Houghton Mifflin, 1942) and *The House on Maple Street* by Bonnie Pryor (Morrow, 1987). These books provide a model for student research and writing. A class book of "My Place" could be developed, with students contributing a one-page description of their own house. Or students might research the history of their house, locating records about it, finding out about its "title," and researching its previous owners. Students might also write about the changes that occur at their house with the changes of the seasons.

Another concept to be explored involves constructing houses. A picture book oftentimes provides a good introduction to what might be a more complex topic. The informational picture book *Building a House* by Byron Barton (Greenwillow, 1981) introduces students to the steps in building a house and the various careers involved in the construction trades. Once this book has been read and discussed, the stages of construction can be explored in greater depth in the informational picture book *Let's Build a House: A White Cottage before Winter* by Russ Flint (Ideals Children's Press, 1990). This book, written from the first-person perspective of a young girl, details the tradespeople involved in construction, from the well driller who must look for fresh water underground, to the workers hanging sheets of drywall. *Pete's House* by Harriet Langsam Sobol (Macmillan, 1978) provides students with the opportunity to follow the construction of a house through photographs. Both of these books provide a wealth of new vocabulary words in a meaningful context, such as *beam, stud, rafters,* and *joist*. Students may visit a nearby construction site to observe the construction of a house in progress. Perhaps some parents in the school who are employed in building-construction occupations, such as stone masons, electricians, or carpenters, could come speak to the class.

As a major project for this aspect of the house theme, students could design, plan, and construct their own dream house out of a variety of materials. Math skills would be stressed here as students measure, compute, and determine scale. Many books can assist the students with the project. *From Idea into House* by architect Rolf Myller (Atheneum, 1974) can be consulted for help with developing plans and figuring scale. The book includes examples of floor plans, working drawings, detail drawings, and scale. *Huts, Hovels, and Houses* by Timothy Fisher (Addison-Wesley, 1977) gives instruction on building houses out of a variety of materials, such as cans, milk cartons, newspapers, and boxes. Similarly, Les Walker in *House-building for Children* (Overlook, 1977) describes the house-building experiences of four girls and six boys between the ages of seven and ten. Specific directions are provided for building various types of houses, such as wood frame or tree houses. The application of math skills is essential for this project in all phases of the construction process. When all houses are complete, the class could hold a Parade of Homes inviting parents and other classrooms to view their creations.

Still another concept to explore centers on the variety of houses around the world. A natural book to introduce this topic is *Shelters: From Tepee to Igloo* by Harvey Weiss (Crowell, 1988). The book describes many types of shelters, such as Bedouin tents, yurts, and Japanese houses. Students might use this book to develop a comparative chart of types of shelters, the climates in which they are found, materials used in construction, cultural group of the people who live in them, and the special features of the shelter. They may also want to divide into groups to research one type of shelter in more depth, perhaps consulting David and Charlotte Yue's *The Tipi: A Center of Native American Life* (Knopf, 1984), *The Pueblo* (Houghton Mifflin, 1986), and *The Igloo* (Houghton Mifflin, 1988), which explore in detail specific types of shelters. Or some children may want to read the picture book *Our Home Is the Sea* by Riki Levinson (Dutton, 1988), which describes life on a houseboat off the coast of Hong Kong. Children may further investigate one aspect of a house. In *Let There Be Light: A Book about Windows,* James Cross Giblin (Crowell, 1988) describes windows in different types of shelters around the world and through history. Student research on this and other topics may lead to the creation of a global village within the classroom.

Another aspect of the house theme deals with animal houses. Children will delight in reading the informational picture book *Is This a House for Hermit Crab?* by Megan McDonald (Orchard, 1990). Students may then generate a list of other types of animal homes. In a classification activity, students classify animals by where they live, such as houses underground, on the ground, above the ground, or in water. Examples of actual animal homes can be brought into the classroom, such as beehives, anthills, aquariums, or tree logs. The class can establish an Animal House Museum for other classes to visit. Poetry integrates well here with a choral reading of the book-length poem *A House Is a House for Me* by Mary Ann Hoberman (Viking Penguin, 1982). Students may look for other poems about animal houses or write their own poems to make a class poetry collection.

I have discussed only five concepts to be developed in the theme of houses, and there are other directions that the theme could take. Historical houses, imaginary houses, houses of the future, or contemporary issues of the homeless, access for the disabled, or group homes for individuals with special needs are additional concepts that might be explored. The possibilities are limitless. Through theme studies, children gain knowledge, extend their knowledge, and share their knowledge with others. They see the interrelationships that exist among topics and across content areas. Nonfiction children's books are a valuable resource to support theme studies in the elementary school.

Reference Works Cited

Abrahamson, Richard, and Robert Stewart. 1982. "Movable Books—A New Golden Age." *Language Arts* 59:342–47.

The American Heritage Dictionary of the English Language. 1981. Boston: Houghton Mifflin.

American Association for the Advancement of Science. 1989. *Science for All Americans.* Washington, D.C.: American Association for the Advancement of Science.

Anderson, C.W. 1987. "Strategic Teaching in Science." In *Strategic Teaching and Learning: Cognitive Instruction in the Content Areas,* edited by B.F. Jones. Alexandria, Va: Association for Supervision and Curriculum Development.

Armbruster, Bonnie B., Charles L. Mitsakos, and Vincent Robert Rogers. 1986. *America's History.* Lexington, Mass.: Ginn and Company.

Berkowitz, Sandra J. 1986. "Effects of Instruction in Text Organization on Sixth-Grade Students' Memory of Expository Reading." *Reading Research Quarterly* 21 (2): 161–78.

Bohning, Gerry, and Marguerite Radencich. 1989a. "Action Books: Pages for Learning and Laughter." *Young Children* 44(6): 62–70.

———. 1989b. "Informational Action Books: A Curriculum Resource for Science and Social Studies." *Journal of Reading* 32 (February): 434.

Braudel, Fernand. 1981. *The Structures of Everyday Life.* New York: Harper and Row.

Britton, James. 1970. "Talking and Writing." In *Explorations in Children's Writing,* edited by E.L. Evertts. Urbana, Ill.: National Council of Teachers of English.

Brodie, Carolyn, and Jim Thomas. 1989. "A Movable Feast: Pop-Ups, Fold-Outs, and Pull Tabs." *School Library Journal* 35 (September): 162–67.

Brown, Hazel, and Brian Cambourne. 1987. *Read and Retell.* Portsmouth, N.H.: Heinemann.

Brown, R.C., W.S. Robinson, and J.T. Cunningham. 1980. *Let Freedom Ring.* Morristown, N.J.: Silver Burdett.

Bruner, Jerome. 1984. "Language, Mind and Reading." In *Awakening to Literacy,* edited by Hillel Goelman, Antoinette A. Oberg, and Frank Smith. Portsmouth, N.H.: Heinemann.

———. 1986. *Actual Minds, Possible Worlds.* Cambridge, Mass.: Harvard University Press.

Byron, Lord George. 1821. Journal entry for January 28, 1821 (quoted in *Bartlett's Familiar Quotations,* 15th ed., 1980).

Cairney, Trevor. 1990. "Intertextuality: Infectious Echoes from the Past." *The Reading Teacher* 43:478–84.

Cambourne, Brian. 1988. *The Whole Story: Natural Learning and the Acquisition of Literacy in the Classroom.* New York: Ashton Scholastic.

Commire, Anne, ed. 1990. *Something about the Author.* Detroit: Gale Research.

Cotterell, Arthur. 1980. *A Dictionary of World Mythology.* New York: G.P. Putnam's Sons.

Cox, Beverly E., Timothy Shanahan, and Elizabeth Sulzby. 1990. "Good and Poor Elementary Readers' Use of Cohesion in Writing." *Reading Research Quarterly* 25:47–65.

Crabtree, Charlotte. 1988. "National Center Set to Improve History Teaching." *New York Times* March 23: B10.

Crook, Patricia R., and Barbara A. Lehman. 1991. "Themes for Two Voices: Children's Fiction and Nonfiction as 'Whole Literature.'" *Language Arts* 68:34–41.

Cullinan, Bernice. 1989. *Literature and the Child.* 2d ed. San Diego: Harcourt Brace Jovanovich.

Cullum, Albert. 1967. *Push Back the Desks.* New York: Citation Press.

Dacey, John S. 1988. *Fundamentals of Creative Thinking.* Lexington, Mass.: Lexington Books, D.C. Heath.

Elleman, Barbara. 1987. "Current Trends in Literature for Children." *Library Trends* 35 (Winter): 421–23.

Englert, Carol Sue, and Elfrieda H. Hiebert. 1984. "Children's Developing Awareness of Text Structures in Expository Materials." *Journal of Educational Psychology* 76 (1): 65–74.

Epstein, Connie. 1987. "Accuracy in Nonfiction." *School Library Journal* 33 (March): 113–15.

Fakih, Kimberly Olson. 1987. "Children's Nonfiction: No Longer a Novelty." *Publisher's Weekly* 23 (June 26): 44.

_____. 1988. "The News Is Nonfiction." *Publisher's Weekly* 33 (February 26): 109.

Feeney, Stephanie, and Eva Moravcik. 1988. "Fostering Aesthetic Development in Young Children." *The Education Digest* 53 (6): 44–47.

Fowler, C.B. 1985. "Art: A Process of Mind." *High Fidelity* (Musical America ed.) 35 (40): 13–15.

Freedman, Russell. 1986. "Pursuing the Pleasure Principle." *The Horn Book* 62 (1): 27–32.

Fritz, Jean. 1988. "Biography: Readability Plus Responsibility." *The Horn Book* 64 (6): 759–60.

Gallant, Mavis. 1955. *The Other Paris: Stories*. Salem, N.H.: Ayer Company Publishing.

Gardner, Howard. 1983. *Frames of Mind: The Theory of Multiple Intelligences*. New York: Harper and Row.

Garraty, John. 1963. "Makers and Shakers in the Pageant of America." *New York Times Book Review* November 10: 6.

Gerhardt, L.N. 1989. "Publishers' Nonfiction Forecast for 1990." *School Library Journal* 35 (November): 34–41.

Giblin, James Cross. 1987. "A Publisher's Perspective." *The Horn Book* 63 (1): 104–7.

_____. 1988. "The Rise and Fall and Rise of Juvenile Nonfiction, 1961–1988." *School Library Journal* 34 (October): 27–31.

Glazer, Joan I., and G. Williams. 1979. *Introduction to Children's Literature*. New York: McGraw-Hill.

Goodman, Ken. 1989. "Whole Language Curriculum: Getting It All Together." Paper presented at the annual convention of the National Council of Teachers of English, November 20, Baltimore.

Graves, Donald H. 1978. *Balance the Basics: Let Them Write*. New York: The Ford Foundation.

_____. 1983. *Writing: Teachers and Students at Work*. Exeter, N.H.: Heinemann.

_____. 1989. *Investigate Nonfiction*. Portsmouth, N.H.: Heinemann.

Hammack, David C. 1990. *U.S. History Report Card: The Achievement of Fourth-, Eighth-, and Twelfth-Grade Students in 1988; Trends from 1986 to 1988 in the Factual Knowledge of High School Juniors*. Washington, D.C.: U.S. Department of Education, Office of Educational Research and Information.

Hardy, Barbara. 1978. "Narrative as a Primary Act of Mind." In *The Cool Web: The Pattern of Children's Reading*, edited by Margaret Meek, Aidan Warlow, and Griselda Barton. New York: Atheneum.

Hirsch, E.D. 1987. *Cultural Literacy: What Every American Needs to Know*. Boston: Houghton Mifflin.

Holman, E. Riley. 1988. *Creativity Potpourri*. Exton, Penn.: Creative and Educational Services.

Huck, Charlotte, Susan Hepler, and Janet Hickman. 1987. *Children's Literature in the Elementary School*. 4th ed. New York: Holt, Rinehart and Winston.

Jaggar, Angela M., Donna H. Carrara, and Sara E. Weiss. 1986. "Research Currents: The Influence of Reading on Children's Narrative Writing (and Vice Versa)." *Language Arts* 63:292–300.

Jett-Simpson, Mary, ed. 1989. *Adventuring with Books: A Booklist for Pre-K–Grade 6*. Urbana, Ill.: National Council of Teachers of English.

Kiefer, Barbara. 1988. "Picture Books as Contexts for Literary, Aesthetic, and Real World Understandings." *Language Arts* 65:260–71.

Kobrin, Beverly. 1988. *Eyeopeners! How to Choose and Use Children's Books about Real People, Places, and Things.* New York: Viking Penguin.

Lasky, Kathryn. 1985. "Reflections on Nonfiction." *The Horn Book* 61 (5): 527–32.

McCarthy, Mary. 1987. *How I Grew.* San Diego: Harcourt Brace Jovanovich.

McGee, Lea M. 1982. "Awareness of Text Structure: Effects on Children's Recall of Expository Text." *Reading Research Quarterly* 17:581–90.

MacLachlan, Patricia. 1987. "The Voice of the Child in a Middle Age Package." Paper presented at Children's Literature '87 Conference, February 6, Columbus, Ohio.

McPhee, John. 1977. "Talk with John McPhee." *New York Times Book Review* November 27: 50.

Meltzer, Milton. 1976. "Where Do All the Prizes Go? The Case for Nonfiction." *The Horn Book* 52 (1): 17–22.

Mersereau, Yvonne, Mary Glover, and Meredith Cherland. 1989. "Dancing on the Edge." *Language Arts* 66:109–17.

Micklos, J. 1990. "Facts Can Be Fun: An Interview with Author Seymour Simon." *Reading Today* February/March: 32.

Moffett, James. 1968. *Teaching the Universe of Discourse.* Boston: Houghton Mifflin.

Moffett, James, and Betty J. Wagner. 1983. *Student-Centered Language Arts and Reading, K-13: A Handbook for Teachers.* Boston: Houghton Mifflin.

Morgan, Ted. 1985. *FDR: A Biography.* New York: Simon and Schuster.

National Association for the Education of Young Children. 1986. "Position Statement on Developmentally Appropriate Practice in Early Childhood Programs Serving Children from Birth through Age 8." *Young Children* 41 (6): 4–19.

National Council of Teachers of English. 1990. Announcement of and Guidelines for Orbis Pictus Award for Outstanding Nonfiction for Children.

National Science Teachers Association. 1986. "Science Education for Middle and Junior High Students." *Science and Children* 24 (3): 62–63.

Norton, Donna. 1987. *Through the Eyes of a Child.* 2d ed. Columbus, Ohio: Merrill Publishing.

Pappas, Christine C., Barbara Z. Kiefer, and Linda S. Levstik. 1990. *An Integrated Language Perspective in the Elementary School.* New York: Longman.

Pearson, P. David, and Robert J. Tierney. 1984. "On Becoming a Thoughtful Reader: Learning to Read Like a Writer." In *Yearbook of the National Society for the Study of Education, 83* (Part 1). Chicago: National Society for the Study of Education.

Perkins, Frances. 1946. *The Roosevelt I Knew.* New York: Viking Press.

Powell, Richard P., and Jesus Garcia. 1988. "What Research Says . . . about Stereotypes." *Science and Children* 25 (5): 21–22.

Pringle, Laurence. 1989. "A Voice for Nature." In *The Voice of the Narrator in Children's Literature,* edited by C. Otten and G. Schmidt. New York: Greenwood Press.

Purves, Alan C., Theresa Rogers, and Anna O. Soter. 1990. *How Porcupines Make Love, II: Teaching a Response-Centered Literature Curriculum.* New York: Longman.

Ravitch, Diane. 1987. "Tot Sociology; or, What Happened to History in the Grade Schools." *American Scholar* 56:343–54.

Ravitch, Diane, and Chester Finn. 1987. *What Do Our 17-Year-Olds Know? A Report on the First National Assessment of History and Literature.* New York: Harper and Row.

Rosenblatt, Louise M. 1989. "Writing and Reading: The Transactional Theory." In *Reading and Writing Connections,* edited by Jana Mason. Boston: Allyn and Bacon.

Rothman, R. 1990. "History and Civics Tests Reveal Knowledge Gaps." *Education Week* 9:5–9.

Rumelhart, D.E. 1980. "Schemata: The Building Blocks of Cognition." In *Theoretical Issues in Reading Comprehension,* edited by R.J. Spiro, B.C. Bruce, and W.F. Brewer. Hillsdale, N.J.: Lawrence Erlbaum.

San Jose, Christine. 1988. "Story Drama in the Content Areas." *Language Arts* 65:26–33.

Santayana, George. 1905. *The Life of Reason,* Vol. I: *Reason in Common* (quoted in *Bartlett's Familiar Quotations,* 15th ed., 1980).

Schlissel, Lillian. 1982. *Women's Diaries of the Westward Journey.* New York: Schocken Books.

Sebesta, Sam L. 1987. "Enriching the Arts and Humanities through Children's Books." In *Children's Literature in the Reading Program,* edited by Bernice E. Cullinan. Newark, Del.: International Reading Association.

Shanahan, Timothy. 1988. "The Reading-Writing Relationship: Seven Instructional Principles." *The Reading Teacher* 41:636–37.

Shanker, Albert. 1990. "Raising the Stakes on NAEP. Where We Stand." *New York Times* July 29: section 4, p. 7.

Shymansky, J.A., W.C. Kyle, Jr., and J.M. Alport. 1983. "The Effects of New Science Curricula on Student Performance." *National Association for Research in Science Teaching* 20 (5): 387–404.

Smith, Frank. 1983. "Reading Like a Writer." *Language Arts* 60:558–67.

Sutherland, Zena, and May Hill Arbuthnot. 1986. *Children and Books.* 7th ed. Glenview, Ill.: Scott, Foresman.

Tierney, Robert J., and M. Leys. 1984. *What Is the Value of Connecting Reading and Writing?* Reading Education Report no. 55. Champaign, Ill.: Center for the Study of Reading, University of Illinois at Urbana-Champaign.

Trelease, Jim. 1985. *The Read-Aloud Handbook.* Rev. ed. New York: Viking Penguin.

Vaughan, J.L., and T.H. Estes. 1986. *Reading and Reasoning beyond the Primary Grades.* Boston: Allyn and Bacon.

Vygotsky, Lev S. 1962. *Thought and Language.* Cambridge, Mass.: MIT Press.

Wagner, Betty J. 1976. *Dorothy Heathcote: Drama as a Learning Medium.* Washington, D.C.: National Educational Association.

Wells, Gordon. 1986. *The Meaning Makers: Children Learning Language and Using Language to Learn.* Portsmouth, N.H.: Heinemann.

Yager, R.E. 1987. "Problem Solving: The STS Advantage." *Curriculum Review* 21 (1): 19–21.

Yolen, Jane. 1981. *Touch Magic: Fantasy, Faerie and Folklore in the Literature of Childhood.* New York: Philomel Books.

Zinsser, William, ed. 1986. *Extraordinary Lives.* New York: American Heritage.

Children's Books Cited

Adler, David A. 1989. *We Remember the Holocaust.* New York: Henry Holt.

Aliki. 1972. *Fossils Tell of Long Ago.* New York: Harper and Row.

_____. 1981. *Digging Up Dinosaurs.* New York: Harper and Row.

_____. 1983. *A Medieval Feast.* New York: Thomas Y. Crowell.

_____. 1985. *My Visit to the Dinosaurs.* Rev. ed. New York: Thomas Y. Crowell.

_____. 1989. *The King's Day: Louis XIV of France.* New York: Thomas Y. Crowell.

Ancona, George. 1987. *Turtle Watch.* New York: Macmillan.

_____. 1989. *The American Family Farm: A Photo Essay.* Text by Joan Anderson. San Diego: Harcourt Brace Jovanovich.

Andersen, Ulla. 1984. *We Live in Denmark.* New York: Bookwright Press.

Andronik, Catherine M. 1989. *Quest for a King: Searching for the Real King Arthur.* New York: Atheneum.

Anno, Mitsumasa. 1975. *Anno's Counting Book.* New York: Thomas Y. Crowell.

_____. 1983. *Anno's U.S.A.* New York: Philomel Books.

_____. 1987. *Anno's Math Games.* New York: Philomel Books.

_____. 1988. *Anno's Mysterious Multiplying Jar.* New York: Philomel Books.

Ardley, Neil. 1989. *Music.* New York: Alfred A. Knopf.

Arnold, Caroline. 1989. *Dinosaur Mountain: Graveyard of the Past.* Photographs by Richard Hewett. New York: Clarion Books.

Arthur, Alex. 1989. *Shell.* New York: Alfred A. Knopf.

Ashabranner, Brent. 1988. *Always to Remember: The Story of the Vietnam Veterans Memorial.* Photographs by Jennifer Ashabranner. New York: G.P. Putnam's Sons.

Bare, Colleen Stanley. 1989. *Never Kiss an Alligator!* New York: E.P. Dutton.

Barth, Edna. 1970. *Lilies, Rabbits and Painted Eggs: The Story of the Easter Symbols.* Illustrated by Ursula Arndt. New York: Seabury Press.

Barton, Byron. 1981. *Building a House.* New York: Greenwillow Books.

_____. 1989. *Dinosaurs, Dinosaurs.* New York: Thomas Y. Crowell.

Bash, Barbara. 1989. *Desert Giant: The World of the Saguaro Cactus.* Boston: Little, Brown.

_____. 1989. *Tree of Life: The World of the African Baobab.* Boston: Little, Brown/Sierra Club.

Bellville, Cheryl Walsh. 1986. *Theater Magic: Behind the Scenes at a Children's Theater.* Minneapolis: Carolrhoda Books.

Better Homes and Gardens, eds. 1981. *Better Homes and Gardens New Junior Cookbook.* Des Moines, Iowa: Better Homes and Gardens.

_____. 1984. *Better Homes and Gardens Step-by-Step Kid's Cookbook.* Des Moines, Iowa: Better Homes and Gardens.

Bjork, Christina. 1987. *Linnea in Monet's Garden.* Illustrated by Lena Anderson. New York: Farrar, Straus and Giroux.

Blumberg, Rhoda. 1985. *Commodore Perry in the Land of the Shogun.* New York: Lothrop, Lee and Shepard Books.

_____. 1989. *The Great American Gold Rush.* New York: Bradbury Press.

Bowler, Peter. 1985. *The Superior Person's Book of Words.* Boston: David R. Godine.

Branley, Franklyn M. 1989. *What Happend to the Dinosaurs?* Illustrated by Marc Simont. New York: Thomas Y. Crowell.

Broekel, Ray. 1988. *Experiments with Water.* Chicago: Children's Press.

Brown, Laurene Krasny, and Marc Brown. 1986. *Dinosaurs Divorce.* New York: Alfred A. Knopf.

_____. 1988. *Dinosaurs Travel: A Guide for Families on the Go.* Boston: Little, Brown.

Bunting, Eve. 1990. *The Wall.* Illustrated by Ronal Himler. New York: Clarion Books.

Burkert, Nancy Ekholm. 1989. *Valentine and Orson.* New York: Farrar, Straus and Giroux.

Burnie, David. 1989. *Plant.* New York: Alfred A. Knopf.

Burton, Virginia Lee. 1942. *The Little House.* Boston: Houghton Mifflin.

Calabro, Marian. 1989. *Operation Grizzly Bear.* New York: Four Winds Press.

Carrick, Carol. 1980. *The Crocodiles Still Wait.* Illustrated by Donald Carrick. Boston: Houghton Mifflin.

_____. 1983. *Patrick's Dinosaurs.* Illustrated by Donald Carrick. New York: Clarion Books.

_____. 1986. *What Happened to Patrick's Dinosaurs?* Illustrated by Donald Carrick. New York: Clarion Books.

Chaucer, Geoffrey. 1988. *The Canterbury Tales.* Adapted by Barbara Cohen. Illustrated by Trina Schart Hyman. New York: Lothrop, Lee and Shepard Books.

_____. 1988. *The Canterbury Tales.* Retold by Selina Hastings. Illustrated by Reg Cartwright. New York: Henry Holt.

Cobb, Vicki. 1987. *Skyscraper Going Up.* Illustrated by John Strejan. New York: Harper and Row.

_____. 1989. *Writing It Down*. Illustrated by Marilyn Hafner. New York: J.B. Lippincott.

Cochrane, Jennifer. 1988. *Urban Ecology*. New York: Bookwright Press.

Cole, Joanna. 1980. *A Frog's Body*. Photographs by Jerome Wexler. New York: William Morrow.

_____. 1982. *A Cat's Body*. Photographs by Jerome Wexler. New York: William Morrow.

_____. 1985. *Large as Life: Daytime Animals Life Size*. Illustrated by Kenneth Lilly. New York: Alfred A. Knopf.

_____. 1985. *Large as Life: Nighttime Animals Life Size*. New York: Alfred A. Knopf.

_____. 1986. *A Dog's Body*. Photographs by Jim and Ann Monteith. New York: William Morrow.

_____. 1986. *Hungry, Hungry Sharks*. Illustrated by Patricia Wynne. New York: Random House.

_____. 1986. *The Magic School Bus at the Water Works*. Illustrated by Bruce Degen. New York: Scholastic.

_____. 1987. *The Magic School Bus inside the Earth*. Illustrated by Bruce Degen. New York: Scholastic.

_____. 1989. *The Magic School Bus inside the Human Body*. Illustrated by Bruce Degen. New York: Scholastic.

_____. 1990. *Large as Life: Animals in Beautiful Life-Size Paintings*. Illustrated by Kenneth Lilly. New York: Alfred A. Knopf.

_____. 1990. *The Magic School Bus Lost in the Solar System*. Illustrated by Bruce Degen. New York: Scholastic.

Cosner, Sharon. 1988. *War Nurses*. New York: Walker.

Courlander, Harold. 1957. *The Hat-Shaking Dance and Other Tales from the Gold Coast*. New York: Harcourt, Brace and World.

Crampton, William. 1989. *Flag*. New York: Alfred A. Knopf.

Crews, Donald. 1978. *Freight Train*. New York: Greenwillow Books.

_____. 1980. *Truck*. New York: Greenwillow Books.

Cutchins, Judy, and Ginny Johnston. 1984. *Are These Animals Real? How Museums Prepare Wildlife Exhibits*. New York: William Morrow.

d'Aulaire, Ingri, and Edgar Parin d'Aulaire. 1939. *Abraham Lincoln*. New York: Doubleday.

dePaola, Tomie. 1977. *The Quicksand Book*. New York: Holiday House.

_____. 1978. *The Popcorn Book*. New York: Holiday House.

_____. 1989. *The Art Lesson*. New York: G.P. Putnam's Sons.

Devlin, Harry. 1967. *To Grandfather's House We Go: A Roadside Tour of American Homes*. New York: Parents Magazine Press.

Dorros, Arthur. 1987. *Ant Cities.* New York: Thomas Y. Crowell.

Dowden, Anne Ophelia. 1990. *The Clover and the Bee: A Book of Pollination.* New York: Thomas Y. Crowell.

Ehlert, Lois. 1989. *Eating the Alphabet.* San Diego: Harcourt Brace Jovanovich.

Ekoomiak, Normee. 1990. *Arctic Memories.* New York: Henry Holt.

Elder, Bruce. 1985. *Take a Trip to Malaysia.* New York: Franklin Watts.

Fisher, Leonard Everett. 1984. *The Olympians.* New York: Holiday House.

Fisher, Timothy. 1977. *Huts, Hovels and Houses.* Illustrated by Kathleen Kolb. Reading, Mass.: Addison-Wesley.

Fitch, Florence. 1944. *One God: The Ways We Worship Him.* Photographs selected by Beatrice Creighton. New York: Lothrop, Lee and Shepard Books.

Fitz-Gerald, Christine. 1986. *I Can Be a Reporter.* Chicago: Children's Press.

Fleischman, Paul. 1988. *Joyful Noise: Poems for Two Voices.* Illustrated by Eric Beddows. New York: Harper and Row.

Flint, Russ. 1990. *Let's Build a House: A White Cottage before Winter.* Nashville: Ideals Children's Books.

Fort, Patrick. 1988. *Redbird.* New York: Orchard Books.

Freedman, Russell. 1961. *Teenagers Who Made History.* New York: Holiday House.

_____. 1980. *Immigrant Kids.* New York: E.P. Dutton.

_____. 1983. *Children of the Wild West.* New York: Clarion Books.

_____. 1985. *Cowboys of the Wild West.* New York: Clarion Books.

_____. 1987. *Indian Chiefs.* New York: Holiday House.

_____. 1987. *Lincoln: A Photobiography.* New York: Clarion Books.

_____. 1988. *Buffalo Hunt.* New York: Holiday House.

_____. 1990. *Franklin Delano Roosevelt.* New York: Clarion Books.

Fritz, Jean. 1969. *George Washington's Breakfast.* Illustrated by Paul Galdone. New York: Coward-McCann.

_____. 1973. *And Then What Happened, Paul Revere?* Illustrated by Margot Tomes. New York: Coward-McCann.

_____. 1976. *Can't You Make Them Behave, King George?* Illustrated by Tomie dePaola. New York: Coward-McCann.

_____. 1981. *Traitor: The Case of Benedict Arnold.* New York: G.P. Putnam's Sons.

_____. 1982. *Homesick: My Own Story.* Illustrated by Margot Tomes. New York: G.P. Putnam's Sons.

_____. 1983. *The Double Life of Pocahontas.* Illustrated by Ed Young. New York: G.P. Putnam's Sons.

_____. 1985. *China Homecoming*. Photographs by Michael Fritz. New York: G.P. Putnam's Sons.

_____. 1986. *Make Way for Sam Houston*. Illustrated by Elise Primavera. New York: G.P. Putnam's Sons.

_____. 1987. *Shh! We're Writing the Constitution*. Illustrated by Tomie dePaola. New York: G.P. Putnam's Sons.

_____. 1989. *The Great Little Madison*. New York: G.P. Putnam's Sons.

George, Jean Craighead. 1988. *One Day in the Woods*. Illustrated by Gary Allen. New York: Thomas Y. Crowell.

Gibbons, Gail. 1981. *Trucks*. New York: Harper and Row.

_____. 1985. *Check It Out! The Book about Libraries*. San Diego: Harcourt Brace Jovanovich.

_____. 1985. *The Milk Makers*. New York: Macmillan.

_____. 1987. *Deadline! From News to Newspaper*. New York: Thomas Y. Crowell.

_____. 1987. *Trains*. New York: Scholastic.

_____. 1988. *Sunken Treasure*. New York: Thomas Y. Crowell.

_____. 1989. *Catch the Wind! All about Kites*. Boston: Little, Brown.

Giblin, James Cross. 1982. *Chimney Sweeps*. Illustrated by Margot Tomes. New York: Thomas Y. Crowell.

_____. 1985. *The Truth about Santa Claus*. New York: Thomas Y. Crowell.

_____. 1988. *Let There Be Light: A Book about Windows*. New York: Thomas Y. Crowell.

Giblin, James Cross, and Dale Ferguson. 1980. *The Scarecrow Book*. New York: Crown Publishers.

Goodall, John S. 1979. *The Story of an English Village*. New York: Atheneum.

_____. 1986. *The Story of a Castle*. New York: Atheneum.

Grillone, Lisa, and Joseph Gennaro. 1978. *Small Worlds Close Up*. New York: Crown Publishers.

Hamilton, Virginia. 1985. *The People Could Fly: American Black Folktales*. Illustrated by Leo and Diane Dillon. New York: Alfred A. Knopf.

Harnett, Cynthia. 1960. *Caxton's Challenge*. Cleveland: World Publishing.

_____. 1984. *The Merchant's Mark*. Minneapolis: Lerner Publications.

Harrison, Ted. 1982. *A Northern Alphabet*. Montreal, Quebec: Tundra Books.

Haskins, Jim. 1987. *Count Your Way through the Arab World*. Minneapolis: Carolrhoda Books.

Hawkes, Nigel. 1985. *Oil*. Fairmont, W.V.: Gloucester Press.

Heller, Ruth. 1983. *The Reason for a Flower*. New York: G.P. Putnam's Sons.

Hoberman, Mary Ann. 1982. *A House Is a House for Me*. Illustrated by Betty Fraser. New York: Viking Penguin.

Hopkins, Lee Bennett. 1987. *Dinosaurs*. Illustrated by Murray Tinkelman. San Diego: Harcourt Brace Jovanovich.

Howe, James. 1981. *The Hospital Book*. Photographs by Mal Warshaw. New York: Crown Publishers.

Hunt, Jonathan. 1989. *Illuminations*. New York: Bradbury Press.

Huynh Quang Nhuong. 1982. *The Land I Lost: Adventures of a Boy in Vietnam*. Illustrated by Vo-Dinh Mai. New York: Harper and Row.

Irwin, Constance. 1980. *Strange Footprints on the Land: Vikings in America*. New York: Harper and Row.

Johnson, Sylvia. 1985. *Rice*. Photographs by Noboru Moriya. Minneapolis: Lerner Publications.

Johnston, Ginny, and Cutchins, Judy. 1990. *Windows on Wildlife*. New York: William Morrow.

Jurmain, Suzanne. 1989. *Once upon a Horse: A History of Horses—and How They Shaped Our History*. New York: Lothrop, Lee and Shepard Books.

Kimmel, Eric A. 1988. *Anansi and the Moss-Covered Rock*. Illustrated by Janet Stevens. New York: Holiday House.

Knight, Joan. 1986. *Journey to Egypt: A UNICEF Pop-Up Book*. New York: Viking Penguin.

Krementz, Jill. 1981. *How It Feels When a Parent Dies*. New York: Alfred A. Knopf.

_____. 1982. *How It Feels to Be Adopted*. New York: Alfred A. Knopf.

_____. 1984. *How It Feels When Parents Divorce*. New York: Alfred A. Knopf.

_____. 1985. *The Fun of Cooking*. New York: Alfred A. Knopf.

_____. 1987. *A Visit to Washington, D.C.* New York: Scholastic.

_____. 1989. *How It Feels to Fight for Your Life*. Boston: Little, Brown.

Kuskin, Karla. 1982. *The Philharmonic Gets Dressed*. Illustrated by Marc Simont. New York: Harper and Row.

LaBonte, Gail. 1989. *The Arctic Fox*. Minneapolis: Dillon Press.

Lanier, Sidney, ed. 1950. *King Arthur and His Knights of the Round Table*. New York: Grosset and Dunlap.

Lasker, Joe. 1976. *Merry Ever After: The Story of Two Medieval Weddings*. New York: Viking Penguin.

_____. 1986. *A Tournament of Knights*. New York: Thomas Y. Crowell.

Lasky, Kathryn. 1983. *Sugaring Time*. Photographs by Christopher Knight. New York: Macmillan.

_____. 1990. *Dinosaur Dig*. Photographs by Christopher Knight. New York: William Morrow.

Latham, Jean Lee. 1955. *Carry On, Mr. Bowditch*. Boston: Houghton Mifflin.

Lattimore, Deborah Nourse. 1991. *The Sailor Who Captured the Sea: A Story of the Book of Kells*. New York: HarperCollins.

Lauber, Patricia. 1955. *Clarence the TV Dog*. New York: Coward-McCann.

_____. 1984. *Life on a Giant Cactus*. Champaign, Ill.: Garrard Publishing Company.

_____. 1981. *Seeds Pop, Stick, Glide*. New York: Crown Publishers.

_____. 1982. *Journey to the Planets*. Rev. ed. 1987, 1990. New York: Crown Publishers.

_____. 1986. *From Flower to Flower: Animals and Pollination*. New York: Crown Publishers.

_____. 1986. *Volcano: The Eruption and Healing of Mount St. Helens*. New York: Bradbury Press.

_____. 1987. *Dinosaurs Walked Here and Other Stories Fossils Tell*. New York: Bradbury Press.

_____. 1989. *The News about Dinosaurs*. New York: Bradbury Press.

Lee, Jeanne. 1985. *Toad Is the Uncle of Heaven: A Vietnamese Folk Tale*. New York: Holt, Rinehart and Winston.

Lester, Julius. 1968. *To Be a Slave*. Illustrated by Tom Feelings. New York: Dial Press.

Levinson, Nancy Smiler. 1990. *Christopher Columbus, Voyager to the Unknown*. New York: E.P. Dutton.

Levinson, Riki. 1988. *Our Home Is the Sea*. Illustrated by Dennis Luzak. New York: E.P. Dutton.

Lewis, Naomi, trans. 1989. *Proud Knight, Fair Lady: The Twelve Lais of Marie de France*. Illustrated by Angela Barrett. New York: Viking Penguin.

Lillegard, Dee, and Wayne Stoker. 1987. *I Can Be a Plumber*. Chicago: Children's Press.

Lines, Kathleen. 1954. *Lavender's Blue: A Book of Nursery Rhymes*. Illustrated by Harold Jones. Oxford: Oxford University Press.

Low, Alice. 1985. *The Macmillan Book of Greek Gods and Heroes*. Illustrated by Arvis Stewart. New York: Macmillan.

Lyon, George Ella. 1989. *ABCedar: An Alphabet of Trees*. Illustrated by Tom Parker. New York: Orchard Books.

Macaulay, David. 1973. *Cathedral: The Story of Its Construction*. Boston: Houghton Mifflin.

_____. 1977. *Castle*. Boston: Houghton Mifflin.

_____. 1988. *The Way Things Work*. Boston: Houghton Mifflin.

McCoy, Joseph J. 1966. *The Hunt for the Whooping Cranes: A Natural History Detective Story*. Maps and illustrations by Rey Abruzzi. New York: Lothrop, Lee and Shepard Books.

McDonald, Megan. 1990. *Is This a House for Hermit Crab?* Illustrated by S.D. Schindler. New York: Orchard Books.

McFarlan, Donald, 1991. *Guinness Book of World Records.* New York: Bantam Books.

MacLachlan, Patricia. 1985. *Sarah, Plain and Tall.* New York: Harper and Row.

_____. 1988. *The Facts and Fictions of Minna Pratt.* New York: Harper and Row.

Maestro, Betsy, and Giulio Maestro. 1986. *The Story of the Statue of Liberty.* New York: Lothrop, Lee and Shepard Books.

Martin, Patricia Stone. 1987. *Reaching for the Stars.* Vero Beach, Fla.: Rourke Enterprises.

Matthews, Downs. 1989. *Polar Bear Cubs.* Photographs by Dan Guravich. New York: Simon and Schuster.

Mayle, Peter. 1982. *As Dead as a Dodo.* Illustrated by Shawn Rice. Boston: David R. Godine.

Meltzer, Milton. 1987. *Mary McLeod Bethune: Voice of Black Hope.* New York: Viking Penguin.

_____. 1989. *Voices from the Civil War.* New York: Thomas Y. Crowell.

_____. 1990. *Columbus and the World around Him.* New York: Franklin Watts.

Meyers, Susan. 1980. *Pearson, A Harbor Seal Pup.* Illustrated by Ilka Hartman. New York: E.P. Dutton.

Musgrove, Margaret. 1976. *Ashanti to Zulu—African Traditions.* Illustrated by Leo and Diane Dillon. New York: Dial Press.

Myller, Rolf. 1974. *From Idea into House.* Illustrated by Henry K. Szwarce. New York: Atheneum.

National Geographic Society. 1986. *A World of Things to Do.* Washington, D.C.: National Geographic Society.

Nelson, Theresa. 1989. *And One for All.* New York: Orchard Books.

Norman, David, and Angela Miller. 1989. *Dinosaur.* New York: Alfred A. Knopf.

Osband, Gillian. 1987. *Our Living Earth: An Exploration in Three Dimensions.* Illustrated by Richard Clifton Dey. New York: G.P. Putnam's Sons.

Overbeck, Cynthia. 1982. *Ants.* Photographs by Satoshi Kuribayashi. Minneapolis: Lerner Publications.

Oxford Scientific Films. 1986. *Hide and Seek.* New York: G.P. Putnam's Sons.

Oz, Charles. 1988. *How Is a Crayon Made?* New York: Simon and Schuster.

Paladino, Catherine. 1990. *Spring Fleece: A Day of Sheepshearing.* Boston: Little, Brown.

Parker, Nancy Winslow, and Joan Richards Wright. 1987. *Bugs.* New York: Greenwillow Books.

Patent, Dorothy Hinshaw. 1989. *Wild Turkey, Tame Turkey.* Photographs by William Muñoz. New York: Clarion Books.

Paterson, Katherine. 1988. *Park's Quest.* New York: E.P. Dutton.

Patterson, Francine. 1985. *Koko's Kitten.* New York: Scholastic.

Peet, Bill. 1989. *Bill Peet: An Autobiography.* Boston: Houghton Mifflin.

Peters, David. 1989. *A Gallery of Dinosaurs and Other Early Reptiles.* New York: Alfred A. Knopf.

Pluckrose, Henry. 1988. *Knowabout Weight.* New York: Franklin Watts.

Prelutsky, Jack. 1988. *Tyrannosaurus Was a Beast: Dinosaur Poems.* Illustrated by Arnold Lobel. New York: Greenwillow Books.

Pringle, Laurence. 1986. *The Only Earth We Have.* New York: Macmillan.

Pryor, Bonnie. 1987. *The House on Maple Street.* Illustrated by Beth Peck. New York: William Morrow.

Quackenbush, Robert. 1980. *Annie, Get Your Gun.* Englewood Cliffs, N.J.: Prentice-Hall.

Ride, Sally (with Susan Okie). 1986. *To Space and Back.* New York: Lothrop, Lee and Shepard Books.

Rinard, Judith. 1985. *Helping Our Animal Friends.* Washington, D.C.: National Geographic Society.

Roop, Peter, and Connie Roop. 1989. *Season of the Crane.* New York: Walker.

Roop, Peter, and Connie Roop, eds. 1990. *I, Columbus: My Journal, 1492–3.* Illustrated by Peter E. Hanson. New York: Walker.

Rutland, Jonathan. 1988. *See inside a Submarine.* Rev. ed. New York: Warwick Press.

Ryden, Hope. 1988. *Wild Animals of America ABC.* New York: E.P. Dutton.

_____. 1989. *Wild Animals of Africa ABC.* New York: E.P. Dutton.

St. George, Judith. 1989. *Panama Canal: Gateway to the World.* New York: G.P. Putnam's Sons.

Sancha, Sheila. 1982. *The Castle Story.* New York: Thomas Y. Crowell.

_____. 1989. *Walter Dragun's Town: Crafts and Trade in the Middle Ages.* New York: Thomas Y. Crowell.

Sattler, Helen Roney. 1983. *The Illustrated Dinosaur Dictionary.* Illustrated by Pamela Carroll. New York: Lothrop, Lee and Shepard Books.

_____. 1989. *Tyrannosaurus Rex and Its Kin: The Mesozoic Monsters.* Illustrated by Joyce Powzyk. New York: Lothrop, Lee and Shepard Books.

_____. 1990. *Giraffes: The Sentinels of the Savannas.* Illustrated by Christopher Santoro. New York: Lothrop, Lee and Shepard Books.

Schwartz, David M. 1985. *How Much Is a Million?* Illustrated by Steven Kellogg. New York: Lothrop, Lee and Shepard Books.

_____. 1989. *If You Made a Million.* Illustrated by Steven Kellogg. New York: Lothrop, Lee and Shepard Books.

Siebert, Diane. 1988. *Mojave.* New York: Thomas Y. Crowell.

Siegel, Alice, and Margo McLoone. 1986. *Kids' World Almanac of Records and Facts.* New York: Pharos Books.

Sills, Leslie. 1989. *Inspirations: Stories about Women Artists.* Niles, Ill.: Albert Whitman.

Simon, Seymour. 1971. *The Paper Airplane Book.* Illustrated by Byron Barton. New York: Viking Press.

_____. 1982. *The Smallest Dinosaurs.* Illustrated by Anthony Rao. New York: Crown Publishers.

_____. 1985. *The BASIC Book.* Illustrated by Barbara and Ed Emberley. New York: Thomas Y. Crowell.

_____. 1985. *Bits and Bytes: A Computer Dictionary for Beginners.* Illustrated by Barbara and Ed Emberley. New York: Thomas Y. Crowell.

_____. 1985. *How to Talk to Your Computer.* Illustrated by Barbara and Ed Emberley. New York: Thomas Y. Crowell.

_____. 1985. *Meet the Computer.* Illustrated by Barbara and Ed Emberley. New York: Thomas Y. Crowell.

_____. 1986. *The Largest Dinosaurs.* Illustrated by Pam Carroll. New York: Macmillan.

_____. 1987. *Icebergs and Glaciers.* New York: William Morrow.

_____. 1987. *Mars.* New York: William Morrow.

_____. 1989. *Storms.* New York: William Morrow.

_____. 1989. *Whales.* New York: Thomas Y. Crowell.

Singer, Marilyn. 1989. *Turtle in July.* Illustrated by Jerry Pinkney. New York: Macmillan.

Sneve, Virginia Driving Hawk. 1989. *Dancing Tepees: Poems of American Indian Youth.* Illustrated by Stephen Gammell. New York: Holiday House.

Sobol, Harriet Langsam. 1978. *Pete's House.* Photographs by Patricia Agre. New York: Macmillan.

Sommerfelt, Aimée. 1961. *The Road to Agra.* Illustrated by Ulf Aas. New York: Criterion Books.

Spier, Peter. 1980. *People.* New York: Doubleday.

Sproule, Anne, and Michael Sproule. 1988. *Know Your Pet: Hamsters.* New York: Bookwright Press.

Stanley, Diane. 1986. *Peter the Great.* New York: Macmillan.

_____. 1988. *Shaka, King of the Zulus.* New York: William Morrow.

Stanley, Diane, and Peter Vennema. 1990. *Good Queen Bess: The Story of Queen Elizabeth I of England.* New York: Macmillan.

Sterne, Noelle. 1979. *Tyrannosaurus Wrecks*. New York: Harper and Row.

Stevens, Carla. 1969. *The Birth of Sunset's Kittens*. Illustrated by Leonard Stevens. New York: Young Scott Books.

Stevenson, Augusta. 1932. *Abe Lincoln: Frontier Boy*. New York: Bobbs Merrill.

Sutcliff, Rosemary. 1981. *The Sword and the Circle: King Arthur and the Knights of the Round Table*. New York: E.P. Dutton.

Tayntor, Elizabeth. 1986. *Dive to the Coral Reefs: A New England Aquarium Book*. New York: Crown Publishers.

Thompson, Peggy. 1985. *Auks, Rocks, and the Odd Dinosaur*. New York: Thomas Y. Crowell.

Thompson, Ruth. 1988. *Look at Hands*. New York: Franklin Watts.

Wakefield, Pat, and Larry Carrara. 1987. *A Moose for Jessica*. New York: E.P. Dutton.

Walker, Les. 1977. *Housebuilding for Children*. Woodstock, N.Y.: Overlook Press.

Webb, Angela. 1986. *Talkabout Soil*. New York: Franklin Watts.

Weiss, Harvey. 1988. *Shelters: From Tepee to Igloo*. New York: Thomas Y. Crowell.

Wexler, Jerome. 1987. *Flowers Fruits Seeds*. Englewood Cliffs, N.J.: Prentice-Hall.

Wheatley, Nadia, and Donna Rawlins. 1989. *My Place*. Long Beach, Calif.: Australia in Print.

Wilcox, Charlotte. 1989. *Trash!* Photographs by Jerry Bushey. Minneapolis: Carolrhoda Books.

Wilcox, R. Turner. 1958. *The Mode in Costume*. New York: Charles Scribner's Sons.

Wilks, Mike. 1986. *The Ultimate Alphabet*. New York: Henry Holt.

Willard, Nancy. 1981. *A Visit to William Blake's Inn: Poems for Innocent and Experienced Travelers*. Illustrated by Alice and Martin Provensen. San Diego: Harcourt Brace Jovanovich.

Wilson, Barbara Ker. 1988. *Acacia Terrace*. Illustrated by David Fielding. New York: Scholastic.

Yue, Charlotte, and David Yue. 1984. *The Tipi: A Center of Native American Life*. New York: Alfred A. Knopf.

_____. 1986. *The Pueblo*. Boston: Houghton Mifflin.

_____. 1988. *The Igloo*. Boston: Houghton Mifflin.

Nonfiction Book Awards

Orbis Pictus Award. The Orbis Pictus Award for Outstanding Nonfiction for Children was established by the National Council of Teachers of English (NCTE) to promote and recognize excellence in the field of nonfiction writing in 1990. The award is named in commemoration of the book *Orbis Pictus (The World in Pictures)* by Johann Comenius, originally published in 1657. It is considered the first informational book written and published specifically for children. The award recognizes that nonfiction has "in recent years . . . emerged as an exciting, attractive and popular genre." The 1990 award winner was *The Great Little Madison* by Jean Fritz; the two honor books were Rhoda Blumberg's *The Great American Gold Rush* and Patricia Lauber's *The News about Dinosaurs.* The 1991 award-winning title was *Franklin Delano Roosevelt* by Russell Freedman; the honor books were Patricia Lauber's *Seeing Earth from Space* and Normee Ekoomiak's *Arctic Memories.* (National Council of Teachers of English, 1111 Kenyon Road, Urbana, IL 61801)

Boston Globe–Horn Book Award. This award was first offered in 1967 for text and illustration; in 1976, an award category for outstanding nonfiction was added. For each category, an engraved silver bowl and cash stipend are awarded. There can be one award winner and up to three honor books in each category. The award is presented annually. (*Boston Globe* and *The Horn Book,* Park Square Building, 31 St. James Avenue, Boston, MA 02116)

Carter G. Woodson Book Award. First presented in 1974 to honor the contribution of the noted black historian and educator Carter G. Woodson, the award is intended to "encourage the writing, publishing and dissemination of outstanding social science books for young readers which treat topics related to ethnic minorities and race relations sensitively and accurately." Thematically appropriate nonfiction books with a U.S. setting published in the year preceding the presentation of the award are eligible. (National Council for the Social Studies, 3501 Newark Street, N.W., Washington, DC 20016)

Children's Book Guild Nonfiction Award. The award was established in 1977 and is presented annually by the Washington, D.C., Children's Book Guild. It is given to an author in recognition of his or her total body of outstanding nonfiction work. A crystal cube and cash award are given. (Children's Book Guild, 7302 Birch Avenue, Takoma Park, MD 20912)

Christopher Awards. The award, a bronze medallion, is given to those books that are representative of the best current fiction or nonfiction. A children's category was established in 1969. Over the years, many nonfiction books have been honored. Award books must be representative of the highest level of human and spiritual values, must enjoy a reasonable degree of popular acceptance, and must have been published in the calendar year for which the award is given. The number of books selected each year varies. (The Christophers, 12 East 48th Street, New York, NY 10017)

Eva L. Gordon Award for Children's Science Literature. The award is presented by the American Nature Society at its annual winter meeting to an author whose works exemplify Dr. Gordon's "high standards of accuracy, readability, sensitivity to interrelationships, timelessness, and joyfulness while they extend, either directly or subtly, an invitation to the child to become involved." A certificate is given. (American Nature Society, 44 College Drive, Jersey City, NJ 07035)

Garden State Children's Book Award. The award was established in 1977 by the Children's Services Section of the New Jersey Library Association to recognize books written for the early and middle grades (2–5). Books must be published three years prior to the year of the award. A certificate is given for Easy to Read, Younger Fiction, and Younger Nonfiction categories "to encourage, stimulate and captivate potential readers through the printed word and good illustrations." The books selected must be popular and have literary merit. (Children's Services Section, New Jersey Library Association, 16 W. State Street, Trenton, NJ 08608)

Golden Kite Award. The Society of Children's Book Writers has sponsored and administered the award since 1977. It is presented annually to a member whose book in the nonfiction category exhibits excellence in writing and has genuine appeal to the interests and concerns of children. A statuette is awarded for nonfiction and for fiction, and there may be one honor book in each category. (Society of Children's Book Writers, P.O. Box 296, Los Angeles, CA 90066)

Janusz Korczak Literary Awards for Children's Books. The award, sponsored by the International Center for Holocaust Studies of the Anti-Defamation League of B'nai B'rith, has been given since 1981. Awards of $1,000 and a plaque are given for the best book in each of two categories: fiction or nonfiction for young readers at the elementary or secondary level, and books for parents/educators on the welfare and nurturing of children. Many nonfiction titles have won this award. Books are judged on the way they exemplify the courage, humanitarianism, and leadership of Dr. Korczak, a Polish physician, educator, author, and administrator of orphanages during World War II. (Janusz Korczak Literary Award Committee, Anti-Defamation League of B'nai B'rith, 823 United Nations Plaza, New York, NY 10017)

Jefferson Cup Award. The award is sponsored by the Children's and Young Adult Round Table of the Virginia Library Association and has been given since 1983. Its purpose is to honor distinguished writing in U.S. history or biography for young people. The winning book may be fiction or nonfiction. (Virginia Library Association, 80 S. Early Street, Alexandria, VA 22304)

New York Academy of Sciences Children's Science Book Awards. This award was established in 1972 by the New York Academy of Sciences to encourage the writing and publishing of books of high quality in the field of science for children. In 1973, three award categories were created: for younger children, for older children, and for the illustrator if different from the author. This award is specifically limited to trade books; decisions are made by a committee of scientists. A citation and $500.00 award are given. (New York Academy of Sciences, 2 East 63 Street, New York, NY 10021)

Please Touch Book Award. The award, made by the Please Touch Museum for Children, was established in 1985 to recognize and encourage the publication of children's books that are of the highest quality and that will help children in the art of enjoying to learn. Award-winning books must be particularly imaginative and effective in clarifying and exploring concepts for children aged three and older. Books must be published in the prior year by an American publisher and must be distinguished in text and illustrations. They must meet the following criteria: (1) be age appropriate, develop concepts, and have a point of view or values; (2) have a design that complements the text and reinforces concepts; and (3) must display overall excellence. Books may be fiction or nonfiction; a medal is given. (Please Touch Museum for Children, 210 N. 21 Street, Philadelphia, PA 19103)

Times Educational Supplement Information Book Awards. This is a prestigious British award. In 1972, the *Times Educational Supplement* established this award for distinction in content and presentation in informational trade books originating in the United Kingdom or its Commonwealth countries. A panel of four judges chaired by the editor of the *Supplement* selects one book in the junior category (up to age nine) and one in the senior category (ages ten to sixteen). (*Times Educational Supplement,* Times Newspaper Ltd., P.O. Box 7, New Printing House Square, Grays Inn Road, London WC1X 8E2, England)

Sources for Selecting Nonfiction Titles

Appraisal: Children's Science Books for Young People. Published quarterly by Children's Science Book Review Committee (605 Commonwealth Avenue, Boston, MA 02215). Reviews are written by children's librarians and subject specialists; ratings, which range from excellent to unacceptable, are also given.

Booklist. Published twice monthly September to June and monthly in July and August by the American Library Association. *Booklist* provides signed annotations and reviews of children's trade books and nonprint materials (video, audio, and computer software) that it recommends for consideration of purchase. Approximate grade levels are given, and there is a separate listing for nonfiction books.

Book Links: Connecting Books, Libraries, and Classrooms. This is a new magazine published six times a year by *Booklist*/American Library Association to help classroom teachers integrate the best children's literature into the curriculum. It offers bibliographies in different genres and subjects and suggests innovative ways to use them in the classroom.

Bulletin of the Center for Children's Books. Published monthly except August by the University of Chicago Press. Its reviews indicate a range from "recommended," "acceptable," "marginal," and "not recommended," to "for special collections or unusual readers only." Grade levels rather than age levels are given in very detailed reviews, and possible curriculum uses are noted. Nonfiction reviews are organized by Dewey classification numbers.

Carter, Betty, and Richard F. Abrahamson. 1990. **Nonfiction for Young Adults: From Delight to Wisdom.** Phoenix: Oryx Press.

Friedberg, Joan B., June B. Mullins, and Adelaid W. Sukiennik. 1985. **Accept Me as I Am: Best Books of Juvenile Nonfiction on Impairments and Disabilities.** New York: R.R. Bowker.

The Horn Book Magazine. Published six times a year by The Horn Book, Inc. Provides articles by noted children's authors, illustrators, and critics on aspects of children's literature, including its use in the classroom. A select number of books recommended as being of the highest quality are offered in signed reviews. Nonfiction books are reviewed in a separate section.

Jett-Simpson, Mary, ed. 1989. **Adventuring with Books: A Booklist for Pre-K–Grade 6.** 9th ed. Urbana, Ill.: National Council of Teachers of English.

Notable Children's Trade Books in the Field of Social Studies. National Council for the Social Studies. Published yearly in a spring issue of *Social Education.* This list of notable books, also available from the Children's Book Council, lists fiction and nonfiction books that are written primarily for children in grades K–8, emphasize human relations, present an original theme or a fresh slant on a traditional topic, are highly readable, and, when appropriate, include maps and illustrations.

Outstanding Science Trade Books for Children. National Science Teachers Association. Published each year in a spring issue of *Science and Children.* This list of outstanding books is also available from the Children's Book Council. The books that are selected are readable, contain information consistent with current scientific knowledge, are pleasing in format and illustrations, and are nonsexist, nonracist, and nonviolent.

School Library Journal. Published eleven times a year by R.R. Bowker. The journal contains articles on all aspects of children's literature, including its use in literacy programs and content areas as well as suggesting cooperative ways that teachers and librarians can work together. All reviews, by school and public librarians, are signed and present recommendations or rejections of new titles. *Star Track* is a new, twice-yearly supplement to the *School Library Journal* that reprints reviews of all starred titles from the prior issues of the journal. In both publications, reviews are divided by fiction and nonfiction and by age: preschool and primary grades, grades 3–6, and junior high and up.

Wilms, Denise M. 1985. **Science Books for Children: Selections from Booklist, 1976–1983.** Chicago: American Library Association.

Index of Authors of Children's Books

Adler, David A.: 93
Aliki: 36, 72, 75, 83, 92, 108-9, 129
Ancona, George: 58, 63, 91
Andersen, Ulla: 40
Andronik, Catherine M.: 73, 75
Anno, Mitsumasa: 51, 99
Ardley, Neil: 79
Arnold, Caroline: 62-63, 110
Arnosky, Jim: 129
Arthur, Alex: 79
Ashabranner, Brent: 23, 50, 70, 129

Bare, Colleen Stanley: 111
Barth, Edna: 21
Barton, Byron: 62, 149
Bash, Barbara: 31, 79
Belleville, Cheryl Walsh: 52
Better Homes and Gardens: 38, 41
Bjork, Christina: 52
Blumberg, Rhoda: 24, 26, 82, 93-94,
    102
Bowler, Peter: 135, 137
Branley, Franklyn M.: 7, 18, 62, 108,
    111
Broekel, Ray: 38, 40
Brown, Laurene Krasny: 35, 80
Brown, Marc: 35, 80
Bunting, Eve: 69-70
Burkert, Nancy Ekholm: 74, 75
Burnie, David: 79
Burton, Virginia Lee: 149

Calabro, Marian: 57-60, 62, 63
Carrara, Larry: 135
Carrick, Carol: 111
Chaucer, Geoffrey: 74, 75
Cobb, Vicki: 35, 102
Cochrane, Jennifer: 41-42
Cole, Joanna: 31, 35, 42, 79, 83, 106,
    111, 124, 126, 127, 129, 135
Cosner, Sharon: 115
Courlander, Harold: 68-69
Crampton, William: 79
Cutchins, Judy: 30, 135

d'Aulaire, Edgar Parin: 5
d'Aulaire, Ingri: 5
dePaola, Tomie: 31, 51-52, 82
Devlin, Harry: 147
Dorros, Arthur: 40
Dowden, Anne Ophelia: 31

Ehlert, Lois: 81
Ekoomiak, Normee: 29-30
Elder, Bruce: 42

Fisher, Leonard Everett: 124, 127, 129,
    141
Fisher, Timothy: 150
Fitch, Florence: 22
Fitz-Gerald, Christine: 36
Fleischman, Paul: 26, 34
Flint, Russ: 149
Fort, Patrick: 35
Freedman, Russell: 2-10, 17-20, 23-25,
    26, 31, 34, 78, 83, 124, 127, 129
Fritz, Jean: 3, 21, 23, 26, 29, 49-50, 68,
    69, 81-82, 92, 124, 125, 127, 129

Gennaro, Joseph: 22
George, Jean Craighead: 102
Gibbons, Gail: 23, 36, 37-38, 42, 100,
    129, 137
Giblin, James Cross: 17-25, 29, 71, 75,
    79, 106, 129, 150
Goodall, John S.: 71, 75
Grillone, Lisa: 22

Hamilton, Virginia: 46
Harnett, Cynthia: 71, 75
Harrison, Ted: 81
Haskins, Jim: 146
Hawkes, Nigel: 43
Heller, Ruth: 82
Hoberman, Mary Ann: 151
Hopkins, Lee Bennett: 135
Howe, James: 22
Hunt, Jonathan: 70-74, 90
Huynh Quang Nhuong: 70, 100

Irwin, Constance: 28

Johnson, Sylvia: 41, 43
Johnston, Ginny: 30, 135
Jurmain, Suzanne: 94

Kimmel, Eric A.: 68-69
Knight, Joan: 35
Krementz, Jill: 38, 50, 80
Kuskin, Karla: 51-52

LaBonte, Gail: 39-40
Lanier, Sidney: 73, 75
Lasker, Joe: 72, 75
Lasky, Kathryn: 24, 26, 29, 41, 46, 110
Latham, Jean Lee: 24, 26
Lattimore, Deborah Nourse: 70-71, 75
Lauber, Patricia: 11-16, 22, 24, 26, 41,
    58, 61, 62, 85, 102, 106, 110, 111,
    129, 135
Lee, Jeanne: 70
Lester, Julius: 20
Levinson, Nancy Smiler: 95
Levinson, Riki: 150
Lewis, Naomi: 73-74, 75
Lillegard, Dee: 38, 40
Lines, Kathleen: 73, 75
Low, Alice: 141
Lyon, George Ella: 81

Macaulay, David: 71, 75, 82
McCoy, Joseph J.: 19-20
McDonald, Megan: 150-51
McFarlan, Donald: 80
MacLachlan, Patricia: 2, 46
McLoone, Margo: 80
Maestro, Betsy: 23, 36, 42
Maestro, Giulio: 23, 36, 42
Martin, Patricia Stone: 115
Matthews, Downs: 91
Mayle, Peter: 111
Meltzer, Milton: 22, 23, 29, 93, 95, 102-
    3, 106, 129

Meyers, Susan: 135
Miller, Angela: 79
Musgrove, Margaret: 81
Myller, Rolf: 150

National Geographic Society: 43
Nelson, Theresa: 70
Norman, David: 79

Osband, Gillian: 35
Overbeck, Cynthia: 38
Oxford Scientific Films: 36
Oz, Charles: 41

Paladino, Catherine: 29
Parker, Nancy Winslow: 35, 42
Patent, Dorothy Hinshaw: 23, 79, 91,
   106, 130
Paterson, Katherine: 69-70
Patterson, Francine: 80
Peet, Bill: 26, 82, 92-93
Peters, David: 63
Pluckrose, Henry: 35-36
Prelutsky, Jack: 108, 112
Pringle, Laurence: 50
Pryor, Bonnie: 149

Quackenbush, Robert: 114

Rawlins, Donna: 149
Ride, Sally: 82, 141
Rinard, Judith: 36
Roop, Connie: 28, 95
Roop, Peter: 28, 95, 106-12
Rutland, Jonathan: 36, 42
Ryden, Hope: 81

St. George, Judith: 93
Sancha, Sheila: 71, 72-73, 75
Sattler, Helen Roney: 30, 63, 130, 135
Schwartz, David M.: 51, 82
Siebert, Diane: 101
Siegel, Alice: 80
Sills, Leslie: 91
Simon, Seymour: 31, 37, 38, 50-51, 79,
   90-91, 101, 106, 108, 110, 125, 127,
   130, 141
Singer, Marilyn: 100
Sneve, Virginia Driving Hawk: 99
Sobol, Harriet Langsam: 149
Sommerfelt, Aimée: 17-18
Spier, Peter: 82, 100
Sproule, Anne: 41

Sproule, Michael: 41
Stanley, Diane: 31
Sterne, Noelle: 108, 112
Stevens, Carla: 22
Stevenson, Augusta: 5-6
Stoker, Wayne: 38, 40
Sutcliff, Rosemary: 73, 75

Tayntor, Elizabeth: 40, 41
Thompson, Peggy: 135
Thompson, Ruth: 38, 40
Wakefield, Pat: 135
Walker, Les: 150
Webb, Angela: 35-36, 40
Weiss, Harvey: 150
Wexler, Jerome: 42
Wheatley, Nadia: 149
Wilcox, Charlotte: 79
Wilcox, R. Turner: 121
Wilks, Mike: 145
Willard, Nancy: 26
Wilson, Barbara Ker: 149
Wright, Joan Richards: 35, 42

Yue, Charlotte: 150
Yue, David: 150

Index of Titles of Children's Books

ABCedar: An Alphabet of Trees: 81
Abe Lincoln: The Great Emancipator: 5-6
Abraham Lincoln: 5
Acacia Terrace: 148, 149
Always to Remember: The Story of the Vietnam Veterans Memorial: 50, 70
American Family Farm, The: A Photo Essay: 91
Anansi and the Moss-Covered Rock: 68-69
And One for All: 70
And Then What Happened, Paul Revere?: 49
Annie, Get Your Gun: 114
Anno's Counting Book: 51
Anno's Math Games: 51
Anno's Mysterious Multiplying Jar: 51
Anno's U.S.A.: 99
Ant Cities: 40
Ants: 38
Are These Animals Real? How Museums Prepare Wildlife Exhibits: 135
Art Lesson, The: 51-52
Arctic Fox, The: 39-40
Arctic Memories: 29-30
As Dead as a Dodo: 111
Ashanti to Zulu—African Traditions: 81
Auks, Rocks, and the Odd Dinosaur: 135

BASIC Book, The: 50-51
Better Homes and Gardens New Junior Cookbook: 38
Better Homes and Gardens Step-by-Step Kid's Cookbook: 41
Bill Peet: An Autobiography: 26, 82, 92-93
Birth of Sunset's Kittens, The: 22
Bits and Bytes: A Computer Dictionary for Beginners: 50-51
Buffalo Hunt: 3-4
Bugs: 35, 42
Building a House: 148, 149

Canterbury Tales, The: 74, 75
Carry On, Mr. Bowditch: 24, 26
Castle: 71, 75
Castle Story, The: 71, 75
Cat's Body, A: 127
Catch the Wind! All about Kites: 100
Cathedral: The Story of Its Construction: 71, 75
Caxton's Challenge: 71, 75
Check It Out! The Book about Libraries: 38, 42, 137
Children of the Wild West: 2-3, 31, 83
Chimney Sweeps: 20
China Homecoming: 69
Christopher Columbus, Voyager to the Unknown: 95
Clarence the TV Dog: 12
Clover and the Bee, The: A Book of Pollination: 31
Columbus and the World around Him: 29, 95
Commodore Perry in the Land of the Shogun: 24, 26
Count Your Way through the Arab World: 146
Cowboys of the Wild West: 25, 83
Crocodiles Still Wait, The: 111

Dancing Tepees: Poems of American Indian Youth: 99
Deadline! From News to Newspaper: 36, 38
Desert Giant: The World of the Saguaro Cactus: 79
Digging Up Dinosaurs: 108, 109
Dinosaur: 79
Dinosaur Dig: 29, 110
Dinosaur Mountain: Graveyard of the Past: 62-63, 110
Dinosaurs: 135
Dinosaurs, Dinosaurs: 62
Dinosaurs Divorce: 80
Dinosaurs Travel: A Guide for Families on the Go: 35
Dinosaurs Walked Here and Other Stories Fossils Tell: 15, 110, 135

Dive to the Coral Reefs: A New England Aquarium Book: 40, 41
Dog's Body, A: 135
Double Life of Pocahontas, The: 68

Eating the Alphabet: 81
Experiments with Water: 38, 40

Facts and Fictions of Minna Pratt: 2
Flag: 79
Flowers Fruits Seeds: 42
Fossils Tell of Long Ago: 108
Franklin Delano Roosevelt: 9-10, 127
Frog's Body, A: 127
From Flower to Flower: Animals and Pollination: 15
From Idea into House: 148, 150
Fun of Cooking, The: 38

Gallery of Dinosaurs and Other Early Reptiles, A: 63
George Washington's Breakfast: 21
Giraffes: The Sentinels of the Savannas: 30
Good Queen Bess: The Story of Queen Elizabeth I of England: 31
Great American Gold Rush, The: 82, 93-94, 102
Great Little Madison, The: 26, 29, 92
Guinness Book of World Records: 80

Hat-Shaking Dance and Other Tales from the Gold Coast, The: 68-69
Helping Our Animal Friends: 36
Hide and Seek: 36
Homesick: My Own Story: 69
Hospital Book, The: 22
House Is a House for Me, A: 148, 151
House on Maple Street, The: 148, 149
Housebuilding for Children: 148, 150
How Is a Crayon Made?: 41
How It Feels to Be Adopted: 80
How It Feels to Fight for Your Life: 80

How It Feels When a Parent Dies: 80
How It Feels When Parents Divorce: 80
How Much Is a Million? 51, 82
How to Talk to Your Computer: 50-51
Hungry, Hungry Sharks: 111
Hunt for the Whooping Cranes, The: A Natural History Detective Story: 20, 25
Huts, Hovels and Houses: 148, 150

I, Columbus: My Journal, 1492-3: 95
I Can Be a Plumber: 38, 40
I Can Be a Reporter: 36
Icebergs and Glaciers: 38
If You Made a Million: 51
Igloo: 148, 150
Illuminations: 70-74, 90
Illustrated Dinosaur Dictionary, The: 135
Immigrant Kids: 83
Indian Chiefs: 20
Inspirations: Stories about Women Artists: 91
Is This a House for Hermit Crab?: 148, 150-51

Journey to Egypt: A UNICEF Pop-Up Book: 35
Journey to the Planets: 13, 15, 22
Joyful Noise: Poems for Two Voices: 26, 34

Kids' World Almanac of Records and Facts: 80
King Arthur and His Knights of the Round Table: 73, 75
King's Day, The: Louis XIV of France: 83, 92
Know Your Pet: Hamsters: 41
Knowabout Weight: 35-36
Koko's Kitten: 80

Land I Lost, The: Adventures of a Boy in Vietnam: 70, 100
Large as Life: Animals in Beautiful Life-Size Paintings: 42
Large as Life: Daytime Animals Life Size: 42, 79
Large as Life: Nighttime Animals Life Size: 42, 79

Largest Dinosaurs, The: 108, 110
Lavender's Blue: A Book of Nursery Rhymes: 73, 75
Let There Be Light: A Book about Windows: 29, 71, 75, 148, 150
Let's Build a House: A White Cottage before Winter: 148, 149
Life on a Giant Cactus: 15
Lilies, Rabbits and Painted Eggs: The Story of the Easter Symbols: 21
Lincoln: A Photobiography: 7-10, 17, 18, 20, 24-25, 26, 34
Linnea in Monet's Garden: 52
Little House, The: 148, 149
Look at Hands: 38, 40

Macmillan Book of Greek Gods and Heroes, The: 141
Magic School Bus at the Water Works, The: 31, 35, 83, 126, 127
Magic School Bus inside the Earth, The: 31, 35, 83, 126, 127
Magic School Bus inside the Human Body, The: 31, 35, 83, 126, 127
Magic School Bus Lost in the Solar System, The: 31, 35, 83, 126, 127
Make Way for Sam Houston: 82
Mars: 141
Mary McLeod Bethune: Voice of Black Hope: 102-3
Medieval Feast, A: 36, 72, 75
Meet the Computer: 50-51
Merchant's Mark, The: 71, 75
Merry Ever After: The Story of Two Medieval Weddings: 72, 75
Mode in Costume, The: 121
Mojave: 101
Moose for Jessica, A: 135
Music: 79
My Place: 148, 149
My Visit to the Dinosaurs: 36, 109

Never Kiss an Alligator!: 111
News about Dinosaurs, The: 58, 61, 62, 85, 102, 111
Northern Alphabet, A: 81

Oil: 43
Olympians, The: 141
Once upon a Horse: A History of Horses—and How They Shaped Our History: 94

One Day in the Woods: 102
One God: The Ways We Worship Him: 22
Only Earth We Have, The: 50
Operation Grizzly Bear: 57-60, 62, 63
Our Home Is the Sea: 148, 150
Our Living Earth: An Exploration in Three Dimensions: 35

Panama Canal: Gateway to the World: 93
Paper Airplane Book, The: 79
Park's Quest: 69-70
Patrick's Dinosaurs: 111
Pearson: A Harbor Seal Pup: 135
People: 82, 100
People Could Fly, The: American Black Folktales: 46
Peter the Great: 31
Pete's House: 148, 149
Philharmonic Gets Dressed, The: 51-52
Plant: 79
Polar Bear Cubs: 91
Popcorn Book, The: 82
Proud Knight, Fair Lady: The Twelve Lais of Marie de France: 73-74, 75
Pueblo, The: 148, 150

Quest for a King: Searching for the Real King Arthur: 73, 75
Quicksand Book, The: 31

Reaching for the Stars: 115
Reason for a Flower, The: 82
Redbird: 35
Rice: 41, 43
Road to Agra, The: 17-18

Sailor Who Captured the Sea, The: A Story of the Book of Kells: 70-71, 75
Sarah, Plain and Tall: 2
Scarecrow Book, The: 22-23
Season of the Crane: 28
See inside a Submarine: 36, 42
Seeds Pop, Stick, Glide: 15
Shaka, King of the Zulus: 31
Shell: 79
Shelters: From Tepee to Igloo: 148, 150
Shh! We're Writing the Constitution: 127

Skyscraper Going Up: 35
Small Worlds Close Up: 22
Smallest Dinosaurs, The: 108, 110
Spring Fleece: A Day of
    Sheepshearing: 29
Storms: 31, 37
Story of a Castle, The: 71, 75
Story of an English Village, The: 71, 75
Story of the Statue of Liberty, The: 36,
    42
Strange Footprints on the Land:
    Vikings in America: 28
Sugaring Time: 24, 26, 41
Superior Person's Book of Words, The:
    135, 137
Sword and the Circle, The: King
    Arthur and the Knights of the
    Round Table: 73, 75

Take a Trip to Malaysia: 42
Talkabout Soil: 35-36, 40
Teenagers Who Made History: 17-19
Theater Magic: Behind the Scenes at a
    Children's Theater: 52
Tipi, The: A Center of Native Ameri-
    can Life: 148, 150
To Be a Slave: 20

To Grandfather's House We Go: A
    Roadside Tour of American
    Homes: 147, 148
To Space and Back: 82, 141
Toad Is the Uncle of Heaven: A
    Vietnamese Folk Tale: 70
Tournament of Knights, A: 72, 75
Traitor: The Case of Benedict Arnold:
    49-50
Trash!: 79
Tree of Life: The World of the African
    Baobab: 31
Truth about Santa Claus, The: 79
Turtle in July: 100
Turtle Watch: 58, 63
Tyrannosaurus Rex and Its Kin: The
    Mesozoic Monsters: 63
Tyrannosaurus Was a Beast: Dinosaur
    Poems: 108, 112
Tyrannosaurus Wrecks: 108, 112

Ultimate Alphabet, The: 145
Urban Ecology: 41-42

Valentine and Orson: 74, 75

Visit to Washington, D.C., A: 50
Visit to William Blake's Inn, A: Poems
    for Innocent and Experienced
    Travelers: 26
Voices from the Civil War: 93
Volcano: The Eruption and Healing of
    Mount St. Helens: 13, 24, 26, 41

Wall, The: 69-70
Walter Dragun's Town: Crafts and
    Trade in the Middle Ages: 72, 75
War Nurses: 115
Way Things Work, The: 82
We Live in Denmark: 40
We Remember the Holocaust: 93
Whales: 90-91, 101
What Happened to Patrick's Dino-
    saurs?: 111
What Happened to the Dinosaurs?:
    62, 108, 111
Wild Animals of Africa ABC: 81
Wild Animals of America ABC: 81
Wild Turkey, Tame Turkey: 79, 91
Windows on Wildlife: 30
World of Things to Do, A: 43
Writing It Down: 102

Editors

Evelyn B. Freeman is an associate professor and coordinator of elementary education at The Ohio State University at Newark. A former elementary school teacher, she now teaches courses and conducts inservice workshops in children's literature, language arts, and reading. Her articles have appeared in *Language Arts, Elementary School Journal,* and *Childhood Education.* She serves on the editorial board of *Language Arts* and on the Children's Book Award Committee for the International Reading Association. She chairs the Buckeye Children's Book Award Committee and is a member of the Executive Board of the Ohio Council of Teachers of English/Language Arts.

Photograph by Hara Person.

Diane Goetz Person is a children's media specialist with experience in public and school libraries. She was the text editor for an elementary-school-level whole language literature series and is currently teaching at Teachers College, Columbia University. She serves on the International Reading Association/Children's Book Council joint committee and the Whole Language Committee of the American Association of School Librarians, and chairs the IRA Special Interest Group on Libraries and Reading. She has presented papers at the national conventions of the National Council of Teachers of English and the International Reading Association, and her writing has been published in *The Reading Teacher* and *Language Arts.*

Contributors

Bette Bosma is a professor of reading and language arts in the Teacher Education Program at Calvin College, Grand Rapids, Michigan. She is the author of *Fairy Tales, Fables, Legends, and Myths: Using Folk Literature in the Classroom.*

Kathleen A. Copeland, a former elementary teacher, currently is an assistant professor at the University of Illinois at Urbana-Champaign, where she teaches courses in language arts education. She received the Promising Researcher Award from the National Council of Teachers of English and serves on the Committee on Language and Learning across the Curriculum.

Bernice E. Cullinan is a professor of education at New York University and past president of the International Reading Association. She has authored *Literature and the Child,* and edited *Children's Literature in the Reading Program* and *Children's Literature in the Classroom: Weaving Charlotte's Web.*

Frances Smardo Dowd is an associate professor in the School of Library and Information Studies at Texas Woman's University, Denton, Texas. Some of her articles have appeared in *School Library Journal, Childhood Education,* and *School Library Media Quarterly.* Her book *Latchkey Children in the Library and Community* was published in 1991.

Barbara Elleman is editor-in-chief of *Book Links: Connecting Books, Libraries, and Classrooms,* a new magazine published by the American Library Association. For eight years she was the children's book editor of *Booklist,* the reviewing journal of the American Library Association, where she previously worked as staff reviewer.

Marjorie Slavick Frank is an adjunct lecturer in the Department of Education at Manhattan College and at Brooklyn College. In addition, she is the author of curriculum materials in the areas of science, social studies, reading, and language arts, and is president of M&H Ideas, an editorial development company specializing in the creation of educational materials across the curriculum.

Russell Freedman has written more than thirty informational books for children. *Lincoln: A Photobiography* received the 1988 Newbery Medal, and *Franklin Delano Roosevelt* was named the 1991 Orbis Pictus Award winner. His books have received much recognition, appearing on the lists of notable books of the National Council of the Social Studies, National Science Teachers Association, and American Library Association.

Patricia Grasty Gaines is a professor of education at West Chester University, West Chester, Pennsylvania, where she teaches courses in literature in the reading program, K–12; elementary language arts methods; and creativity. She is a consultant and workshop leader in creativity, creative dramatics, and poetry for children.

James Cross Giblin was editor-in-chief at Clarion Books for twenty-two years. His book *Chimney Sweeps: Yesterday and Today* received the 1983 American Book Award and the Golden Kite Award for nonfiction. He has received many honors for his nonfiction books for children on a variety of topics, such as Santa Claus, windows, the Rosetta Stone, and milk.

M. Jean Greenlaw is a Regents Professor at the University of North Texas, Denton. She is book review editor for *The New Advocate* and is the author of books, journal articles, and textbooks. She has been active for many years in the National Council of Teachers of English, the International Reading Association, and the American Library Association.

Nancy DeVries Guth is a supervisor of reading and language arts for Stafford County, Virginia. She has previously taught in Brazil and on a Zuni reservation in New Mexico. She received her master's degree in elementary education and reading from the University of New Mexico.

Judith W. Keck is assistant director of staff development for the Licking County, Ohio, schools. She has been a book reviewer since 1985 for *The ALAN Review,* and a member of the committee of the National Council of Teachers of English that produced the 1988 edition of *Your Reading,* an annotated booklist for junior high/middle school readers.

Patricia Lauber is the author of more than eighty books for young people. Her many science books range from earthquakes to earthworms. Her book *Volcano: The Eruption and Healing of Mount St. Helens* was a 1987 Newbery Honor Book, and her book *The News about Dinosaurs* was a 1990 Orbis Pictus Honor Book. In 1988, she was the recipient of the American Nature Society's Eva L. Gordon Award.

Peter Roop has been an elementary teacher for seventeen years and is currently teaching first grade in the Appleton, Wisconsin, schools. His efforts in bringing children and books together were recognized when he was named Wisconsin State Teacher of the Year in 1986. He is also an award-winning author of nonfiction for children.

Rosemary A. Salesi is a professor of education at the University of Maine at Orono. She has served as treasurer and president of the New England Reading Association and as treasurer and membership chair of the Children's Literature Assembly of the National Council of Teachers of English. She currently co-edits the "Book Beat" column for the *New England Reading Association Journal.*

Sylvia M. Vardell is currently an assistant professor of reading/language arts at the University of Texas at Arlington, where she teaches undergraduate and graduate courses in reading and language arts. Her research has focused on children's development of reading and writing abilities, and her articles have appeared in *Language Arts, English Journal,* and *The Horn Book.*